D1593941

STUDIES IN GERMAN LITERATURE,
LINGUISTICS, AND CULTURE

VOL. 9

STUDIES IN GERMAN LITERATURE, LINGUISTICS, AND CULTURE

Vol. 9

CAMDEN HOUSE
Columbia, South Carolina

TWENTIETH CENTURY ODYSSEY

DODERER WITH THE MANUSCRIPT OF *DIE DÄMONEN*

Twentieth Century Odyssey

a study of Heimito von Doderer's *Die Dämonen*

ELIZABETH C. HESSON

CAMDEN HOUSE
Columbia, South Carolina

Set in Garamond type and printed on
acid-free Glatfelder paper.

Acknowledgments

IT IS A PLEASURE to acknowledge my debt to those who have been of assistance to me during my work. I am extremely grateful to Dr. Kenneth H. Segar, St. Edmund Hall, Oxford, for his invaluable suggestions regarding form and content of the original thesis that was the basis for this book, and for his unfailing encouragement. I am indebted to Dr. Wendelin Schmidt-Dengler of the University of Vienna for facilitating my researches on unpublished material in the Österreichische Nationalbibliothek in Vienna and for allowing me to benefit from his vast knowledge of the author and his work.

I should like to express my gratitude to the author's widow, Frau Maria von Doderer, for granting me permission to consult her late husband's papers in the Österreichische Nationalbibliothek, and for allowing me to quote from this material. To Doderer's publishers, C.H. Beck'sche Verlagsbuchhandlung, Munich, I am grateful for permission to publish the "Aide-mémoire zu 'Die Dämonen der Ostmark'" in its entirety and to quote from unpublished material in Doderer's *Nachlaß*. Herr Horst Wiemer, for many years reader with this firm, also provided valuable information based on his personal knowledge of Doderer. I likewise wish to thank the Biederstein Verlag for permission to reproduce the portrait of Doderer.

Finally, I am indebted to the Social Sciences and Humanities Research Council of Canada for awarding me a Doctoral Fellowship for the year 1977-78; to the Board of Regents of Memorial University of Newfoundland for granting me leave to pursue my research; to the Vice-President's Research Fund, for financial assistance; and to my husband, both for his unstinting assistance in the preparation of the manuscript and for his constant support.

Contents

x

Introduction

WHEN HEIMITO VON DODERER'S novel *Die Dämonen* was published in 1956,[1] it marked the culmination of the work of a quarter of a century. Such a protracted genesis must necessarily affect both the form and the content of the final version of the novel and cannot be disregarded in any interpretation of the work.

The impetus to make a genetic study of the novel came from a remark of Wendelin Schmidt-Dengler, who is at present the foremost authority on Doderer. Discussing Doderer's posthumous papers, Schmidt-Dengler writes:

> From a literary-historical point of view, the chief concern today is to make manifest the complex and critically incisive genesis of the great later novels. This would not only elucidate the structure of Doderer's *oeuvre*, but would also constitute a paradigm for the elucidation of the unique process of artistic creation.[2]

Those critics who have so far studied *Die Dämonen* have not been primarily concerned with the genesis of the novel. Anton Reininger examines "Die Dämonen der Ostmark," the seventeen chapters of the novel which Doderer wrote in the 1930s, and the material related to it, only insofar as they form part of his critique of ideology in Doderer's work. Hans Joachim Schröder seems more concerned with the novel as an expression of Doderer's "reactionary" thought, while Dietrich Weber's interpretation of the novel is based almost exclusively on its final version and is a formal analysis rather than a genetic inquiry. As Lutz-Werner Wolff points out in the preamble to his study of *Roman No 7*, the dissertations of Franz-Peter Haberl and Elisabeth Stengel are based on the published texts, do not take account of unpublished material and disregard Doderer's theoretical writings.[3] For a complete understanding of the novel all of these factors must be taken into account.

A genetic study such as I propose affords an insight into how Doderer tackled the task of literary creation and illustrates how theory and practice are not infrequently at variance. As Doderer considered that the raw material for his novels originated in his diaries,[4] and often stressed their importance for him, these diaries, in particular those of 1951 to 1956,[5] the years during which Doderer was completing the novel, bear close scrutiny. They furnish a wealth of information as to how the novel actually evolved. Doderer was a highly conscious literary artist whose art consists in a careful fusion of inspired creativity and studied reflection. The diaries are the medium in which this reflection most conspicuously occurs. In addition to the diary material an examination of unpublished materials relating to the genesis of the novel corrects widespread misinterpretations of the work.

There has as yet been no systematic attempt to chronicle the development of the entire novel, perhaps because of the sheer bulk of the material involved. Roswitha Fischer, who made a comprehensive genetic study of *Die Strudlhofstiege*, writes:

> Auch zu den "Dämonen" gibt es Konvolute von Dokumenten und Vorstudien, deren Aufarbeitung eine Reihe neuer Aspekte und Erkenntnisse sowohl hinsichtlich der Arbeitsweise des Autors als auch hinsichtlich einer Gesamtinterpretation dieses Werkes beibringen würde.
>
> Allerdings ist dieses "Dämonen"-Manuskript (einschließlich der Skizzen) auf Grund der verschiedenen Fassungen derart umfangreich, daß eine solche Aufarbeitung von einem Einzelnen kaum bewältigt werden könnte.[6]

Indeed, a close textual study of the genesis of the novel, along the lines of Fischer's approach to *Die Strudlhofstiege*, would run to several volumes. Fischer's material for *Die Strudlhofstiege* was much less diffuse and more easily analyzed than the material for *Die Dämonen*. While conceding the merits of her approach to the problems of the novel's genesis, it is not the method I have chosen to adopt. The correlation of the "Probetexte,"[7] the manuscript versions, the typescript of the novel, the proofs and the printed text, would amount to the preparation of a critical edition of the novel. I have accordingly chosen to give an account of the genesis of the novel along chronological lines, using the material in the diaries, both published and unpublished, to illuminate the novel's development. I consider the business of the actual composition of the novel to be more interesting and more revelatory of the author's creative process than a comparative study of various versions of the text. Hence my reluctant decision to disregard certain aspects of the genesis of the novel, such as material expurgated from the manuscript, the examination of marginal notes in the manuscript composed between 1952 and 1956, and the reproduction and detailed analysis of diagrammatic material.[8] My intention is to show how the novel took shape, what factors played a critical role in determining its structure, how its material came to accommodate Doderer's changing attitudes, and how it mediates the author's personal experiences and his interpretation of reality.

The present study is divided into five chapters, which together form an analysis of the genesis, structure and purport of the novel. Chapter one consists of a brief biographical introduction, a synopsis of the novel's contents and some data on the historico-political content of the work. All of this material is helpful to the reader who is not familiar with the facts of Doderer's life or with the Austrian scene in the 1920s and 1930s. Chapter two is a factual account of the genesis of *Die Dämonen*, over a period of twenty-five years. I examine the reasons for this protracted genesis as well as Doderer's personal problems which had a decisive influence on the work. Chapter three examines technical devices employed by the author to resolve the tensions between form and content. Chapter four is a detailed study of how Doderer composed the climax of the novel, the chapter "Das Feuer." This chapter is highly complex, but Doderer's mastery of formal techniques allows him to shape its immense and involved contents and to achieve his goal of having the form of the chapter convey the atmosphere of confusion in Vienna on 15 July 1927. Chapter five examines Doderer's Thomist interpretation of reality, his anti-political thought, and his view of history and its role for the novelist. Although Doderer was a member of the NSDAP between 1933 and 1938, the years when it was a proscribed movement in Austria, he later rejected fascism, and the novel represents to some degree his attempt to come to terms with his fascist past. He endeavors to explain his "Dummheit" in Thomist terms, as a rejection of the *analogia entis*. The majority of the characters in *Die Dämonen* are living in a "second reality," a state in which they are prey to some obsession or ideology, and the novel illustrates how this spurious "second reality" disintegrates when forced into a confrontation with empirical reality. The major historical event portrayed in the novel, the rioting in the streets of Vienna on 15 July 1927, which culminated in the burning of the Palace of Justice, allows Doderer to formulate his thesis that the individual is more important than the historical process. This idea determines the form of the concluding portions of the novel.

Die Dämonen is a highly complex structure with a multiplicity of characters and a profusion of plots and subplots. Doderer devoted almost one-third of his eventful life to this work. He was either working on it, or for fifteen of these twenty-five years he was trying to find a means of continuing the first part of the novel, which he completed in 1936. During these fifteen years he was struggling with problems that were not only of a literary nature but fundamental to his own existential situation. That Doderer completed the novel is no mean achievement; in aesthetic terms it is the transmutation of his own existence, an interpretation of the human situation.

ABBREVIATIONS USED BY DODERER IN HIS DIARIES

A —"Textmasse A," = Part II of the novel, except that Chapter 9 is Dicke Damen and not Der Sturz vom Steckenpferd

A1 —Am anderen Ufer

A2 —Im Osten

A3 —Der Triumph der Rahel

A4 —"Neudegg" sequence, Die Falltür, Die Kavernen von Neudegg, Dort unten, Am Strom

A4, Vignette —Am Strom

A5 —Dicke Damen, also referred to as CS = Chronique scandaleuse

B —"Textmasse B," = Chapters 1-5 of Part III of the novel, except that Chapter 1 is Der Sturz vom Steckenpferd and not Dicke Damen

B1 (E) —Im Haus "Zum blauen Einhorn"

Be —Überm Berg

Br —Brandgeruch

C —"Textmasse C," infrequently used, = Chapters 6-12 of Part III

CS —Chronique scandaleuse

DD —Dicke Damen/*Die Dämonen*

DD I —Part I of the novel

DD II/1 —Auf offener Strecke; sometimes referred to as II/XVIII or II/XIX

DDO —Die Dämonen der Ostmark; the title of the seventeen chapters of the novel which Doderer had completed in 1936. With alterations and additions they became Part I of the novel

E —Im Haus "Zum blauen Einhorn"

E/G —Einhorn/Gyurkicz

F —Das Feuer

F 1, 2, 3 —the chapter Das Feuer was originally conceived of as three separate chapters

G —Gyurkicz

K 1	—Die Entstehung einer Kolonie I
K 2	—Die Entstehung einer Kolonie II
Ka	—Kampferduft
Kaps	—Frau Kapsreiter
KK	—Kurze Kurven
LP	—Leuchtpunkt
LPM	—Leuchtpunkt Mayrinker, the Mayrinker episode in Das Feuer, DD, pp. 1280-87
LPN	—Leuchtpunkt Neuberg, the Neuberg episode in Das Feuer, DD, pp. 1299-306
Ms I-III	—the three volumes of manuscript of the novel, started in 1952
N	—Nachtbuch
Q	—Quapp
R I	—Auf offener Strecke
R II	—Der Sturz vom Steckenpferd
R III/a	—Vor verschlossenen Türen
R III/b	—Auf der Schanze
R 7	—*Roman No 7*
R 7/I	—*Die Wasserfälle von Slunj*
R 7/II	—*Der Grenzwald*
RP	—Reifepunkt
Sp	—Spalt, original title of the chapter Kurze Kurven
W	—Schlaggenberg's Wiederkehr

1

Prolegomena to a
Study of *Die Dämonen*

I. The Man and His Work: a Brief Synopsis

THE CLOSE RELATIONSHIP between Doderer's life and work makes a knowledge of biographical data particularly valuable to his readers. Although it is possible to offer a purely text-related interpretation of the contents of *Die Dämonen*, its richness, diversity and complexity are more fully appreciated by the reader informed of the circumstances of Doderer's eventful personal history. His life is truly an Odyssey, although not even Odysseus lived through two global conflicts, spending ten years under arms or in captivity.

It is not always easy to find details of Doderer's personal life, for he eschewed autobiographies, and when asked by his publisher to prepare one at the time of his seventieth birthday, he wrote instead *Meine neunzehn Lebensläufe und neun andere Geschichten*,[1] a collection of aphorisms and short stories, one of which is a parody of an autobiography. In his diaries and essays the autobiographical content is almost always rigorously filtered and it is his imaginative writings which offer most biographical data, although the mature Doderer was critical of what he termed "Direkt-Autobiographisches," and claimed that he was hampered by it when writing *Die Dämonen*. Although he used autobiographical material in his later novels it was in a more objective and sublimated fashion. The most reliable source of biographical information is to be found in Weber's study, as this life-history was established with Doderer's collaboration.[2]

Heimito von Doderer was born in Weidlingau near Vienna on 5 September

1896, the youngest of the six children of the construction engineer Wilhelm Ritter von Doderer and his German-born wife, Luise Wilhelmine von Hügel. The relationships within Doderer's family closely parallel those portrayed in the Stangeler family in the novels *Die Strudlhofstiege* and *Die Dämonen*, where the father is a dominant patriarchal figure who inspires feelings of inferiority and alienation in the son.

After graduating from the Landstraßer Gymnasium in Vienna in 1914 Doderer studied law for a year at the University of Vienna. His studies were interrupted by World War I, in which he saw service in Russia and was captured by the Russians after the Battle of Olesza in 1916. The four years spent in various prisoner-of-war camps in Siberia significantly influenced his development both as an individual and a writer. On his first and only furlough from the front in 1916 he had made an attempt at writing and he continued with his efforts during his years of imprisonment. He later lost or destroyed this material, except for the fragment "Szene zu 'Katharina'" which he wrote in August 1918 and which was found in his posthumous papers. In Siberia he made the acquaintance of Rudolf Haybach, who became his first publisher. Doderer's contacts with his fellow-officers of the Imperial Army imbued him with strongly partisan feelings for the Austro-Hungarian Empire, destined shortly to be dissolved. He later viewed the Third Reich from the standpoint of this "Reichsidee" and this may have contributed to his attraction to fascism in the 1930s.

On his return to Vienna in 1920 he did not resume his law studies but enrolled as a student of history and psychology. He carried on research toward a doctorate out of deference to the wishes of his father; his choice of subjects was dictated by his decision to become a writer: "Zweifellos, das Studium der Geschichte ist das am allermeisten bildende erst recht für den werdenden Romancier, indem es ganz vorzüglich geeignet ist, ihm den Begriff des Schicksals sachlich und unerbittlich vor Augen zu rücken."[3]

In 1925 Doderer received his doctorate for a dissertation titled "Zur bürger-lichen Geschichtsschreibung in Wien während des 15. Jahrhunderts." He did not seek to pursue a career in the academic field, especially after strong disagreements with members of the prestigious Institut für Österreichische Geschichtsfor-schung, where he had commenced studies. His ambitions remained literary, but he was to achieve only meagre success in the field of literature during the following years.

In 1921 Doderer began an affair with Gusti Hasterlik, a Jewess. Theirs was a love-hate relationship and although they married in 1930, they separated in 1932 and were divorced two years later. The ups and downs in their liaison had various causes. As a struggling writer, Doderer could not support himself, much less a wife. Her relatives suggested that he turn to journalism to augment his income and he did so, although he never considered this work as truly part of his *oeuvre*.

The fact that she was a Jewess was also a source of friction, as Doderer seemed to feel, rightly or wrongly, that his lack of success as a writer was due to Jewish domination of the publishing world. He used his wife as a model for both Camy von Schlaggenberg and Grete Siebenschein in the novel and the Camy/Schlaggenberg, Grete/Stangeler relationships are based on his own personal situation.

During his student years Doderer published a slim volume of poetry, *Gassen und Landschaft*, in 1923, and in the following year his first prose-work, *Die Bresche*.[4] In the 1920s he experimented with formal composition and wrote several "Divertimenti," which, as their name suggests, used a musical structure for a short piece of literature. These "Divertimenti," with the exception of "Divertimento V," were not published during Doderer's lifetime.[5] He continued to see close links between literature and music, and several of his major works illustrate this preoccupation. In fact, he solved the pressing problem of the structure of *Die Dämonen* in 1955 by analogy with the symphonic form. He already had an "Ouvertüre," composed in 1935, and he now divided the novel into three parts, which he called movements. In the years before his death in 1966 he was working on *Roman No 7*. This was actually his tenth novel, but he renumbered it out of admiration for Beethoven and his Seventh Symphony and made strenuous efforts to embody in the work the elements of the musical composition.

1929 marked a decisive stage in Doderer's development as a writer. While in captivity in Siberia he read *Die tanzende Törin*, a novel by the artist-writer, Albert Paris von Gütersloh.[6] Gütersloh was one of the early Impressionists and Doderer's early works, *Die Bresche*, the fragment *Jutta Bamberger*, and the novel, *Das Geheimnis des Reichs*, show marked Impressionist traits, undoubtedly influenced by his admiration for Gütersloh.[7] When Doderer finally became acquainted with Gütersloh in 1924, he was at first not favorably impressed. But when it was suggested to him in 1929 by his publisher, Rudolf Haybach, that he write a book on Gütersloh he agreed to do so. In the course of his preparations for the book he read Gütersloh's *Die Bekenntnisse eines modernen Malers*.[8] Over thirty years later he wrote that for him this was not simply a book, but that these were quite literally pages from his own life. Although one may view his ecstatic account of the book's effect on him with some scepticism, he undoubtedly saw in the work a confirmation of his own position as a writer, a reinforcement of his belief in his own abilities. From this time onwards he considered Gütersloh his mentor, remained on close friendly terms with him, and did not waver in his admiration, even when Gütersloh scurrilously attacked him in the novel *Sonne und Mond* in 1962.[9] Gütersloh appears in *Die Dämonen* in the figure of Schlaggenberg's teacher, Albert Scolander, whose name comes from Lenz Scolander, a character in one of Gütersloh's unpublished works.

1929 also marked the beginnings of what eventually became the novel *Die*

Dämonen. Its original title was "Dicke Damen," and stemmed from an idiosyncrasy of Doderer, a fascination with mature females of generous proportions. This obsession was the main theme of the novel in its early stages, embodied in Schlaggenberg's "Chronique Scandaleuse." In the course of its development the content of the novel became more political and its title was changed to "Die Dämonen der Ostmark."

In 1930 Doderer published his book on Gütersloh, *Der Fall Gütersloh*,[10] which did not have wide public appeal, and the novel, *Das Geheimnis des Reichs.* The latter work was based on his experiences as a P.O.W. in Siberia, but there is also a disproportionate amount of historical content which is not successfully integrated into the action of the novel. Doderer was aware of the shortcomings of *Das Geheimnis des Reichs* and treated the historico-political content of *Die Dämonen* in much different fashion. The fact that he returned to his Siberian experiences over thirty years later in *Der Grenzwald* underscores the tremendous influence exerted on him by this happening.[11]

In 1933 Doderer joined the NSDAP, which was proscribed in Austria by Chancellor Dollfuß on 19 June 1933. It is not clear just when Doderer's membership began, but it was probably after the Party was banned, as its illegality could well have been one of the features which attracted him to it. It may also have been a way of further distancing himself from his family which, though favoring the union of Austria and Germany, was not fascist. In the 1920s Doderer had frequented a bohemian group on the fringes of Viennese society and had also had contacts with criminal elements in Vienna. This was his way of expressing his feeling of not belonging to his bourgeois milieu. It also provided him with background for the group "Die Unsrigen" in the part of the novel written in the 1930s and for characters such as the criminal, Meisgeier, and the prostitutes, Anny Gräven and Anna Diwald, introduced into the novel in the 1950s.

In 1936 Doderer completed chapter seventeen of "Die Dämonen der Ostmark" and with it Part I of the novel. He experienced great difficulty with his attempts to continue to Part II and he was also unable to find a publisher in Vienna. He decided to move to Munich, partly to use some funds belonging to his mother, which were available to him there, and partly in the hopes of finding a publisher. He could not find accommodation in Munich itself, so took up residence in Dachau, where the notorious concentration camp was already in existence.[12] He had an introduction to the firm of C.H. Beck which published *Ein Mord den jeder begeht* in 1938 and *Ein Umweg* in 1940.[13] Doderer also signed a contract with Beck for *Die Dämonen*, but refused to allow the work to be published at this time. Beck, the later Biederstein Verlag, published all of Doderer's major works and continued to do so after his death.

His stay in Germany between 1936 and 1938 was sufficient to shatter any illusions that he might have had that Hitler's new regime in any way corresponded to his own "Reichsidee," and after the Anschluß on 13 March 1938 he resigned his Party membership. At that time this was a courageous, even foolhardy, act, and Doderer later claimed that only his military service in the Luftwaffe saved him from persecution. His rejection of National Socialism was followed by his conversion to Catholicism in the winter of 1939/40, another bold step in the prevailing political situation. In April 1940 he was conscripted into the Luftwaffe at the age of forty-three. During the war years *Die Dämonen* disappeared, in his words, into his diaries. The manuscript of "Die Dämonen der Ostmark" was destroyed when Beck's publishing house was bombed in 1944. Luckily Doderer had in his possession two typescripts, one of which is now in the *Nachlaß*.[14] It was on these that he worked when he modified the 1930s material so that it could eventually become the first part of the entire novel. Doderer saw service in various European theatres of war until his capture by the British in Norway on 7 May 1945.

On his return to Vienna from captivity Doderer found himself in straitened circumstances. In addition to the hardships faced by all people in occupied countries he had to face the added punishment of being forbidden to publish any of his work because of his Party membership in the 1930s. His first two post-war articles, both on Gütersloh, appeared under the pseudonym of René Stangeler in 1948.[15] Between 1946 and 1948 he completed *Die Strudlhofstiege* and between 1948 and 1950 he again pursued studies at the Institut für Österreichische Geschichtsforschung. He was accepted as a Member in 1950 on completion of a "Hausarbeit" titled "Die Abtwahlformel in den Herrscherurkunden bis zum 10. Jahrhundert." Doderer claimed that he undertook these studies in order to prepare himself intellectually for resumption of work on *Die Dämonen*.

When the ban on publishing was lifted in 1951 the simultaneous publication of *Die erleuchteten Fenster*[16] and *Die Strudlhofstiege* marked Doderer's breakthrough as a writer of stature. The latter novel caused Doderer some headaches when he resumed work on *Die Dämonen* in mid-1951, because a large number of the same characters are involved in both novels. The action of *Die Strudlhofstiege* ends shortly before the events narrated in Geyrenhoff's chronicle begin. Although both works might be seen as "Stangeler"-novels, as this autobiographical figure is a central character in each of them, Doderer wanted each novel to be an autonomous structure and made strenuous efforts to achieve this goal.

A preliminary to the writing of *Die Dämonen* was a first version of the tract "Sexualität und totaler Staat," which Doderer composed in 1948 and which deals in theoretical terms with the problem of fascism.[17] Doderer had now taken up an anti-political position and was also endeavoring to prove that totalitarian regimes find their sustenance in any form of deviant sexual behavior. Doderer makes this rather contentious mode of thought into one of the central themes of *Die Dämonen* and links it to his concept of the "second reality." At the beginning of 1951 Doderer wrote *Die Posaunen von Jericho* which he later considered his most important work as well as the one which finally enabled him to resume work on *Die Dämonen*.[18]

The composition of *Die Dämonen* was his prime interest between 1951 and 1956, although he also worked, in less sustained fashion, on *Die Merowinger*, which was completed after the publication of *Die Dämonen* in 1956 and published in 1962.[19] In 1952 Doderer married Maria Emma Thoma, whom he had known for a number of years. Doderer had written to her almost daily during the war years and Frau von Doderer has in her possession all of these letters. After his marriage Doderer divided his time between his wife's home in Landshut in Germany and his little bachelor apartment in Vienna.

On completion of *Die Dämonen* Doderer began to prepare for publication his diaries for the years 1940 to 1950 and they appeared in 1964 titled *Tangenten. Tagebuch eines Schriftstellers 1940-1950*. In 1959 he published *Grundlagen und Funktion des Romans*,[20] which is in part an account of his theory of the novel as it evolved during his work on *Die Dämonen*, and in part his establishment of the theory of the "roman muet," which was to be the basis of his projected tetralogy, *Roman No 7*. He completed the first part of this work, *Die Wasserfälle von Slunj*, in 1963,[21] but the second part, *Der Grenzwald*, was incomplete at the time of his death in 1966 and was published posthumously in 1967.

During the last decade of his life Doderer achieved international recognition and saw his works translated into the major European languages. On 23 December 1966 he died of cancer and was buried in the cemetery of Grinzing on 2 January 1967. Due in no small part to the efforts of his widow, the Österreichische Nationalbibliothek was able to acquire his *Nachlaß* in 1968 and so ensured that it did not leave Austria, meeting the fate of those of several other famous Austrian writers such as Broch, Kafka, Musil, and Schnitzler. Doderer's correspondence, mainly letters received by him but also letters to his mother, his sister Astri von Stummer and Gütersloh among others, is in the Autographensammlung in the Nationalbibliothek. Dr. Wendelin Schmidt-Dengler of the University of Vienna was entrusted by Frau von Doderer with the publication of her husband's diaries for the last fifteen years of his life. The first volume, entitled *Commentarii 1951 bis 1956. Tagebücher aus dem Nachlaß*, appeared in 1976, and is indispensable in tracing the genesis of *Die Dämonen*. The diaries for the years 1957 to 1966, which accompany the genesis of *Roman No 7*, have not yet been published.

II. A Summary of the Novel

If the account of the genesis of *Die Dämonen* might be called an Odyssey, the summary of its contents could be looked on as an Ariadne's thread to guide the reader through the veritable maze of characters and events. In most novels there is a plot which serves this function, but in *Die Dämonen* the main plot, that of Levielle's attempt to defraud Quapp of her inheritance, is convoluted, and is further complicated by a whole series of subplots. The "Ouvertüre," which acts as an introduction to the novel, was written in the 1930s and is an exposition only of Geyrenhoff's chronicle, not of the entire novel.

The plot-structure is complicated; the chronology of the novel is fragmented; the setting is not always Vienna. If there is a unifying feature in the work it is the thematic content. The main theme of the novel is that of the "second reality." The individual who is subject to some form of obsession is, in Doderer's eyes, living in a "second reality" and only a forced confrontation with empirical reality (Doderer calls this the "first reality") will allow him to break free of it. This is the main theme of the part of the novel which was written in the 1950s, but fortunately for Doderer the majority of the characters that were created in the 1930s as members of the group "Die Unsrigen," suffered from a form of delusion or neurosis. Thus the 1930s material was easily accommodated to Doderer's changed political thinking and the whole of Part I eventually assumed an expository role. When Doderer became disenchanted with fascism in the late 1930s he became highly critical of any form of ideology and he also adopted the view that thinking according to ideologies is closely linked to sexual behavior of a deviant kind. The title of his tract "Sexualität und totaler Staat" makes the connection quite explicit, and in *Die Dämonen* Doderer uses Schlaggenberg's "Dicke-Damen-Doktrinär-Sexualität" (p. 851) and introduces the episode of Jan Herzka and his 15th century ancestor, Achaz von Neudegg, to illustrate his thesis.

According to the subtitle of *Die Dämonen* the work is a novel based on the chronicle written by Georg von Geyrenhoff. Geyrenhoff starts by writing an eyewitness account of events involving the group of people, who, borrowing from Dostoevsky's novel, *The Possessed* (German title, *Die Dämonen*), adopt the title "Die Unsrigen." These events take place between November 1926 and 14 May 1927. Geyrenhoff becomes so involved personally with what is happening to his friends that he breaks off writing and from then onwards only keeps notes, which he and the author, who is Doderer himself, use as the basis of the novel twenty-eight years later. Like many of the other characters in the novel Geyrenhoff is living in a "second reality." His premature retirement from the Civil Service is a form of retreat from life, and writing about the lives of others is also a substitute for attempting to come to terms with the reality of his own situation. Increasing personal involvement with these people and falling in love with Friederike Ruthmayr allow him to break free of his "second reality" and to become a fully-integrated person.

When Geyrenhoff embarks on his literary career he is aided by the professional writer, Kajetan von Schlaggenberg, and the young historian, René von Stangeler. Schlaggenberg agrees to help Geyrenhoff if he is allowed to include in the chronicle his own "Chronique Scandaleuse." This is the rather scabrous account of his obsession with mature women of ample proportions, an obsession which is determining the pattern of his existence. Separated from his wife, Camy, he is enjoying meagre success as a writer and is earning a precarious living through journalism. Stangeler is equally unhappy. He has no career prospects, and his relationship with his lover, Grete Siebenschein, is a stormy one. He is under pressure from her family to marry her, but he can think of nothing more repugnant: "Professor sein und verheiratet, das ist für mich eine geradezu grausliche Vorstellung" (p. 206). The characters of Schlaggenberg and Stangeler are highly autobiographical and their sexual relationships are based in part on Doderer's own relationship with Gusti Hasterlik.

Schlaggenberg's sister, Charlotte, nicknamed Quapp, is also divorced from reality. She has aspirations to become a professional violinist but lacks the necessary talent. Her problem is solved when she inherits two large sums of money from the estates of her natural parents. Quapp is the illegitimate daughter of the rich landowner, Georg von Ruthmayr, who was killed in World War I, and Baroness Claire von Neudegg. She was adopted at birth by the Schlaggenbergs and the true facts of her parentage were kept a closely-guarded secret, but one known to the financier, Levielle. He became the executor of Ruthmayr's will, drawn up by Ruthmayr just before his death, bequeathing Quapp a large sum of money. Levielle is the financial advisor of Ruthmayr's widow, Friederike, and he suppresses the fact of the legacy to Quapp. Levielle's duplicity is eventually unmasked, thanks to the efforts of Geyrenhoff and to a sort of *deus ex machina*, in the person of Alois Gach, who was the witness of Ruthmayr's will.

Quapp's relationship to Claire von Neudegg, which comes to light when she inherits from the estate of her maternal grandfather, Achaz von Neudegg, links her with two important subplots in the novel. Claire von Neudegg was the woman who soured Geyrenhoff's relations with the opposite sex and contributed to his inability to live life fully. The wheel turns full circle when Geyrenhoff falls in love with Friederike Ruthmayr, who married Ruthmayr after his affair with Claire von Neudegg came to an end. The second plot involving the Neudegg family concerns the businessman, Jan Herzka. Herzka's mother was a Neudegg and when Achaz von Neudegg dies in March 1927 his estates pass to Herzka. Herzka is the heir because Claire has predeceased her father. Herzka is living in a "second reality," a victim of his sadistic tendencies. In Schloß Neudegg are found not only the dungeons in which his 15th century ancestor, Achaz von Neudegg, conducted a form of witch trial which pandered to his sexual depravity, but also a manuscript which purports to be an eye-witness account of these happenings.

Herzka asks René von Stangeler to prepare the manuscript for publication and Stangeler's edition of it allows him to achieve scholarly success. It also ensures a stable relationship with Grete Siebenschein. Herzka himself breaks free of his "second reality" because of the actions of the prostitute, Anny Gräven, and of his secretary, Agnes Gebaur, whom he marries.

Quapp's sudden wealth coincides with her falling in love with the Hungarian diplomat, Géza von Orkay, and the end of her affair with Imre von Gyurkicz, a mythomaniac. The son of lower-class Austrian parents, he claims to be a scion of the old Hungarian aristocracy. He purportedly took part in an abortive coup in Hungary and to add credence to his claims he keeps in his room a skull and a bayonet on a belt. The skull is supposed to be that of his best friend, to whom the bayonet belonged. Everything is fabrication. But Gyurkicz is unable to sustain his confrontation with reality. His affair with Quapp ends, his career as an artist runs into difficulties and he is shot by the police on 15 July 1927. Even his death cannot be taken at face-value. He was shot because he seemed to be inciting the workers to revolt, brandishing a revolver, but his political sympathies actually lay on the Right and he had been involved with the fascists in Burgenland.

Quapp, Schlaggenberg, Gyurkicz and Stangeler are the four central characters in the group "Die Unsrigen." The leader of the group is the hard-drinking, womanizing, Otto von Eulenfeld, a former German infantry major. He and Geyrenhoff's nephew, Dr. Körger, are fascist sympathisers and Körger is an anti-Semite. Another member of the group is the young historian, Dr. Neuberg, who, like Stangeler, is having problems with his career and with his fiancée, Angelika Trapp. The group is very close during the winter of 1926-27. They go on ski-trips, have parties, live in each other's pockets, but by the spring of 1927 they are starting to go their separate ways and the table-tennis evening at Siebenscheins' on 14 May 1927 marks the break-up of the group. It also marks the end of Part I of the novel, completed in 1936, and written throughout in the form of Geyrenhoff's chronicle. When Doderer resumed work on the novel in 1951 he changed the narrative mode from that of the first-person narrator to that of the omniscient author and he also added a significant group of new characters.

The first of these new, positive characters, intended as a counterweight to "Die Unsrigen," are the American lepidopterist, Dwight Williams, and the secretary, Emma Drobil, who comes from Prague. Williams makes the acquaintance of Stangeler and is introduced by him to "Die Unsrigen." Before coming to Vienna Williams lived in London and there fell in love with the portrait of Mary K. The astute Drobil tracks down the real Mary K. and when Williams is confronted with her in person he realizes that his feelings for her were in fact fantasy and that he really loves Emma. His obsession was not so deep-seated or neurotic as that of Schlaggenberg and his healthier attitude to reality is intended to emphasize how obsessed Schlaggenberg really is.

Mary K. herself is, in Doderer's eyes, one of the most admirable characters in the novel. In September 1925 she lost her right leg in a traffic accident. This catastrophe formed part of the climax of *Die Strudlhofstiege*. In *Die Dämonen* she overcomes this trauma, remaining an integrated person despite physical mutilation. Her relationship with Leonhard Kakabsa is a crucial element in her physical and spiritual regeneration. Kakabsa is a young worker who, through the study of Latin, achieves self-realization. His knowledge of this language affords him greater insight into his own language, which is restricted by his lack of education and use of dialect. When he breaks through this language-barrier, as Doderer terms it, he is firmly on the path to what Doderer considers a more fulfilled life. Although he did not start his process of self-education in the hopes of improving his material situation, he eventually becomes a doctoral candidate, librarian to Prince Croix and the lover of Mary K. He embodies Doderer's philosophy of life, his conservative view that evolution within the individual is of greater value to society as a whole than is revolutionary change from without.

All of these subplots develop more or less independently of each other although they occasionally overlap, for example when Stangeler becomes associated with Herzka. The action of all of them is resolved on 15 July 1927, the climax of the historico-political action of the novel. Friederike Ruthmayr accepts Geyrenhoff's proposal of marriage; Quapp and Orkay become engaged; Leonhard and Mary K. become lovers; even those whose relationships fall apart completely, Schlaggenberg and Camy, Neuberg and Angelika Trapp, are reconciled to their situation. The "Platzregen von Banalitäten" (p. 1337) in which the novel ends makes ironically clear the fact that Austria's political future is uncertain. The problems of the novel's characters are resolved, but there is no happy ending to the conflict between the parties of the Left and the Right. In fact, 15 July 1927 greatly weakens the position of the Socialists as a political force in the country and marks the emergence of the right-wing paramilitary Heimwehr as a dominant faction in Austrian politics.

In addition to the various plots and subplots there are three important interpolations in the novel's contents, all of which reinforce the main theme, the "second reality." Schlaggenberg's "Chronique Scandaleuse" illustrates graphically his perverted sexuality, and with its overtones of Nazi terminology it links sexual aberration to political ideology. The supposed 16th century manuscript of Achaz von Neudegg's witch trials indicates that perverted sexual thinking is not an exclusively 20th century phenomenon; Doderer's emphasis on the dungeons of Schloß Neudegg underscores his belief that demonic forces are lurking in the depths of society, irrational forces which society is powerless to combat. The third, and to some critics seemingly extraneous, interpolation is the most mystifying of the three. Entitled "Das Nachtbuch der Kaps," it is the account of her dreams kept by Frau Kapsreiter, the tenant of the "Haus zum blauen

Einhorn." This account, however, serves several useful purposes. In her dreams Frau Kapsreiter can foresee the events of the real world and this device is used by Doderer to create suspense in the reader's mind. At this metaphorical level the author can also explicate the novel's content. Frau Kapsreiter has dreams about the sewers, in which an octopus lurks, an illustration of the theme of the "Einbruch von unten." Doderer also makes use of the character of Frau Kapsreiter to link the fictional happenings of the novel to the actual political happenings. Her brother, Mathias Csmarits, and her ten year old nephew, Pepi Grössing, are the victims of the shootings in Schattendorf on 24 January 1927. This is a mixture of fact and fiction,[22] but it serves to show that the historical process can intrude on the life of the individual, that the "Alltag" may be threatened by "anonymes Geschehen." Frau Kapsreiter is a character who is immensely important to Doderer, and even after her death her spiritual presence dominates the concluding portions of the novel. Frau Mayrinker, her successor as the tenant of the "Haus zum blauen Einhorn," also plays an important symbolic role. On 15 July, acting independently of outside help, Frau Mayrinker extinguishes a potentially dangerous fire in her kitchen. Afterwards nothing has been destroyed for her and life can go on as before. This is an illustration of Doderer's belief that everyday reality continues, despite the assault on it by the impersonal forces of history.

This résumé has touched, if only briefly, on the most significant parts of the novel's content. Several less crucial, but nonetheless interesting, subsidiary plots have been disregarded. Joseph Frank said of James Joyce that he cannot be read— he can only be reread;[23] this dictum is axiomatic for *Die Dämonen*. A summary of this novel cannot do justice to the contents; it can at best offer a few guidelines to point the reader in the direction of the center of the maze and head him off from a series of dead-ends. More should not be expected of it.

III. The Historical Facts

The historico-political content of the novel, although it does not determine the novel's structure, may be confusing to the reader who is unfamiliar with the confused situation of Austrian politics in the 1920s and 1930s. Doderer himself lived through these events and, like so many of his fellow-Austrians, fell victim to fascist ideology. The spread of fascism in Austria was greatly facilitated by the freedom of movement granted to the paramilitary units of the Right after the events of 15 July 1927. This is the political happening which Doderer chose to make the climax of his novel. Historians differ in their view of the significance of this event. Alfred Doppler calls it an insignificant incident as far as world history is concerned,[24] but C. Earl Edmondson considers that "the political effects of the bloodshed in Vienna on 15 July, 1927, and of the nationwide strike that followed, were so enormous that the crisis must be seen as a turning point in the history of the First Republic."[25] A brief account of the history of the First Republic not only helps to explain this divergence of opinion but also clarifies certain sections of Doderer's novel which may perplex the uninformed reader.

The defeat in World War I of the Dual Monarchy was followed by the dissolution of the Habsburg Empire, the setting up of the First Republic, and the establishment of sovereign states in the Balkans. A truncated Austria found herself demoted from the status of a world power and faced with immense reparation payments to the victorious powers of the Entente. On her doorsteps were communist Russia and, from the early 1920s onwards, fascist Italy and semi-fascist Hungary. The chaos within Austria herself sparked the creation of paramilitary groups of the Left and the Right, and increasing class conflict was the dominant feature of these years. From 1920 onwards the ruling party in the country was the clerical, conservative Christian Socials. Their main support came from rural areas, and from all those who feared the spectre of communism. The opposition party, the Social Democrats, held power in urban areas and Vienna, in particular, was a "red" stronghold. In the 1920s the Socialists consistently enjoyed the support of roughly 40% of the population. Smaller political factions were the Monarchists, the Pan-German movement, the fascists and the communists.

The greatest threat to public security was posed by the paramilitary groups, the right-wing Heimwehr and the socialist Republikanischer Schutzbund. One area where there were frequent confrontations between them was in Burgenland, the province southeast of Vienna, adjoining Hungary, which was under the extreme right-wing regime of Admiral Horthy. It was in the village of Schattendorf in Burgenland that the Schutzbund staged a march on 30 January 1927. Shots were fired from the village-inn by supporters of the right-wing Frontkämpfer, and two of the marchers, a war veteran and a young boy, were fatally wounded by shotgun blasts. Two men were arrested and charged with murder. When they were brought to trial they were acquitted on 14 July, the fifth occasion on which crimes of violence perpetrated by right-wing groups had gone unpunished. The Socialists looked on the verdict as a denial of justice to the proletariat and their leaders decided to record their protest in peaceable fashion by staging a strike and a workers' march in Vienna on 15 July. They refused to sanction the release of arms to Schutzbund members, a decision which had tragic consequences. In spite of their intentions, the peaceful protest march turned to violence. The marchers set fire to the Palace of Justice, the symbol of a judicial system which to them seemed biased in favor of the bourgeois élite; the police fired on the unarmed marchers. Over a thousand people were injured and there were eighty-nine deaths, only four of them policemen. The Christian Social Chancellor, Ignaz Seipel, took ruth less measures to squash the workers' revolts and gave the Heimwehr even greater license to crush its socialist opposition. The real victors of the day were thus the forces of reaction.

In the late 1920s and early 1930s the political situation remained highly volatile and even before Hitler's accession to power in 1933 Austrian Nazis were becoming increasingly militant. On 20 May 1933 Chancellor Dollfuß formed the "Vaterländische Front," in a vain attempt to create a viable alternative to Nazism. It was supposedly non-partisan and Dollfuß even hoped to attract to it the more moderate Social Democrats, but in reality it was essentially semi-fascist. On 12 February 1934 at the outset of the short-lived civil war (12-15 February 1934) Dollfuß dissolved the Social Democrat Party. The government's policy of destroying Social Democracy in order to be free to combat Nazism inside Austria had fatal consequences for the country. This destruction annihilated the one political faction that could have offered effective opposition to Hitler's Anschluß in 1938.

Doderer decided in the 1930s that the burning of the Palace of Justice would play a prominent part in the novel. He intended the events of the day to illustrate his belief that society was being ripped apart because of the pernicious influence of the Jews within it. Twenty years later he uses the events of 15 July 1927 as the climax of the novel, but interprets them in the light of his changed political thinking. He now uses the happenings of the day to illustrate his thesis that the anonymous historical event does not condition the life of the individual. In the novel the burning of the Palace of Justice and the rioting actually take place on the periphery of the action involving the main characters and do not determine their course of action. Geyrenhoff afterwards describes the day as the Cannae of Austrian freedom (p. 1328), but it must be admitted that one has to read between the lines of the novel to reach this conclusion. Doderer supplies some historical data in the novel, principally concerning the shootings in Schattendorf, but his account of the events of 15 July is aimed at capturing the atmosphere of the day, not at offering an analysis of the political situation. His treatment of the historical content of the novel springs from his view of the different roles of the historian and the novelist. The historian is concerned with impersonal forces; the novelist with the "business of living." Doderer has been criticized for not condemning in the novel the excesses of the police on 15 July. He would counter that it was not his intention to write a historical novel but instead to use this political happening as a canvas on which to portray his own personal view of the situation. In this aim he has succeeded admirably.

2

The Genesis
of *Die Dämonen*

IN AN INTERVIEW which took place only a year before his death in 1966, Doderer was asked if he could explain why he had achieved success so late in life. He replied, "Ich habe dafür die Erklärung, daß der Roman überhaupt die Form der späteren Männlichkeit ist."[1] Wealth of experience is, in his eyes, a prerequisite to the creation of a work of art. The involved and complex genesis of *Die Dämonen* is paralleled by the equally eventful personal history of its author. The traumatic nature of certain of his experiences clearly exerted a formative effect on the content of the novel and determined the thematic structure of the work.[2] I now propose to trace the development of the novel, linking it to Doderer's life and illuminating it with Doderer's reflection on it as found in his diaries.

The genesis of the novel will be examined chronologically, and is divided into three sections, each of which corresponds to a significant stage in the novel's development. These are:

    I. "Die Dämonen der Ostmark" (1929-1936)
    II. "Gedächtnis-Distanz" (1936-1951)
    III. *Die Dämonen* (1951-1956)

I. "Die Dämonen der Ostmark" (1929-1936)

Most critics consider that Doderer conceived the idea for *Die Dämonen* in 1931, probably because he read Dostoevsky's novel, *The Possessed*, in that year, and it is assumed that it was this reading of the work of the Russian novelist that gave the impetus to his own novel. Doderer himself said over thirty years later, "Hier [in der Pfarrwiesengasse] begann ich, 1931, die 'Dämonen,' und zwar mit jenem Kapitel des ersten Teiles, das 'Topfenkuchen' heißt."[3] However, our examination of the genesis of the novel will indicate that this is an over-simplification of its initial stages and that almost two years of preparatory work preceded the writing of this chapter.

The beginnings of the work actually go back to 1929, when Doderer inserted the following advertisement in the columns of the *Neue Freie Presse:*

> Junger Doktor aus guter Familie, finanziell unabhängig, tadellose Erscheinung, sucht Anschluß an ca. 40 jährige distinguierte *israelitische Dame* (Wienerin) von nur sehr starker korpulenter größerer Figur und schwarzem Haar. Strengste Diskretion. Unter "Neue Jugend Nr. 47302" an das Ankündigungs-Büro des Blattes 47302.[4]

Doderer received ten replies to his curious advertisement[5] and in "Studien Va" he lists all ten of his correspondents in order of merit. Among them are:

> 1. Anita B., reizend aber nicht Typus.
> 4. Hermine Bergmann, eventuell brauchbar.
> 7. Rose Hartmann, böhmische Jüdin.

It is easy to see in this the embryonic form of Kajetan von Schlaggenberg's "Chronique Scandaleuse" in which he catalogues the statistics of the well-endowed females with whom he is obsessed. "Studien Va" has several sections of narrative headed "CS" ("Chronique Scandaleuse"), dealing with the replies of the "Dicke Damen" to the advertisement and with the correspondence which ensues with a certain Selma, "Die Frau von Gestern." However, in the "CS" sections of "Studien Va," it is not Schlaggenberg but René von Stangeler who is involved in the "Annoncen-Campagne." The following is the description of the scene in a café after René has picked up the replies to his newspaper advertisement:

> CS: Er vermochte kaum, die ganze Fülle, die ihm da aus dem Schalter herausspritzte, zu bändigen, in den Taschen zu verstauen. Beflügelten Schrittes eilte René in's nächste Caffeehaus und schüttelte die Beute neben sich auf die Polsterbank in der Nische, worin er sich zurückgezogen hatte...Die große Annoncen-Exposition lag ja hier in nächster Nähe und es wäre wenig wünschenswert gewesen, sich vom Herrn "Ober" erraten zu lassen.[6]

The chronology of the advertisement in the newspaper and the composition of the novel can leave no doubt in one's mind as to which of the following alternatives one should choose, and leads one to wonder if Doderer's statement was perhaps made with tongue in cheek:

> So hat sich auch Doderer eine Zeitlang durch Zeitungsinserate und auf andere

Weise die oft intime Bekanntschaft mit ungewöhnlich dicken Frauen zu verschaffen gewußt. Es bleibt eine Frage der Auslegung, ob Doderer hier Detailstudien betrieb, um die Marotte des Kajetan von Schlaggenberg genau beschreiben zu können, oder ob dem Kajetan hier nur ein Kapitel aus Doderers Biographie auferlegt worden ist. Sicherheitshalber fordert aber Doderer im Gespräch: "Verwechseln Sie doch nicht die Ansichten meiner Romanfiguren mit den meinen."[7]

It is quite clear that the "Dicke Damen" started out as a personal idiosyncrasy of Doderer and developed, by a happy coincidence, as the novel progressed, into a particularly apt illustration of his "second reality" and of his theory of the direct link between sexual aberration and political ideology. Thus the definition of the "Dicke-Damen-Intermezzo" as a "schonungslose Parodie aller Weltanschauungen"[8] is a *post factum* interpretation which, although correct, does not correspond to the author's original intentions for the episode.

It is not ascertainable when Schlaggenberg took over the role played here by René, but as both figures are *alter egos* of the author this substitution does not involve any significant changes in the structure of the novel. However, although these are embryonic stages in the novel's development, they do clearly indicate what is going to emerge as the main theme of the first part of the work. Schlaggenberg's fascination with older women of ample proportions will become a mania which distorts his view of the reality around him.

The novel really began to take shape in 1930, after the completion of *Der Fall Gütersloh* and *Das Geheimnis des Reichs*. In "Studien Va" we find, undated, under the heading "DD Programm," the following outline of the projected novel. "DD" is here the abbreviation for "Dicke Damen," although it is by chance also the abbreviation for the later title of the novel, *Die Dämonen*. The opening chapter of the work was to be "Rückblick auf eine große Liebe." Several other suggestions for possible chapter headings were noted, not all of which were used as the novel progressed, but some developed into chapters which remained substantially unchanged in the final version of the novel over a quarter of a century later. At this juncture the novel was conceived in two parts and a journal entry for 1 December 1930 indicated that he had almost completed the plan for it: "Ich stehe unmittelbar vor dem Abschluß der Composition DD."[9] Nine days later he was writing text for the novel and by the end of the month he was making satisfactory progress: "Wir haben in der Herbstsaison die Composition DD gewonnen, wie ich glaube, günstig... Mit Text DD sind wir soweit im Flusse."[10]

Personal problems now intervened and impeded progress on the novel. Doderer's relationship with his wife, Gusti, whom he married on 28 May 1930, after a long liaison, had become very acrimonious and deteriorated rapidly during the winter months of 1930-31:

Winter von 30 auf 31: Der Winter selbst verdarb zu Teil die "ewige" und unverbesserliche Complication in meiner Ehe. Die Leistung fiel dementsprechend minimal aus: *etwa hundert Seiten Text DD.*[11]

In the following year he broke off work on the novel to write the first version of *Ein Umweg*, which he composed between mid-June and September 1931.

After this break in the composition of the novel he experienced difficulty in resuming work on it:

> Noch immer halte ich nicht bei der Wiedereroberung von DD. Zwar ist mir diese Erzählung jetzt weit näher als vor 3 Wochen,...aber die Composition habe ich noch nicht wieder erfaßt.[12]

However, on 18 October 1931 he outlined a plan for the composition of the novel which remained more or less unchanged as the work developed. He listed eight chapters, which he termed "exponierende Kapitel":

1. Rückblick, etc.
2. Topfenkuchen
3. Der Freiherr von E [ulenfeld]
4. Ruthmayr
5. Der Winter*, etc.
6. Streitereien (3-teilig)
7. Concil
8. Des Frühlings Einzug
   *eventuell nach "Streitereien": Ein Winter mit Q. Fortsetzung.[13]

He still had the intention of writing a two-part novel and went on to say:

> Es gibt also zwei Teile:
> 1. Teil: Dicke Damen oder die große Chronique Scandaleuse—zerfällt in 8 exponierende Kapitel (etwa) 10 CS Kapitel
> 2. Teil: Die Frau von Gestern, oder das verwandelte Ziel—bringt die Durchführung aller in 1. vorgebauten erzählerischen Möglichkeiten.[14]

Despite this plan, however, the novel had not yet adopted a definitive form. In a letter of 3-4 June 1932 to Dr. Bergmann of Eugen Diederichs Verlag in Jena he spoke of his novel's being in a state of "Um- und Neubildung."[15] He described the work as "ein großer Zeitroman, der das sozusagen 'unterirdische' Werden eines neuen Deutschlands...in seiner Vorgeschichte gestalten will."[16] This is the first mention of a political content in the novel. The "Dicke Damen" theme merely illustrated one of Doderer's own sexual idiosyncrasies and did not yet have any political connotations.

Doderer now felt that his fortunes as a writer were at a very low ebb. He even contemplated taking up residence in Germany because he believed that he had no prospect of a successful career in Austria: "Was hab' ich in Wien? Kaum eine

Redaktion, kaum einen Verleger mehr. Fast alles jüdisch und daher jetzt zergehend wie Eis in der Hand."[17] Although 1933 also proved to be a period of low creativity,[18] due in part to emotional upheavals in his relationship with his wife, a relationship which ended in divorce in 1934, he continued to work on the novel. In 1933 Doderer joined the National Socialist Party which was proscribed by Chancellor Dollfuß in June of that year.

As yet there had been no mention of a title for the novel. Doderer had used "DD" and "CS" to refer to the work in its earliest stages, but now "Dicke Damen oder die große Chronique Scandaleuse" had become the title of the first part of the novel. However, on 20 March 1933 Doderer referred to the work as "Dämonen I,"[19] and on 19 July of the same year he mentioned "Die Dämonen der Ostmark,"[20] which was now established as the title of the novel. Although he had not added much new text to the novel in the preceding months, he felt that recognizable contours were emerging: "Der Gesamtballen 'Dämonen' löst sich rückwärts von dem vorliegenden Teil der Vergangenheit und vorwärts von dem nachklingenden Teil der Zukunft, wird rund und steigt."[21]

In 1934, while writing "Die Dämonen der Ostmark," Doderer was also working on the second version of *Ein Umweg.* This novel might be said to typify Doderer's lack of success in having his works published. He sent a copy of the first version to a publisher in Jena in 1932. They turned it down, as did the firm of Hesse & Becker the second version two years later. Doderer's dismay at this rejection was still felt twenty years later: "So deprimierte es mich 1934 außerordentlich, daß mein 'Umweg' von Hesse & Becker in Leipzig nicht akzeptiert wurde."[22]

In November 1934 the idea of an "Ouvertüre," with which to begin the novel, suggested itself:

> In der Tat gälte es nur, den Faden an einer beliebigen Stelle aus dem Geweb' des Lebens zu ziehen, und er liefe durchs Ganze, und in der nun breiteren offenen Bahn würden auch die anderen, sich ablösend, einzelweis sichtbar. (So will ich denn auch jene "Ouvertüre" zu den "Dämonen" angreifen.) Mit Scolander [Gütersloh] sprach ich einst darüber, daß ein Roman ganz auf diese Art müßte geschrieben werden. Denn im kleinsten Ausschnitte...[23]

Up to this point the novel began with the chapter "Rückblick auf eine große Liebe und auf die Mondsucht."

A document, three letters from Doderer to his friend Fritz Höpfner, which throws light on his plans for the continuation of the novel is his "Aide-mémoire zu 'Die Dämonen der Ostmark'."[24] Although Doderer did not carry into practice all the suggestions made in these letters, one must take account of them as representing an intermediate stage in the development of the novel. The letters are undated, but their contents suggest that they were written in 1934, a fact that is borne out by an entry in Doderer's "Notizheft 1953:" "DD Material. Aide mémoire 1934."[25] In the first letter Doderer summarizes the content of Part I of the novel. According to the second letter, this part now bears the title "Die roten Lichter," its earlier title, "Dicke Damen," being the title of the projected second part. In the second letter Doderer provides more specifics about certain chapters of Part I, particularly "Rückblick..." and "Die Entstehung einer Kolonie," in which he sees Schlaggenberg exaggerating his problematic relationship with his wife Camy and making out of his personal situation a form of ideology which he seeks to impose on others. In Part II Schlaggenberg's mania for fat females leads him into a Jewish milieu and the proposed content of Part II is of a very anti-Semitic nature. The burning of the Palace of Justice on 15 July 1927 puts an end to Schlaggenberg's erotic obsession. This is the end of Part II.

Doderer continues his second letter by touching on the contents of a projected third part of the novel and says that its main theme will be "die Zerlegung der Gesellschaft durch die Entscheidung jenes...Komplexes, den man gemeinhin mit dem Worte Judenfrage zu bezeichnen pflegt."[26] He goes on to suggest that the events of 15 July 1927 will act as a catalyst and consolidate the division of Viennese society into two racially opposed factions. Having already said that Part II of the novel will end on 15 July 1927, he now indicates that 1932 will mark the end of Part III.

The third letter continues with an account of the unappetizing situations into which Schlaggenberg is led by his neurotic obsession, and mentions a reception which Friederike Ruthmayr is going to give in April 1929. Although Friederike would appear to embody all the qualities demanded by Schlaggenberg's ideology, he nonetheless tries to interest her in René Stangeler. This is an opportunity to translate into reality his belief that mature women are the most suitable partners for those young men who have come through the hardships of World War I. To achieve this end Schlaggenberg resolves to break up Stangeler's relationship with Grete Siebenschein, a Jewess.

The last few pages of the "Aide-mémoire" deal briefly with the potential development of the various plots and subplots in the novel and relationships are created along racial lines. For example, Angelika Trapp gives up the historian Neuberg, a Jew, and becomes engaged to the toilet-paper manufacturer Dulnik. By so doing she shows clearly "daß sie eine solide Versorgung innerhalb der eigenen Kreise dem romantischen und anstrengenden Überhüpfen einer gott-gewollten Rassenkluft, gut bürgerlich, vorzieht."[27] Schlaggenberg and his es-tranged wife Camy are briefly reconciled, then irrevocably parted. The last chapter of the novel is entitled "Schlaggenberg's Wiederkehr."

The tone of strident anti-Semitism which permeates the "Aide-mémoire" grates on the reader and tends to obscure the deep-seated problems which

Doderer's projected plan for the novel reveals. The first difficulty is the temporal structure envisaged in such a plan. Part I of the novel covers a period of only a few months, from November 1926 until May 1927. Part II will cover an equally brief period, the summer of 1927. Part III, however, is intended to cover a period of five years, a fact that causes one to wonder how Doderer would have dealt with such an extended temporal framework within the compass of the novel form, given the fact that Part I will itself eventually consist of over 700 typed pages. In addition, by extending the action of the novel to 1932 he is making its content almost contemporaneous with his own personal situation, and thus eliminating the possibility of the narrator's reflecting upon the political content of the work.

In the first half of 1935 Doderer wrote the "Ouvertüre," which he later described as "für das Schicksal des ganzen Buches entscheidend."[28] It must have been at this time that he decided to use Geyrenhoff's chronicle with its first-person narrator as the basic narrative mode of the novel. It appears that the earlier versions of the novel were narrated by the author himself: " 'Vieles hinter sich lassend,' so tritt der Held meiner 'Dicken Damen' in den zweiten Teil seines Romans."[29] The novel started out as the account of Stangeler's attempt to make the acquaintance of fat females through his insertion of advertisements in newspapers. This role was then assigned to Schlaggenberg and he is the hero referred to here. The introduction of Geyrenhoff as the narrator serves two purposes. The fiction of his chronicle gives the novel a recognizable form and as a figural narrator he stands between the author and his narrative.[30] That Geyrenhoff was a later addition to the novel might explain the omission of his name from the "Namenverzeichnis," a list of the *personae* of the novel which was drawn up at about the same time as the "Aide-mémoire,"[31] and might also account for the word "Autor" in the following list of characters drawn up on 16 September 1932:

> DD I, 8 Grande Szene
> Personage
>
> 1. Schlaggenberg
> 2. Quapp
> 3. Stangeler
> 4. Eulenfeld
> 5. Faddy
> 6. Glöckner
> 7. Neuberg
> 8. Holder
> 9. Autor
> 10. Höpfner[32]

Although the idea of the "Ouvertüre" seemed to be a solution to the problem of

giving the novel a coherent structure, Doderer did not find the introduction of the
first-person narrator to be without difficulty. He said of the novel that it

> ...birgt immer noch Formprobleme, die mich mitunter auf's äußerste mit Unruhe
> erfüllen. Die Verschmelzung (Verzahnung) der IE [Ich-Erzählung] mit dem
> "objektiven" Bericht ist zwar durch die Ouvertüre erst ermöglicht worden, erfor-
> dert aber weiterhin den ganzen Takt des Erzählers.[33]

The introduction of the first-person narrator also involved the reworking of
those chapters which he had written up to this point. Nonetheless, he appeared
confident of producing Part I of the novel within a short period of time: "Und
dazu noch die 'Dämonen,' deren *erster* Teil bereits in einigen Wochen fertig
vorliegen wird."[34]

In June 1935 he reworked chapters two and three, "Rückblick...," and "Alle
Wege führen nach Düsseldorf," in accordance with the changed narrative form of
the novel. He experienced problems with the conclusion of chapter three, but
seemed convinced that his new approach to the novel would result in an improve-
ment on the earlier version of the chapter.

The first mention of Geyrenhoff by name occurred on 1 July 1935 and on 15
July Doderer noted "Von D liegen mit heutigem Tage die ersten 8 Kapitel
definitiv (bis inclusive S. 268 im Manuscript). Ich bearbeite heute noch das 8.
Kapitel ('Streitereien')."[35]

In the second half of 1935 Doderer continued to make alterations to the novel,
interpolating as many as ten pages on occasion, so as to remodel it in accordance
with the plan set down in the "Ouvertüre." On 12 December 1935 he read aloud
before a gathering of friends the "Ouvertüre" and chapter thirteen of the novel,
"Die Allianz." In his introductory remarks to this reading, "Vor-Rede zu einer
literarischen Abend-Unterhaltung," he made reference to the political events of
the previous four years and said that they were relevant to the main theme of the
social novel he was engaged in writing. The type of novel which he wished to
create must have as its prime function the representation of life in its entirety,
and "diese Totalität [muß] auch in irgendeiner Weise aus jedem einzelnen
Splitter uns anhauchen und erahnt werden können, sei's im Schweren, sei's im
Leichten."[36] These remarks clearly indicate that Doderer's thoughts were turning
toward the idea of the "total novel," a concept he repeatedly treated in the coming
years.

In the middle of January 1936 Doderer finished revising the chapters written
before the composition of the "Ouvertüre." He had been obliged to rewrite those
chapters "deren alte Fassung sich als völlig unbrauchbar erwies, und die darum
jetzt auch ein Vielfaches an Umfang haben."[37] He had not been composing new
material and so the novel itself appeared at a standstill. But he felt that he now
had a clearer idea of the form and content of the novel and "hätte ich mir

gestattet, weiterzuschreiben, ehe ich diese Ordnung hinter mir hergestellt: es wäre zu ihr vielleicht nicht mehr gekommen."[38] There remained only one chapter of Part I to be written, "Der Eintopf." He began writing it in January 1936 and completed it, and along with it Part I of the novel, on 18 June 1936. The titles of these seventeen chapters are: 1. Ouvertüre 2. Rückblick auf eine große Liebe und auf die Mondsucht 3. Alle Wege führen nach Düsseldorf 4. Topfenkuchen 5. Friederike Ruthmayr 6. Der große Nebelfleck oder Vorbei an Friederike Ruthmayr 7. Ein Winter mit Quapp 8. Streitereien 9. Die Entstehung einer Kolonie 10. Ein entzückendes Konzil 11. Der Herr Kammer-Rat 12. Bei den Unsrigen 13. Die Allianz 14. Die Sache mit Altschul 15. Literarische Unterhaltungen 16. Wieder daheim 17. Der Eintopf.

Our study of the genesis of "Die Dämonen der Ostmark" reveals that the form of the novel underwent considerable modification during the course of its development, not all the stages of which can be documented, because the manuscript of these earlier stages is not in Doderer's Nachlaß, and may well have been destroyed by him. The work started out as an impersonally narrated account of Schlaggenberg's fixation with fat ladies, a theme intimately related to an idiosyncrasy of the author. Also of major significance was Schlaggenberg's relationship with his Jewish wife, and the related idea of the division of Viennese society into Jew and Aryan, the "Wasserscheide" theme as Doderer called it. With the composition of the "Ouvertüre" in 1935 Geyrenhoff was introduced as the first-person narrator. In 1936 this new orientation of the novel seemed a successful stratagem and Doderer did not appear to doubt his ability to continue with the novel along the lines established in Part I.

II. "Gedächtnis-Distanz" (1936-1951)

I have chosen this expression, coined by Doderer,[39] to describe the interim between "Die Dämonen der Ostmark" and Die Dämonen because it sums up very succinctly the prime function of these fifteen years. This period of enforced gestation, created partially by his own inability to complete the novel and partially by external circumstances, allowed him to stand back from the work to determine the method that would enable him to continue it.

After the completion of Part I in June 1936 Doderer immediately started on Part II by collecting material relevant to the events of 15 July 1927. On 25 June 1936 he noted: "Es kann die Aufgabe hier nicht darin liegen, um die Feststellung eines bestimmten Verlauf's, also um Tatsachen zu ringen...Manches Anekdotische ist mehr wert, z.B. 'das verwüstete Junggesellenheim eines jungen Doktors der Philosophie.'"[40] This remark is indicative of his view of history and politics.

He is concerned with the lives of individual characters caught up in the historical process, not with the interpretation of historical events. He decided to use as his sources three newspapers: the *Neue Freie Presse*, the *Arbeiter-Zeitung* and the *Reichspost*. He hoped that by consulting the editions for July 1927 he would be able to check on the veracity of their reports, all of which might be colored by their political affiliations.

On 30 June 1936 Doderer jotted down some preliminary notes for Part II of "Die Dämonen der Ostmark" and the next few pages of the "Commentarii 1935/36" contain notes about the weather in July 1927 and about the Schattendorf shootings on 30 January 1927. There is also an eye-witness account of the burning of the Palace of Justice, as seen from the window of an apartment on the Schmerlingplatz. Doderer's source was his friend, Gaby Murad, on whom the character of Renate von Gürtzner-Gontard in the novel was based. It was her father who actually was a spectator of these events. Doderer used the substance of this report when he wrote the chapter "Das Feuer" in 1955.

A letter of 21 July 1936 to Gerhard A.[41] throws some light on Doderer's motives for writing *Die Dämonen*. Gerhard A. had asked Doderer for biographical data, perhaps in order to write an article about him, and Doderer gives this information in the first part of the letter. He then goes on to reflect bitterly on the role of Jews in Viennese society and on the immense influence which he considers they are able to exert in politics, commerce, and the arts. He claims that he started writing *Die Dämonen* toward the end of 1930 because: "Ich hatte unzweideutig erkannt—aus einer außerordentlichen Fülle privater, gesellschaftlicher und beruflicher Erfahrungen—daß dem Judentume in Österreich und besonders in Wien bei Entscheidungen, deren Heran-Nahen man damals schon fühlte, eine geradezu überwältigende Bedeutung werde zukommen müssen."[42] He asserts that his novel will make his readers aware of the fact that the seam holding together the fabric of Viennese society is being steadily torn apart, resulting in the formation of Semitic and non-Semitic factions. This is the theme referred to by Doderer as the "Wasserscheide." He states that for the last three years it has been his intention to have his novel end in 1932, the year before Hitler's accession to power in Germany. The novel is to be a two-part work, the second part concerned with the political situation in Austria in the 1920s and the early 1930s. Particularly important are the collapse of the major banks in 1930 and 1931 and "jene marxistischen Gärungen die im Juli des Jahres 1927 ihren blutigen Ausbruch fanden."[43]

He considers the significance of his novel to lie in the fact that, as he claims, this is the first time that a non-Jewish author has undertaken to treat the situation of the Jews in Austria. Those who have already done so, Schnitzler and Wassermann, for example, were themselves Jewish. He has chosen to illustrate his thesis of "pernicious" and all-pervasive Jewish influence on Viennese social life at three different levels in society; in family life, in the newspaper world, and in the commercial sphere, particularly in banking circles.

Doderer closes his letter by saying that he intends to devote the next year of his life to Part II of *Die Dämonen*, but wishes that there were a greater distance between him and the events which he is portraying in the novel, so that this work could be accepted for what it really is, a historical novel.[44] His wish to distance himself from the era in which his novel is set was destined to be fulfilled, although not in circumstances of his choosing. Almost thirty years would separate the events of 1927 from their narration in the novel of the 1950s.

On 31 July 1936 Doderer arrived in Munich and took up residence in a studio found for him in Dachau by his friend, Gaby Murad. His move to Germany may have been dictated by two factors: the feeling that his talents were not recognized in Austria,[45] and the fact that as an unsuccessful independent writer he was living in an impoverished condition and was unwilling to accept financial support from his father. However, his mother had some German funds which could only be drawn upon within Germany and these would be available to him in Munich. Thirty years later Doderer said that he went to Germany in search of a publisher.[46]

On arrival in Munich he decided to suspend work on *Die Dämonen* and to take up instead *Ein Mord, den jeder begeht*. He later offered as a reason for his not finishing *Die Dämonen* the fact that he discontinued work on it to write *Ein Umweg* and *Ein Mord...*, but the real reasons were considerably more complex. Despite stating his intention of working on *Ein Mord...* he did not immediately do so. Instead, on 3 September 1936, he resumed work on "Divertimento VII," later titled *Das letzte Abenteuer*, the idea for which was conceived in 1917 and on which he worked in 1923. His work for the next two years, as noted on 14 September 1936, was as follows:[47]

3 Divertimenti (VII, VIII, IX und eventuell weitere, nebst Variationen)	200 Seiten
"Ein Mord, den Jeder begeht"	300 Seiten
"Dämonen," *zweiter* Band	700 Seiten
	1200 Seiten

Doderer's friend, Rudolf Haybach, who had published some of his earlier works, put him in touch with the Munich publishing firm of C.H. Beck. Doderer gave Beck the manuscript of "Die Dämonen der Ostmark"[48] but then chose not to publish the novel. A compelling reason for his reluctance to publish may have been the growing realization of his inability to continue with the novel at that time. Premature publication of Part I might have resulted in the work's remaining incomplete.

Doderer's plan for the continuation sustains this thesis. In an entry of 25 November 1936[49] we find a draft of a rather strange scene between Schlaggenberg and his estranged wife, Camy, which seems to suggest that she, a Jewess, has become assimilated into Aryan society. Doderer describes this encounter as an "apokalyptische Szene,...die den letzten Band von 'Die Dämonen der Ostmark' schließt."[50] He now thinks in terms of a five-part novel, each part moving forward in time:

1. Der Eintopf [ends May 1927]
2. An der Wasserscheide [will end in 1932]
3. Nach dem Siege (Österreich Februar 1933 bis Juli 1934)
4. Ein Maskenball (Österreich Juli 1934 - bis etwa 1936)
5. Die Heimkehr oder "Im Spital, zum deutschen Geist" (spielt im Reich 1936)[51]

Doderer was moving back to his original intention of illustrating the emergence of a new Germany, a plan that had been superseded by the idea of portraying Austria, where the *status quo* was menaced by Judaism within and communism without. However, this expansion in the spatial content of the novel was not so vital as the extension of the temporal framework and its implications for the eventual dimensions of the work. Had Doderer treated the last three parts of his novel in similar fashion to the first two parts ("Der Eintopf" consisted of over 700 typescript pages and he projected another 700 for "An der Wasserscheide"), the work would have assumed Proustian and possibly unmanageable proportions. In addition to this problematic chronological structure, Doderer also intended to make the action of the last segment of the novel contemporaneous with the time when the novel was written. This intention was to present increasing problems as Doderer moved away from, and eventually rejected, National Socialism.

Another factor which undoubtedly contributed to Doderer's inability to complete the second part of "Die Dämonen der Ostmark" in the time he had projected was the composition of *Ein Mord, den jeder begeht*. He started work on this novel in the spring of 1937 and completed it on 17 May 1938. He was under constant pressure while writing it because he had a deadline to meet. His concentration on the smaller novel meant that, for all practical purposes, "Die Dämonen der Ostmark" had to be shelved.

At the end of August 1938 Doderer returned to Vienna. At the time of the Anschluß on 13 March 1938 he had resigned his membership of the NSDAP and his disillusionment with fascist politics led him to adopt not just an apolitical but an anti-political stance. The shattering of his political ideals was clearly a key factor in the stagnation of "Die Dämonen."

But in January 1939 he was working on the eighteenth chapter of the novel,

"Auf offener Strecke." The following month his publishers sent him a contract for *Die Dämonen* asking him to fill in a deadline. In his letter of 17 February 1939 to Dr. Heinrich Beck Doderer wrote that he first thought of spring 1940 as a possible date for completion but had chosen the date of November 1940 instead. Although he mentioned having sketches and material for the novel he faced the daunting prospect of writing 700 pages of narrative in less than two years. When one considers that he had spent six years on the composition of the first part of the novel, also 700 pages in length, one becomes aware of the enormity of his task. Doderer seemed to realize, however, that distancing himself from the events which formed the content of his novel could only be of benefit both to the form of his literary creation and to his perspective as its author:

> Evident ist mir heute dieses Eine: hätte ich nicht "Ein Umweg" und "Ein Mord" zwischendurch geschrieben, dann wäre der Roman "Die Dämonen" heute längst fertig—und endgültig gescheitert...Die Prüfung der Festigkeit einer bereits histori-schen Distanz von jenen Räumen, in welchen meine Figuren sich bewegen, belehrt mich in einem darüber, daß diese Distanz heute zulänglich ist, damals unzulänglich war: was den Zusammenbruch meines Baues zur notwendigen Folge hätte haben müssen.[52]

Doderer's figural narrator, Geyrenhoff, stood too close to the events he was chronicling and Doderer himself did not possess sufficient "Gedächtnis-Distanz" to be able to evaluate the social and political climate in which his novel was set.

In March 1939 Doderer reread the manuscript of the first part of the novel and the "Aide-mémoire" and noted certain remarks about the contents and projected changes in several chapters.[53] The proposed changes were not very extensive, but what is interesting is the fact that he could see possible links between the themes already present or hinted at in the first part ("DD" and "Wasserscheide") and the new theme which he was proposing for the second part.[54] He was starting to elaborate on this theme, to which he referred as "Genf," in his diary. By this term he meant his belief that any form of doctrinaire thought, whether of religious or political nature, could lead to the establishment of a spurious system of values, a state which Doderer considered to be a form of surrogate reality.

In the winter of 1939-40 Doderer converted to Catholicism. No matter how one views his conversion, whether as an act of defiance in Nazi Austria, or a form of cathartic process in his rejection of fascism, or as a deeply felt personal need, it had the effect of giving him a form of metaphysical support in his anti-political, anti-ideological frame of mind. God created the universe: man's attempts to change it are a rejection of the Divine Being. He stated this view explicitly on 13 December 1939: "Das heißt, wir können Gott nur lieben, indem wir die Apper-ception des Lebens nicht verweigern."[55] Doderer had not yet become acquainted with the writings of St. Thomas Aquinas, but he would find in the doctrine of the *analogia entis* support for his theory of the intrinsic goodness of reality, a goodness which is not perceived by those misguided beings who seek to change reality in accordance with their own obsessions. Man's refusal to accept God-given reality can result only in the creation of a less perfect reality, a "geminderte Wirklichkeit."[56] Doderer did not yet employ the term "second reality," but this was the logical development from his elaboration on the idea of an impaired reality. The individual controlled by his obsession or ideology refuses to perceive the reality around him and creates instead a surrogate reality. Breaking free from his obsessive thinking also enables him to escape from his "second reality."

While Doderer was attempting to grapple with the consequences of his political *volte face*, the novel itself remained at a standstill. But in July 1939 he began theorizing on a possible form for the work. He was now of the opinion that what he termed a "total chronicle" was the ideal form for the novel.[57] He continued to reflect on the problems which he faced and in January 1940 he undertook a complete examination of the novel as it stood and of its potential future development. He realized that the form of the novel had been dictated by its thematic content, "Dicke Dämen" and "Wasserscheide," but now felt that this method of approach to the novel had proved unfruitful and should be discarded: "Hier ist nun der Punkt, an welchem ich einsehe, daß ein Roman auf 'thematische' Art und Weise überhaupt nicht entstehen kann."[58] Using the characters and situations already present in the novel, he now aimed to write "einen neuen Roman im totalen Sinne."[59] A major obstacle to continuation of work on the novel was the fact that his rejection of the "Wasserscheide" theme effectively cancelled his plan for Part II and undermined the importance of characters such as Schlaggenberg. The only escape from this depressing situation seemed to be offered by the "total novel": "Über dieser ganzen Katastrophe aber erlischt mir nicht mein Stern neuer totaler Prosa, und wenn ich ihn nur sehe, der dem zweiten Himmel meines Lebens angehört, wird sich ein Weg aus dieser Wirrnis und diesem Trümmerhaufen finden."[60] Moreover, a "total novel" would not prevent him from using Geyrenhoff as narrator. All that would be required would be to broaden the scope of Geyrenhoff's chronicle and make it more representative of the totality of life: "Die Entthronung des Themas 'Wasserscheide' hindert nicht—so erkannte ich heute—diesen Einfall des Sektionsrates als Nährboden eines totalen Romans für möglich zu halten. Man müßte nur in diesem Netze mehr—nämlich das Leben telle qu'elle est—fangen wollen."[61]

Doderer's interest in the "total novel" was probably stimulated by Gütersloh. In 1935 the latter started work on what has been described as his *Summa*, the novel *Sonne und Mond*. He did not complete the work until 1962, but Doderer was certainly cognizant of its development.[62] In the novel itself Gütersloh describes the work as a universal chronicle, and this aspect of the "total novel" seems to be the most attractive to Doderer as he seeks a literary form which will enable him to continue with the composition of "Die Dämonen der Ostmark." However, it should not be surprising that Doderer's attraction to the "total novel" in the sense in which it was propounded by Gütersloh was of relatively short duration. Implicit in Gütersloh's conception of the genre is a formlessness, a principle which is at variance with Doderer's strongly held views on the primacy of formal considerations in the creation of a work of literature. By 1945 Doderer was starting to question the suitability of the "total novel" as a vehicle for his literary expression, precisely on formal grounds: "Wenn er [Gütersloh] beinahe ohne Komposition doch immer noch erzählt, muß ich trotz der Komposition immer wieder improvisieren."[63] By the following year he was expressing more clearly the fact that the idea of the "total novel" had been attractive to him, but that this attraction was short-lived and occasioned by external circumstance:

> Die Theorie vom totalen Roman war für meinen Horizont sehr erweiternd; aber sie blieb als fruchtbare Anwendung verknüpft mit einer Zeit, während welcher ich umgetrieben leben mußte,...mit meinen Notizen und Journalen nistend und jederzeit bereit und gewärtig, wieder abbrechen zu müssen.[64]

Intrinsically he could not reconcile himself to a mode of expression totally liberated from the constraints of form. A later section of the diary entry just cited mentions the fact that he is preparing to make a sketch to plan the composition of *Die Strudlhofstiege*: "Kurz vor meiner Abreise nach Wien hab' ich schon ein Reißbrett bespannt gehabt, um eine Kompositionszeichnung zu machen!"[65]

In later years Doderer said that he greatly admired "das ständige Brandungsgeräusch der Totalität des Lebens" which Gütersloh was able to convey in *Sonne und Mond*,[66] and it was this effect that he wished to achieve in his own work. Where he differed from Gütersloh was in his view of *how* the novelist should transfer the raw material of human existence into an aesthetic form. Weber's description of *Die Dämonen* as "komponierte Kompositionslosigkeit"[67] best sums up how Doderer adapted Gütersloh's "total novel" to suit his own artistic purposes. Perhaps the most important contribution made by the idea of the "total novel" was the fact that by seeming to offer Doderer a way out of the *impasse* his novel had apparently reached in 1936 it sustained his faith in his ability to complete the work despite the passage of time and despite fundamental changes in its form and content.

Between 15 February and 2 May 1940 Doderer wrote the eighteenth chapter of the novel, "Auf offener Strecke." Chronologically this chapter picks up where chapter seventeen left off, but its contents indicate how Doderer's political views have changed and also are evidence of his desire to make his novel embrace a wider range of character and situation. The character of Gürtzner-Gontard is introduced, and he expounds a view of the human situation which parallels Doderer's own changed political thinking and marks his transition from the partisan politics of National Socialism to an anti-political stance. Gontard also supplies a significant amount of information about the Stangeler family, which leads one to suppose that it is Doderer's intention to give them a prominent place in the novel.

Before leaving for his visit to Gürtzner-Gontard, Geyrenhoff reads a letter which he has received from Camy von Schlaggenberg, Kajetan's estranged wife. She is now living in London, in the home of Mrs. Libesny, who is herself Viennese. Although the fact is not emphasized at this point, Doderer is here extending the scope of the work, making it more of a "total novel." The Anglo-Viennese relationship is destined to play a significant role as the novel unfolds and will involve a considerable number of important characters.

At this point World War II interrupted Doderer's work on the novel. With his conscription into the Luftwaffe in April 1940 the novel disappeared into his diary.[68] This is a reversal of the usual relationship between his diaries and his creative writings. The function of the diary is normally to supply the raw material for the literary work. It may serve a critical function, but this, in Doderer's eyes, is not its prime task. He reproached Gütersloh with failing to recognize the role which his diaries play for him: "Er vergißt nur die Funktion meiner Tagebücher als Mutterkuchen, Placenta, und daß sie entleert zurückbleiben. Mein Weg geht vom explicite zum implicite, nicht umgekehrt."[69]

The fact that Doderer's opportunities to work on the novel were greatly curtailed during the war years was not the sole reason for his consigning the nascent second part of the novel to his diary. If this were the case, one would wonder how he then found the time to complete a major portion of a new work, *Die Strudlhofstiege*. Although the idea of the "total novel" had seemed to be the panacea for which he had been searching, it did not really solve the more practical problems which he faced. How was he to reconcile his approbatory attitude toward the emergence of a fascist regime in Germany and his tacit approval of some of the anti-Semitic opinions expressed by certain of the novel's characters with his new anti-political, anti-ideological stance? Could he succeed in doing this without discarding the entire 700 pages of "Die Dämonen der Ostmark?" He was also concerned about the narrative mode of the novel, as he felt that the perspective of the first-person narrator, Geyrenhoff, was too limited. Yet another disturbing feature was the close temporal proximity of the narrator, and of the author himself, to the events being chronicled.

During the years 1940 to 1944 Doderer continued to reflect on these problems, collecting his thoughts in his diary under the title "Die Epiloge des Sektionsrates Geyrenhoff."[70] He intended this to be the nineteenth chapter of the novel and referred to it as a fragment of a "total novel." If formlessness is a criterion of a "total novel" then this material is truly representative of the genre. These pages contain two cycles of poems, extracts from the novel *Das Geheimnis des Reichs*, a formulation of Doderer's theory of the novel, particularly with respect to the importance of the role of memory for the literary artist, an analysis of the character of René Stangeler, himself an *alter ego* of the author—the list of disparate elements is a long one.[71] Despite his reaffirmation of these pages as potential novel material, they eventually became part of his diary: "Sollte dies ein Tagebuch werden? Nein, es ist ein auf sein Mindestmaß an Ausbreitung reduzierter Romantext."[72]

What is most significant for the future development of the novel is Doderer's assessment of Geyrenhoff's function as narrator. He had considered that the interpolation of a figural narrator between the author and his text lent a certain objectivity to the narration: "Auch sein Autor hat den Sektionsrat delegiert und sich auf diese Weise vor einem ihm noch zu nahen Sachverhalte zurückgezogen."[73] However, with the passage of time he no longer felt the need for this form of counterpoise, for this "seltsamste Durchdringung zwischen einer Person und einer Fiktion, diese Reservation des Objektiven mitten in einer aus den Angeln gehängten Erzählung."[74] The author himself would now narrate *in propria persona*, but would preserve the fiction of Geyrenhoff's chronicle by allowing him on occasion to become the narrative voice.

Although this reflection on the novel seemed to have cleared up the problem of the narrative mode and although the idea of the "total novel" had suggested a means of escape from the circumscribed content of "Die Dämonen der Ostmark," Doderer did not yet seem to have any fixed idea as to how he would resume work on the novel. He still rejected the idea of a radical modification of "Die Dämonen der Ostmark," but wondered if an approach to this material from another angle might have a cathartic effect and allow him to redeem those aspects of the content which were now distasteful to him. He felt that there were two possibilities which might facilitate this approach. The first was that he should introduce an episode which occurred before the events recounted in Geyrenhoff's chronicle. Such an episode might concern Stangeler's elder sister, Etelka Grauermann. Mention had been made of her in the chapter "Auf offener Strecke," when Gontard asked Geyrenhoff if he was acquainted with the Stangeler family, in particular with Etelka Grauermann:

> "Ja," sagte ich, "freilich, die Etelka Stangeler, die hat doch den Pista Grauermann geheiratet. Sie ist viel älter als der René."
> "Merkwürdig, daß man ihr schon als Kind einen ungarischen Namen gegeben hat," bemerkte er, "später hat sie dazu noch einen Ungarn geheiratet und heute lebt sie in Budapest."[75]

But in the time between writing "Auf offener Strecke," mentioning in the

"Epilog" the possibility of including Etelka in a more major role in the novel, and actually writing new material for the work in 1951, Doderer wrote *Die Strudlhofstiege*. This novel climaxes in the twin catastrophes of Etelka's suicide, based factually on the suicide of Doderer's elder sister, Helga, in Budapest on 17 January 1927, and Mary K.'s loss of her right leg in a traffic accident. Both fictional events take place in September 1925. Thus, although for over a year Doderer considered using Etelka's tragedy as a point of departure for resumption of work on *Die Dämonen* and having her suicide coincide with the swift upturn in René's fortunes,[76] he was forced eventually to discard this idea because of the changes in the fictional circumstances brought about by the events of *Die Strudlhofstiege*.

Doderer did not go into any detail about the second possibility which he considered might offer an avenue of approach to the novel. He suggested that it might be connected to the plot involving Quapp's inheritance, a suggestion which could foreshadow the introduction of Alois Gach, who helps reveal Levielle's duplicity by telling Geyrenhoff of Ruthmayr's battlefield will. This, however, is a hypothesis, with no concrete data to sustain it.

While *Die Dämonen* lay dormant in his diaries during the war years *Die Strudlhofstiege* continued to take shape. The relationship of the two novels raised yet another problem for Doderer. He had decided to introduce into *Die Dämonen* the character of Mary K., whose traumatic accident occurred in September 1925. This meant that there would be a rather lengthy break in the chronology of the two novels, *Die Strudlhofstiege* and *Die Dämonen*, as the events of Geyrenhoff's chronicle did not begin until November 1927. Doderer solved this problem by having *Die Strudlhofstiege* continue on until the day in late fall 1925 when Melzer married Thea Rokitzer and by interpolating the chapter "Draußen am Rande" after the "Ouvertüre" in *Die Dämonen*.[77] The action in this new chapter takes place in the summer of 1926 and there is also a flashback to events which took place in October 1925.

Doderer finished writing *Die Strudlhofstiege* on 9 June 1948. A letter of this period to his sister, Astri von Stummer, reveals strong feelings of dissatisfaction, yet at the same time expresses confidence that he will succeed in finishing *Die Dämonen*:

> Hab' doch einiges leisten können im Leben, die 1000 Seiten "Strudlhofstiege" von 1946-48, den "Mord," den "Umweg," den "Zihal," aber nichts hat's mir genützt in diesem Lande hier, nicht einmal ein Kripperl findet sich für mich...Ich bin schon fast verbittert. Dabei fühl' ich außerordentliche Kräfte und eine große geistige Zukunft...Die "Dämonen" fertig zu machen und mein großes Wörterbuch ["Repertorium"] wär' allein für Einen genug.[78]

In 1948 he worked on the first version of "Sexualität und totaler Staat" and embarked on a course of study at the Institut für Österreichische Geschichtsforschung. He looked on this study as a form of mental preparation for resuming work on *Die Dämonen*:

> Ich leb' in einer Schinderei; es deprimiert mich; aber doch nützt es mir enorm, vor den "Dämonen" noch einmal intellektuell und disziplinär durchgewalkt zu werden....Ein Jahr noch, kaum mehr soviel, eigentlich, nur ein Dreivierteljahr.[79]

In October 1949 Doderer's precarious financial position was slightly improved when C.H. Beck offered him the position of reader. This was a position he continued to hold even after he achieved success with his writings and financial problems were no longer pressing.

Between the end of January 1951 and mid-April 1951 Doderer wrote *Die Posaunen von Jericho* and between 21 April and 26 October of the same year he worked on the second version of "Sexualität und totaler Staat." He was trying to come to terms with his Nazi past, which he described as a "Dummheit," as a "pseudological misadventure." He made no attempt to deny his fascist sympathies in the 1930s or to try to excuse his behavior, but one wonders if his explanation of his actions in Thomist terminology is completely convincing. He considered his political aberration as a rejection of the *analogia entis*, as "Apperzeptions-Verweigerung." However, the fact that Doderer could rationalize his behavior in this fashion, whatever the weaknesses in his argument, seemed to free him from the constraints imposed on him psychologically by his guilt-complex and allowed him to resume work on *Die Dämonen*.

Although only one chapter was added to the novel between 1936 and 1951, these fifteen years were of crucial importance for the development of the novel in its final form. This lapse of time allowed Doderer to distance himself from his literary creation and to reflect on both the political content of the novel and on his own political shortcomings. There was a complete shift in emphasis in the content of the novel. "Die Dämonen der Ostmark" had a strong thematic content, overtly political in nature. Doderer now rejected completely the "Wasserscheide" theme and his intention was to write a novel, which, in its attack on any form of ideology, he clearly wished to be quite unambiguously anti-political. Gütersloh's idea of a "total novel" also exerted an influence on Doderer during these years and suggested to him new dimensions for his novel. However, unlike Gütersloh, he was unwilling to attempt to mediate the totality of existence in the work of literature without the aesthetic refinement of a clearly-established form. Doderer's decision that the author himself should take over the narration from the first-person narrator, Geyrenhoff, also had far-reaching implications for the form and content of the novel. The omniscient narrator is not subject to the temporal and spatial limitations of the figural narrator and can therefore encompass the totality of life, not just a narrow segment of society.

Die Strudlhofstiege had demonstrated to Doderer that he was capable, despite the vagaries of fate, of creating a work of literature. His research at the Institut für Österreichische Geschichtsforschung had strengthened his intellectual resolve. His Thomist philosophizing had clarified his misgivings about a dubious political past. Conditions seemed at last to be favorable for resumption of work on the novel.

III. *Die Dämonen* (1951-1956)

Doderer resumed work on "Die Dämonen der Ostmark," to which he now referred as D I, on 17 April 1951, by subjecting these seventeen chapters to a thorough review.[80] His notes clearly indicate that it was not his intention to make any radical changes to this material. With respect to the "Ouvertüre" he said that it could remain as it was, but that it could accommodate additions in order to make it an exposition of the entire novel. However, when he reworked Part I of the novel in 1956, the "Ouvertüre" remained unchanged and is, in essence, a rather limited exposition of Geyrenhoff's chronicle.[81]

Doderer finished his review on 8 August 1951 and on 24 August he jotted down some ideas for Part II of the novel. The main theme of the novel was now going to be the "second reality." Doderer's main concern, to illustrate how damaging to the individual and to society any form of obsessive thinking can be, compelled him to make this issue the central theme of the novel, despite the fact that the "total novel" is by definition athematic,[82] and despite his own previous quite unequivocal statement that his novel could not be constructed on a thematic basis.

While working on projected ideas for Part II and carrying out the review of Part I, Doderer was also concerned with the practical implications of illustrating the theme of the "second reality." As a counterbalance to the group, "Die Unsrigen," who were living in a "second reality," Doderer had decided to introduce a new set of characters, who, in his eyes, possessed a much healthier attitude to reality. Such positive characters he termed "Genies in Latenz,"[83] among them being Melzer, whose self-realization was the main theme of *Die Strudlhofstiege*. He actually wrote a section on Melzer in the chapter "Draußen am Rande," but expunged it shortly afterwards. Another exemplary character was Mary K., whose triumph over personal disaster singled her out as an individual worthy of emulation and admiration.

When Doderer composed the first new text for Part I on 21 October 1951, he introduced to this chapter, "Draußen am Rande," two hitherto unmentioned characters, Dwight Williams and Emma Drobil, as protagonists of the "ideologically uninfected" group. As strangers to Vienna they are not affected by the evils of anti-Semitism or radicalism. These two characters were of tremendous importance to Doderer, for with them he seemed to have found the means of access to his novel: "Von Drobil und Dwight aus trete ich in den Roman ein, ich weiß es heute."[84] These two characters are on the periphery of the main action of the novel, as the title of the chapter itself suggests. They move in the orbit of the central characters, but they do not determine their course of action. The technique of adopting a peripheral approach to the novel is one which became increasingly important to Doderer.

Doderer finished work on "Draußen am Rande" on 12 December 1951, and did not write any material for Part II until 19 April 1952. This chapter, "Am anderen Ufer," contains one of the focal points of the novel. Leonhard Kakabsa is a young worker who has been studying Latin. His aim in doing so was not to change his station in life, but rather to achieve self-realization. When he breaks through the "dialect barrier" (p. 532) he affects a change in his social position. For him the "Grenzen der Sprache" are the "Grenzen des Seins" (p. 570) and they can be broken down and self-realization achieved without seeking to impose a change on the rest of society, as is the aim of the revolutionary. Kakabsa was, in Doderer's eyes, the anti-revolutionary figure par excellence and embodied his conservative world-view.

In the course of 1952 Kakabsa became one of Doderer's favorite figures. He was a new addition to the novel, although his sister Ludmilla, Friederike Ruthmayr's maid, was mentioned in "Die Dämonen der Ostmark." Doderer first mentioned Kakabsa on 3 April 1952 when he decided to add a section on him to the chapter "Der große Nebelfleck oder Vorbei an Friederike Ruthmayr," which was chapter six of "Die Dämonen der Ostmark."[85] When he completed "Am anderen Ufer" he took up this interpolation and worked on it until 8 September 1952. He seemed almost to become obsessed with the character of Kakabsa, apostrophizing him in the *Commentarii* as "der Mensch von heute,"[86] and referring to him in the novel as "unser Vortrefflicher" (p. 532).

The addition of the Leonhard insert to "Der große Nebelfleck..." illustrates how far Doderer had moved from the linear narration of "Die Dämonen der Ostmark." This chapter was one of the shortest in the novel and was concerned solely with the incident involving Friederike Ruthmayr and Eulenfeld and his drunken friends in the garden of the Ruthmayr mansion in the early hours of 9 January 1927. Using Ludmilla Kakabsa as a link, Doderer merely appended the Leonhard material to this episode and the reader was given the impression that the incidents involving Leonhard took place after Friederike's encounter with Eulenfeld. There is chronological detail in the Leonhard interpolation, the ages of Leonhard and his landlady are mentioned, but in itself this detail is meaningless for it is not related to the temporal framework. When Doderer finally says: "Man sah von hier in den Garten hinab—in den rückwärtigen, nicht in jenen an der

Straße, über dessen Gitter dereinst (genauer: kein ganzes Jahr später) Eulenfelds 'Troupeau' unter Gesang und Lautenspiel klettern sollte" (p. 143), it becomes obvious that the Leonhard episode is taking place in the spring and summer of 1926, that is, prior to the incident in the garden.

When Doderer completed the Leonhard interpolation he returned to work on "Auf offener Strecke," the concluding section of which he considered to be of cardinal importance to the novel: "Ich meine, ich muß in DD wieder auf II 1 Schluß (letzte Periode) zurück; es ist dies, wohl möglich, wirklich der Drehpunkt des Ganzen."[87] He had now decided to make of this incident what he called an "Anatomie des Augenblickes." This is a concept which assumed great significance for Doderer not only in his literary practice but also in his philosophical thinking. In terms of his writing he considered the "Anatomie des Augenblickes" to be a molecule of the novel, which in one given instant of time summarizes in its essentials the complex situation of the entire novel. As Geyrenhoff stands outside the home of Gürtzner-Gontard, he is suddenly confronted with a situation which makes him doubt his abilities to be the chronicler of the group, "Die Unsrigen." This concentration on a single moment enabled Doderer, among other things, to condense the narrative, by making the moment represent a much longer period of time. It also made the narrative more static, as it halted its progress in time. Doderer made frequent use of the concept in his diaries and tried on several occasions to use it as a narrative device in the novel. He henceforward referred to the three chapters in which Geyrenhoff is the figural narrator as R I, R II and R III, the abbreviation signifying "Raffung in der Anatomie des Augenblickes."

At this stage Doderer encountered difficulty with the novel's structure and spent some time reflecting on the problems which he faced. Finally, on 8 April 1953 he commenced work on the chapter "Die Falltür," but even here it was not smooth sailing. Doderer had decided to make the businessman, Jan Herzka, who was mentioned only briefly in "Die Dämonen der Ostmark," into one of the major characters of the novel. Herzka is living in a "second reality," obsessed by his sadistic desires. Some five years previously he had brutally attacked his lover, Magda Güllich. Herzka, Güllich and the Russian musician Slobedeff were the main characters in *Die Bresche*, which Doderer wrote in 1924. This fact illustrates the close relationship which exists between Doderer's writings and contributes to his entire *oeuvre* becoming an organic whole.

Not only does Herzka offer an illustration of an individual living in a "second reality" and eventually breaking free of it, his inheritance of Schloß Neudegg allows Doderer to exemplify his idea of evil lurking in the depths of society. Herzka's ancestor, Achaz von Neudegg, was also a sexual pervert and conducted "witch trials" in the dungeons of his castle. Doderer gave the title "Dort unten" to the chapter which deals with the chronicle of these happenings, and linked these events with the happenings of 15 July 1927, the blame for which he ascribed to the criminal classes of Viennese society. However, despite the fact that the Herzka sequence was to be a key episode in the novel, Doderer was unable to continue work on it because he had not solved his problems with the composition.

But March 1953 marked an upturn in the fortunes of the novel. On 12 March Doderer made the first mention of Alois Gach, who was to be instrumental in resolving the plot concerning Ruthmayr's suppressed will. Gach is a peripheral figure, as are Williams and Drobil, but his is a crucial role: "Gach ist der richtige Einschlag in R II: excentrisch—muß bis dahin ganz am Rand gehalten werden... —und zentral zugleich."[88] Doderer had now found a compositional technique which was to assume increasing importance, that of using peripheral characters, and a tangential approach to the novel as a whole, as a determining factor in its composition. As we saw, the title of the chapter "Draußen am Rande" hinted at this method of composition. Doderer eventually came to ascribe so much significance to events on the periphery of the historical happening that he saw the climax of the novel not as the burning of the Palace of Justice on 15 July 1927, but as the extinction by Frau Mayrinker of the fire in her kitchen: "Doch ist LPM-fin der Kern des Satzes, und mir ahnt' es schon vor längerem, daß hier im Randlichen, in den LP's, die eigentliche Essenz des Werks liegt."[89] Frau Mayrinker succeeds in putting out her fire; the Palace of Justice resists the efforts of the firemen, who are impeded by the demonstrators. Thus Doderer exemplifies his view that the individual holds the key to his own salvation; there is no political solution to the problems of society.

Having spent some time on compositional problems Doderer was now ready to resume work on that part of the novel which he designated as "Textmasse A." While working on Part II of the novel in 1952 Doderer divided its projected contents into three blocks. "Textmasse A" comprised the eight chapters of the eventual second part of the novel. The chapter "Dicke Damen" was originally intended to be the fifth chapter of this section (A5), but was moved by Doderer to "Textmasse B," which comprised mainly the chapters concerning Frau Kapsreiter, Gyurkicz and Quapp. "Textmasse C" began with the chapter "Vor verschlossenen Türen." Strangely enough, Doderer made very little use of the term "Textmasse C" in the *Commentarii*, which would seem to suggest that his initial division of the material for Part II into three blocks was overshadowed by his decision in 1955 to split the entire novel into three, as opposed to two parts. He certainly used the designators A1, A2, etc. for the chapters in "Textmasse A," B1 was used to refer to the "Einhorn" sequence, but none of the chapters in "Textmasse C" was ever referred to by a C designator.[90]

From 8 April 1953 onwards Doderer wrote new text almost daily, and there were very few breaks in the composition of the novel.[91] He was able to write in such continuous fashion because of the six months of reflection devoted to the novel between September 1952 and April 1953. A form for the work had now suggested itself to him as a basis for further composition, and he could devote his attention to the shaping of his material.

On 8 April 1953 Doderer took up work on the Herzka episode. He referred to this section of narrative as A5, and it eventually developed into four chapters, "Die Falltür," "Die Kavernen von Neudegg," "Dort unten," and "Am Strom," which he described as a "Nachtakt" to the Neudegg sequence. Less than a week after commencing work on A5 Doderer wrote:

> Wer hätte des gedacht! Als ich wieder begann, nach dem Jahr 1950 und der Institutszeit, hatt' ich in Bezug auf DD kaum Grund unter den Füßen, keine knetbare Masse in der Hand. Und heut'—alles ist zwar noch in den ersten Anfängen, die paar hundert Seiten neuer Texte nicht nennenswert...
> ...Dennoch: es strampelt und rührt sich, wie einige Leute, die unter einem großen Tuch sich balgen...[92]

Despite the introduction of so many new characters and the multiplicity of incident which this involved, the novel was cohesive, the threads of the narrative were beginning to be woven together. At this point, however, Doderer made a change in the order of the chapters in "Textmasse A." He reversed the order of A4, which he also designated as CS ("Chronique Scandaleuse"), and A5. For some time afterwards he referred to the Neudegg sequence of chapters as A5(4), but from 25 July 1953 onwards the chapter was referred to as A4. The two entries in the *Commentarii* when Doderer decided to reverse the order of the chapters in question do not make his reasons for the change very explicit:

> DD: Neudegg...wird nun dort ein Bild Quapp's gefunden, in einer Kassette mit Photographien? Oder ist das zu viel der Beziehung zum nahen A4?

> DD - A5/A4: Quapp-Photo: als Vorhalt gut, als Nachtakt nicht zu brauchen. A5 vor A4 stellen?![93]

In the finished version of the novel there is no such motivational link between the two chapters. Chronological considerations probably played a more influential role in his decision. The Neudegg sequence takes place between 16 May and 19 May 1927 and when Doderer came to write the chapter "Der Triumph der Rahel," which precedes the Neudegg sequence, he deliberately led it up to this point in time. CS, on the other hand, is much more closely linked, thematically and from the point of view of the content, to Part I of the novel. (This may explain why Doderer did not write the chapter, although he had abundant material for it, until 1956, when he was adapting "Die Dämonen der Ostmark.") Thus, although for some time to come Doderer continued to consider CS as part of "Textmasse A," and referred to it as A5, he eventually placed it in "Textmasse B," after the Geyrenhoff chapter R II.

While working on A4 Doderer gradually amassed material for those chapters of "Textmasse A" which had still to be written. Chief of these was the chapter entitled "Dort unten," the fictitious 16th century manuscript of the witch trials in the dungeons of Burg Neudegg.[94] Despite the trouble which the introduction of this manuscript caused him, particularly the fact that he decided to write it in Late Middle High German which could not possibly be familiar to all his readers, he felt that this was a valuable addition to the novel. It added another dimension to the temporal structure: "Doch bekommt das Buch noch eine Dimension hinzu, mit diesem in die Tiefe der Zeiten gestreckten Strang. Und—vom Rande her, vom Rande her!"[95] The insistence on time as an important element in the structure of the novel is one of the major differences between "Die Dämonen der Ostmark" and *Die Dämonen*. Geyrenhoff's chronicle was written simultaneously with the events, and time and memory played no part in the creation of the novel. The ultimate lapse of twenty-eight years between the events of Geyrenhoff's chronicle and their narration in the novel, and the accompanying expansion of the temporal perspective of the narrator, is foreshadowed in the fact that Achaz von Neudegg's page, Ruodlieb, who was an unwilling participant in the witch trials, did not write his chronicle of them until 1517, fifty-three years after they took place: "Ruodlieb kommt—durch das bei dem 'Process' vor ihm liegende weiße Papier—schon damals (1464) auf den Gedanken, Aufzeichnungen zu machen, die er dann 1517 zu Augsburg benützt."[96] This is the same procedure which Geyrenhoff adopts after he "falls from his hobby-horse" (p. 839). He uses the notes which he made in 1927 when he writes his chronicle twenty-eight years later.

Doderer worked without interruption on "Textmasse A" over the summer of 1953, and on 20 August 1953, the day on which he completed A4, he noted:

> Ich streue diesen Roman aus, und mache mit der Composition eine Probe: ob sie, wie ein Elektromagnet, wenn der Strom eingeschaltet wird, sogleich jeden Feilspan an seinen Platz reißt, so daß ein klares Bild der Kraftlinien hervortritt.[97]

The analogy is well-chosen. Although his method of composition appears totally unstructured, each apparently unconnected incident has its assigned place in the scheme of things, and despite the seeming discontinuity in the chronology, a well-defined chronological pattern is present.

Over the fall and winter of 1953 Doderer worked on the "Einhorn" sequence, which was concerned mainly with Frau Kapsreiter and the "Haus zum blauen Einhorn," but also with the affair between Quapp and Gyurkicz, and with the latter's contacts with the fascists in Burgenland.[98] He completed the chapter on 2 February 1954, except for what he termed its "Nachtakt," which he wrote on 19 February 1954 (pp. 953-55).

On 3 February 1954 he resumed work on A2 ("Am anderen Ufer"). He initially experienced difficulties with this chapter, difficulties no doubt due in part to the four months' break in its composition, even though he had been reflecting on its form and contents in his diary during these months. He now decided that toward the end of the chapter he would foreshadow the happenings of "Das Feuer:"

> Es wäre denkbar in A2, vorletzte Periode, F (1,2,3) aus Textmasse C, als deklarierten, und vielleicht verstärkten, Vorhalt einzusetzen, stark instrumentiert sogar! Analog zur Vorwegnahme von Mary's Bein-Verlust am Anfang der "Stiege" (und an anderen Stellen dort noch). Man könnte so weit gehen, hier sogar Expositives einzubauen, in extenso, was dann bei Einsatz F eben schon erledigt wäre![99]

The introduction of this material would serve two purposes. First, the anticipation of coming happenings would indicate that the events of 15 July 1927 will be instrumental in solving the murder of the prostitute, Hertha Plankl. The cryptic nature of this remark is intended to create suspense. The reader already knows that Plankl was killed by Meisgeier but is puzzled by the fact that a political disturbance will reveal this fact to the police. The remark is also intended to demonstrate that it is not the historical event *per se* that is important but its consequences for the individual.

The second purpose which is served by the introduction of historico-political content is of greater import for the narrative structure of the concluding and climactic segment of the novel. Although *Die Dämonen* is a social rather than a historical novel, the fact that Doderer chose as the climax of his work a historical event, the rioting in the streets of Vienna on 15 July 1927, which resulted in the deaths of eighty-nine people, compelled him to furnish the reader with certain data on the events which led up to this catastrophe.[100] By giving the relevant information here in A2 he avoided the necessity of doing so later, where it might retard the flow of the narrative. The essence of the chapter "Das Feuer" is the random nature of the happenings, the fact that the main protagonists never become directly involved in the events of the day, that they are mere onlookers divorced from the political situation. The author conveys this sense of remoteness from reality by the use of short, causally unconnected segments of narrative. Only a terse presentation of the salient details of the historical events is given. An exposé of the facts here in A2 enabled Doderer to prune the informative sections of "Das Feuer," which in turn allowed him to maintain the pace of the narrative. Thus, Doderer uses a chronological excursus as a means of achieving economy of narrative at a crucial point in the novel.

On completion of A2 on 12 April 1954, Doderer turned his attention to the composition of A3, "Der Triumph der Rahel." Although Doderer described the first meeting of Mary K. and Leonhard Kakabsa in the second part of A3 as one of the most crucial points in the novel, he seemed impatient to complete the chapter, and with it "Überm Berg" and the conclusion of "Am Strom," so that he could proceed to work on those chapters which were more relevant to the main theme of the novel, that of the "second reality." Doderer had not lost sight of the fact that this was the main theme of the novel. He had illustrated it in the Herzka episode, but his intention was that Schlaggenberg and his "Dicke Damen" would offer its prime illustration. Doderer completed A3 within a month of starting work on it and by the end of May he had also completed "Überm Berg" and "Am Strom," except for the concluding section of the latter chapter, which he did not write until 5 April 1955.

There was now a break of seven weeks before Doderer started writing R III, "Vor verschlossenen Türen," on 21 July 1954. These weeks were devoted to the compositional problems which he faced in leading up to the climax of the novel, the events of 15 July 1927. In purely chronological terms there was a gap, a "Spalt" as Doderer termed it, between "Textmasse A," "Textmasse B," and R III, the first chapter of "Textmasse C," on the one hand, and F, "Das Feuer," which is the climax of the novel, on the other. The former chapters take place in May 1927; the events of the latter chapter take place two months later on 15 July 1927. In terms of the narrative Doderer wanted this gap to be kept as narrow as possible, so that it would not retard the climax of the novel. He saw this as one of the functions of the two chapters A5 and R III: "Es müssen A5 und R III ('Vor verschlossenen Türen') den 'Spalt' (nach R III) weitgehend vorwegnehmen, so daß er schmal gehalten werden kann. Sodann F 1, 2, 3 (wozu sich schon die Substrate sammeln)."[101] It was at first his intention to write A5, but he decided instead to work on R III. Although A5 had an important role to play it did not contribute as much to the forward movement of the narrative and to the thematic content of the novel as did R III. In addition to considering "Spalt" quite literally as a break in the chronology of the novel, Doderer also conceived it in more abstract terms, and spoke of "den unüberbrückbaren Spalt zwischen individuellem und anonymem Geschehen."[102] The events of 15 July are an anonymous happening which impinges on the life of the individual,[103] and in "Das Feuer" Doderer intended to show the reaction of the individual, when faced by the irruption into his life of the historical event. He decided to use R III to illustrate the schism between the individual and external reality, and did so by a sort of reversal of the process by which the relationship will be illustrated in "Das Feuer." In R III Geyrenhoff discards his role of passive observer and becomes an active participant. But his attempts to contact Quapp, Schlaggenberg and Stangeler end in failure; Quapp is in Burgenland, Schlaggenberg in Styria, and Stangeler in Carinthia. In "Das Feuer" the individuals do not seek involvement in the political happenings, but are powerless to prevent the intrusion of these events into everyday reality.

Although a definitive form for the concluding chapters of the novel had not yet emerged, Doderer thought that a possible order for what he was careful to term "units of composition" rather than chapters might be: "R III Sp F post F."[104]

This was a wise choice of terminology, as R III and Sp were each eventually split into two chapters. Despite this seeming achievement of a formal structure for the concluding part of the novel, Doderer was not yet ready to begin work on R III. He spent some time working out the legal details of the plot involving Ruthmayr's suppressed will and reflected further on the links between R III and Sp. On 21 July 1954 he commenced writing R III, feeling that he had exhausted all the compositional possibilities of the situation. That this was not in fact the case is revealed by the following remark: "Seit vorgestern läuft wieder Text. Sich dem Textlauf anvertrauen, die Composition improvisieren, geöffnet sein und schmerzbereit in dieser Hinsicht."[105] Such a remark suggests that the composition of the chapter had taken on an *ad hoc* nature, that content was taking priority over form. The reason was that Doderer had assigned yet another purpose to R III. It was to function as a repository of material from which facts could be extracted at a later stage in the composition of the novel. Such a conception of the function of this chapter within the narrative framework of the novel must necessarily subordinate form to content and explains Doderer's seeming reversal of his normal insistence on the prime importance of formal considerations.

In marked contrast to the length of time which was devoted to the composition of the chapter, the time required for actually writing R III was comparatively short, as it was completed within a period of four weeks. Sp, on the other hand, proved much more problematic, as the chapter seemed to defy Doderer's efforts to contain it within a formal structure. At the root of his compositional problems with the chapter lay not only the function he assigned to it, but also the complex nature of the chapter "Das Feuer" which followed it. Quite apart from the political happenings, 15 July 1927 marked the culmination of a series of personal relationships which were focal points in the novel. The problematic nature of these relationships had tended to be obscured as the novel progressed. For example, when Doderer decided to open Sp with the Mary K./Leonhard Kakabsa relationship, it was because it had not been mentioned in over 300 pages of the novel! The task of Sp consisted in reintroducing these relationships into the main body of the work, and developing them to such a point that their resolution in F would require no further expository material in the chapter itself. How formidable a task this was became apparent only as Sp developed.

Doderer started writing Sp on 21 August 1954 and four weeks later he had completed Sp 1(a,b), Sp 2, Sp 3 (a,b,c). (Doderer's use of designators is at first confusing. The chapter is divided into episodes, Sp 1, Sp 2, etc., each of which corresponds to one of the main plots or relationships in the novel. Each episode may in turn be broken down into subsections, 1a, 1b, etc., in which the respective partners in the relationship are featured. For example: Sp 1a deals with Mary K., Sp 1b deals with Kakabsa. Doderer projected in total seven episodes for Sp.) He had also found what he considered to be an appropriate title for the chapter. He obviously did not wish to use "Spalt" as a title, as his intention had always been to minimize the gap between R III and F. He thus chose another title, "Kurze Kurven," which had symbolic significance for him.[106] The writing of the remaining half of the chapter was not completed until 1 December 1954.

Doderer added no new text to the chapter between 4 October and 26 October. There were two reasons for this break. First, on 6 October he went to London to research the Williams/Libesny episode *in situ*, and spent some time in Landshut and St. Veit before returning to Vienna on 18 October. Second, he devoted quite some time to the composition of Sp 5 (Herzka, Gebaur, Gräven) because of the significant role this episode has to play not only in the main theme of the novel, the "second reality," but also in the corollary to this theme, which Doderer terms the "General-Thema,"[107] namely, the fact that every "second reality" must disintegrate when forced into a confrontation with empirical reality. The individual lives in a "second reality" because of his refusal to perceive reality, because of "Apperceptions-Verweigerung." When he is compelled by external circumstances to a sudden awareness of reality as it actually exists, his "second reality" collapses and becomes incomprehensible to him. This is what happens to Herzka in the hotel-room, where he has an assignation with the two prostitutes, Anny Gräven and Anita. Anny's refusal to act out his sexual fantasies for him reveals their phantasmagoric nature to him. This "shock therapy"[108] brings him to his senses and enables him to find in his secretary, Agnes Gebaur, the means of his transposition "aus einer zweiten in eine wirkliche und erste Realität" (p. 1045).

Doderer completed "Kurze Kurven" on 1 December 1954, but seemed to regard this stage only as a provisional conclusion to the chapter, for two days later he mentioned the possibility of making further additions to it.[109] Although he considered that he now had all preparations in hand for "Das Feuer," this was far from being the case. He would spend another ten months in preparation for this chapter and commence writing it only on 22 September 1955.

On 12 December 1954 Doderer started writing II/15, "Auf der Schanze," but he ran into difficulties, and even though he did not seem to regard them as insurmountable, they caused him to break off work on the chapter between 14 January 1955 and 22 March 1955. Doderer's difficulties did not relate solely to II/15, but to the composition of the entire concluding section of the novel and to the structure of the novel as a whole. His intention up to this point had been to write a two-part novel. Although the second part was to be the more significant of the two, he seemed to be striving for a balanced structure, with each part consisting of around 800 pages and each divided into eighteen chapters. Doderer clearly felt that the sheer mass of material which he was compelled to add to these concluding chapters not only shifted the emphasis to them, but also caused the narrative form to lose its contours.[110] He felt himself constrained to adopt a compositional method which ran counter to his normal practice of shaping the content of the novel to fit a pre-established form. This is the problem with which Doderer wrestled during the early months of 1955 and to which he found the solution in the sphere of music, in particular in the symphonic form.

When one looks at the *Commentarii* for 1954 one might almost anticipate Doderer's turning to music to find a way out of his difficulties. In that year he made ever-increasing use of musical terminology in connection with the novel. Indeed, he even spoke of using "symphonic units" in constructing the closing sections of the novel.[111] He later considered Geyrenhoff's room in II/15 as being the "Zentrum des kommenden symphonischen Satzes."[112] If one part of the novel could be called a symphonic movement, the logical inference would seem to be that the novel itself should be considered as a symphony *in toto*. An "Ouvertüre" already existed; Part I was clearly indicated as the introductory movement: "Durchgang I gestern beendet. Dieses Buch ist aus klar abgesetzten Baumassen errichtet. 1-17 rollen als Treppe hinauf."[113] By 17 February Doderer was able to divide the novel into its three symphonic movements:[114]

DD Gen[esis] in 3 Sätzen:

Ouvertüre	Draußen–	(1) Strecke–	(10) Berg–
	Eintopf	(9) Sturz	(17) Wiederkehr
	ca. 300	ca. 400	ca. 400

This schema clearly provided a much more symmetrical structure for the novel, and also allowed Doderer the necessary freedom of movement which he required in constructing the closing sections of the work. It would allow him to more than double the length of II/15, to make both "Kurze Kurven II" and "Das Feuer" exceptionally long chapters, and yet keep them within the established narrative framework.

A division into three parts also appeared eminently satisfactory from a thematic point of view. In Part I the theme of the "second reality" was established; in Part II the Neudegg sequence offered graphic illustration of the theme;[115] in Part III the corollary of the main theme was to be portrayed, the waning of the "second reality," illustrated in Herzka's return to reality and the end of Schlaggenberg's mania for fat ladies. A further consequence of the division into three parts was Doderer's decision to move A5 (CS) to the beginning of Part III, where it could act as an intermezzo, in which the theme of the "second reality" would still be dominant, but about to be replaced in Part III by the new theme of the individual's breaking free of the "second reality" in which he had been living.

When Doderer resumed work on II/15 on 22 March 1955 the new format of the novel was an established fact. His decision to adopt a tripartite structure brought him a marvellous sense of relief, although he felt that he had devoted a tremendous amount of time to solving his structural problems.[116] He worked steadily on II/15 and completed it on 28 April 1955. He immediately started writing "Kurze Kurven II." That this chapter required almost nine months to complete was not due to the fact that it presented Doderer with any major compositional problems, but was because of its inordinate length. Its main purpose was to lead up to the climax of the novel and it was thus in both form and content similar to "Kurze Kurven I." "Kurze Kurven II" also brings the novel to the eve of 15 July and ends with the "Vollmond des heutigen 14. Juli" (p. 1201).[117]

Another new departure in KK II, which prefigured the form of "Das Feuer," was the fact that a significant portion of the chapter was narrated by Geyrenhoff: "KK II erstmalig Ich-Stimme und 'objektiv' in einem Kapitel!"[118] The four Geyrenhoff chapters, "Auf offener Strecke," "Der Sturz vom Steckenpferd," "Vor verschlossenen Türen," and "Auf der Schanze" are separate entities in the main body of the narrative. However, the form of "Das Feuer" precludes this rigid segregation of the two narrative modes, first-person narrator and omniscient author. Geyrenhoff chronicles only what he observes from the window of Gontard's home and his own actions on 15 July 1927. But these are themselves part of the totality of the day's events and cannot be set apart from them. Thus Geyrenhoff's report must be integrated with the account of the author himself, and it is this confluence of the two narrative modes, hitherto kept separate from each other, which Doderer anticipates in KK II.

When Doderer completed KK II on 7 September 1955, he required less than a week to write the chapter N II, "Das Nachtbuch der Kaps II." Although he had completed the original "Nachtbuch" chapter on 21 February 1954 he obviously intended to add more material to it. On 15 July 1954 he wrote a "Probetext" which he called a "Nachtbuch-Anschluß," and "Probetexte" for almost all the contents of N II are to be found in his diaries for 1954 and 1955. On 29 April 1955 he mentioned the possibility of making the continuation of N into a separate chapter and interpolating it between KK II and F.[119] When he did this on 14 September 1955 all the material was at hand, which explains the speed with which he was able to write the chapter.

The actual writing of the chapter "Das Feuer" went very smoothly, an accomplishment due in no small part to the length of time Doderer prepared for writing it. In fact, things seemed to be going so well that he even thought in terms of the completion of the entire novel. He finished writing "Das Feuer" on 11 January 1956 and then spent over two weeks on what he called the "Exaratio" and the "Reihung" of the chapter, a process which involved the splitting up and reordering of the various episodes into which the chapter was divided.

The last stages in the composition of the novel had been reached. Doderer now turned his attention to DD I, "Die Dämonen der Ostmark," and on 4 February 1956 he noted the procedure he would follow in dealing with these seventeen chapters:

DD I: 1) Notizen-Sammlung.
       2) Ausscheidung.
       3) Katalog der Substrate.

Dann erster Versuch eines Graphicons.[120]

On 6 February he carried out the "Ausscheidung," that is, he eliminated from the manuscript all the material that was no longer appropriate to his changed approach to the novel. He had decided a year previously that he would prune DD I drastically, and he now worked out in detail exactly how he was going to do so. He realized from the outset what a difficult task he faced: "Gestern erste technische Griffe an DD I...Dabei wird die Schwierigkeit, ja Schwere der Sache sichtbar. Mich drückte es zunächst nieder."[121] He now proceeded to draw up a list of the main details of the contents of DD I.[122] These "Substrate," as he called them, were either to be a constituent of the revised version of each chapter or to be discarded as no longer essential to the novel. On 13 February, the day before he started writing new text for Part I of the novel, he drew a sketch which showed exactly how he intended to remodel the seventeen chapters of "Die Dämonen der Ostmark."[123]

The most extensive changes were made to the chapters "Rückblick auf eine große Liebe und auf die Mondsucht" and "Alle Wege führen nach Düsseldorf," which were amalgamated into the chapter "Die Entstehung einer Kolonie I." Doderer had to write substantial amounts of new text for this chapter. There were two reasons for this. First, he was reducing Schlaggenberg's role as a character and, second, he was making Geyrenhoff the narrator of this chapter. The original chapters were not written as first-person narrative (they were supposedly based on material supplied to Geyrenhoff by Schlaggenberg and Stangeler), except for a portion of "Rückblick," although they were part of Geyrenhoff's chronicle.

On 24 March 1956 Doderer completed the writing of "Die Entstehung einer Kolonie II." He then turned his attention to CS, "Eine Chronik Scandaleuse," for which he had amassed a substantial amount of material, an amount which he himself felt was disproportionate to the length of the chapter: "Gestern erster Text CS, nach nicht geringer Mühe: diese Massen von Material (für solch kleines Segment!)."[124] However, he was able to write the chapter very quickly between 1 April and 7 April 1956, and felt that this was because he had delayed working on this chapter until he was involved with the reworking of the manuscript of "Die Dämonen der Ostmark": "CS war unbedingt im Connex mit I zu bearbeiten, dies sah ich richtig, wie sich zeigt."[125] The reason is that the two are closely connected thematically and are illustrations of the "second reality."

With the writing of CS and the completion of the reworking of DD I on 11 June

1956, only the final chapter, W, "Schlaggenberg's Wiederkehr," remained to be written. This chapter functions as an epilogue, or, to use Doderer's musical terminology, a coda to the novel. By sustaining two leitmotifs which were used in the concluding chapters of the novel—the odor of mothballs and an autumnal feeling—the chapter emphasizes the fact that everyday existence has been unaffected by the historical event. Just as the characters in the novel have broken free from their "second reality," so the author too has freed himself from his past: "W muß aus der zweiten Wirklichkeit schon herausragen: so endet diese Symphonie autobiographisch."[126] Having been guilty of "Apperceptions-Verweigerung" Doderer now sees, and this is the message of "Schlaggenberg's Wiederkehr," that "ein ganz neu beginnendes apperceptives Leben ist zu führen."[127] With the completion of the chapter on 26 July 1956 the end of the novel was reached.[128]

Doderer seemed almost unable to believe that he had successfully completed the task of writing the novel, after the fluctuations in its fortunes over the previous five years:

> Ich muß bekennen, daß mir 1951 das Werk nur ein Vorsatz war: mit "Draußen am Rande" allerdings erschienen schon "zarte Verbündete." Die folgenden Jahre brachten—unaufhörliche und umfängliche—Versuchs-Würfe. Erst nach jenen ersten Julitagen des Jahres 1955 schoss alles von allen Seiten zu Kristall.[129]

It was only to be expected that he should experience both mental and physical after-effects following the completion of so monumental a task. Over a year later he wrote to a friend: "Die Vollendung der 'Dämonen'...lehrte mich hintnach, daß man nicht ungestraft 25 Jahre gegen den Strom (der Zeit nämlich!) schwimmt, das heißt, eine gewisse Erschöpfung war bei mir weit über ein halbes Jahr lang sehr zu spüren: und so blieb vieles dahinter."[130] Nonetheless, he almost immediately began preparing his diaries of 1940 to 1950 for publication, and shortly thereafter expressed his desire to write "ein Divertimento mit fest abgesetzter eigener Sprachrhythmik jedes Satzes."[131] This is the germ of *Roman No. 7*. Doderer was now moving toward the creation of what he termed the "roman muet," which he looked on as the ultimate expression of his craft as a writer. It was to mark a radical change from *Die Dämonen*: "Nach den 'Dämonen' mußte ein absolut Neues kommen."[132]

"Die Entstehung eines großen Romanes ist holpernd, stoßweise, ein organisches Gewächs."[133] Our examination of the genesis of *Die Dämonen* between 1951 and 1956 shows that it corresponds more closely to the above description than to Doderer's later, more facile assertion that the novel's "Dreiteiligkeit samt dem dynamischen Konzept übrigens ganz ebenso als apriorische Form gegeben waren."[134] It is obvious that when Doderer resumed work on the novel in 1951 he had no preconceived idea as to the formal structure of the work. With respect to

Part I he clearly envisaged no extensive changes to "Die Dämonen der Ostmark," but intended merely to interpolate into it the chapter "Draußen am Rande" and the Leonhard insert.[135] The decision to condense drastically these seventeen chapters was taken, as was the change from a two-part to a three-part structure for the novel, at a much later date. One must therefore view remarks such as the following with some scepticism:

> Bevor er einen Roman beginnt, entwirft er ausgedehnte Planskizzen, auf denen die Stationen der Handlung und die Beziehungen der handelnden Personen zuein- ander, ja zuweilen sogar bereits die Seitenzahlen der Kapitel genau vorausbestimmt sind.[136]

This description corresponds more closely to that of an *ex post* sketch, which, as the name implies, was constructed *after* the composition of the chapter or segment to afford the author an overview of all the compositional data. In the 1950s Doderer made several sketches during the composition of *Die Dämonen*, but the earliest of these date from the late summer of 1952, that is, almost a year after Doderer wrote the first new text for the novel. I agree with Schmidt-Dengler that "der Wert dieser Skizzen von Doderer überschätzt wurde, der seinerseits viel dazu beitrug, daß die Kritik gläubig in ihm einen Autor vermutete und immer noch vermutet, der seine Romane auf dem 'Reißbrett konstruierte,' sich aber über das Wie dieses Vorgangs keinerlei Gedanken macht."[137]

Just as critics have unreservedly accepted Doderer as a formal perfectionist with a mania for graphic planning and detail, so too they have tended to accept his solution of the dialectic of form and content, "Die Form ist die Entelechie des Inhalts," as paradigmatic for the creation of *Die Dämonen*. This analysis of the genesis of the novel shows, however, that Doderer's attitude toward this problem was much more ambivalent than his theoretical utterances would lead one to believe. His *Grundlagen und Funktion des Romans* is a rationalization of his theory of the novel that obscures the practical difficulties which presented themselves during the writing of *Die Dämonen*.

The foregoing account of the genesis of *Die Dämonen* has sought to remain factual in nature, so that by presenting relevant data a basis can be established for an interpretation of the novel. A secondary aim has been to demonstrate that a knowledge of the various stages in the protracted development of the novel is essential if the critic is not to run the risk of trying to sustain a thesis which is not borne out by the facts.

3
Narrative Techniques

OUR EXAMINATION OF THE DEVELOPMENT of the novel between 1951 and 1956 reveals that a major problem faced by Doderer during these years was that of the tension between form and content. His decision in the 1940s to have the omniscient author take over the narrative function from the figural narrator, Geyrenhoff, meant that the authorial perspective was no longer restricted to an individual consciousness, but could range freely in time and space. Although this decision allowed Doderer to resume work on the novel after a break of fifteen years in its composition, it also confronted him with a previously unencountered difficulty. As Geyrenhoff's chronicle, narrated almost simultaneously with the events as they unfolded, the novel had a clearly-established form and a relatively circumscribed content. As the work of the omniscient author, the novel knew no barriers in time and space; characters could be introduced who had only tenuous connections with the group of characters about whom Geyrenhoff was writing. The incorporation of so much new material, although adding considerably to the richness of texture of the work, exerted constant pressure on the novel's form. One means used by Doderer to solve this problem was to employ narrative devices, aimed at condensing the contents and tightening the structure of the novel by drawing together totally unconnected portions of narrative. I now propose to study Doderer's use of three techniques, "Reifepunkte," "excentrische Einsätze" and "Kontraktionsglieder," which resulted in a contraction of the novel's contents, and a fourth, and very significant technique, termed by Doderer the "Fenster-Technik," which resulted in a dramatic expansion of these contents without detriment to the novel's form.

When Doderer resumed work on the novel in the early 1950s he seemed to be aware of the fact that experimentation with literary techniques might allow him to reach a successful conclusion to the work of over twenty years: "Wie ist das nun mit dem Roman? Es wird ein Zeichen seines Werdens sein, wenn man im Technischen zu Kühnheiten sich anschickt: und es wird heute bestimmt kein neues Buch entstehen, ohne daß auch solche Hürden dabei genommen werden."[1]

While Doderer employed certain narrative techniques prior to the composition of *Die Dämonen*, some others proved themselves particularly appropriate to the type of narrative structure he sought to create and others were elaborated in the course of the development of the novel. Not all of these devices are especially innovative, although Doderer seemed to desire to be experimental, but they do have an important role to play in a novel of such vast proportions. Doderer's skillful manipulation of his material is due in no small part to narrative devices.

I. "Reifepunkte" and "excentrische Einsätze"

One technical device by which Doderer laid great store was the one which he termed a "Reifepunkt." This might be described as a literary stratagem in which the author directs the narrative to a critical point and then breaks off, leaving the reader to deduce the ensuing course of events from the given facts. When the author resumes the narration, at however great a distance, the reader, who has made the necessary connections, experiences no difficulty in picking up the thread of the narrative. Doderer defines the technique in *Grundlagen und Funktion des Romans* as "das Verfahren, einen Vorgang nicht ganz bis zum Ende zu erzählen, sondern ihn nur bis zu einem Reifepunkt zu führen: den letzten Vollzug besorgt der Leser selbst und wird zustimmen, wenn er den Sachen später und in anderem Zusammenhange schon auf diesem Punkte begegnet."[2] By encouraging the active participation of the reader in the development of the novel Doderer sustains his interest and creates a degree of tension in his mind, as he waits to see whether or not events will unfold in the manner which he has anticipated. Moreover, it allows for economy of narrative, an important consideration in a novel of the magnitude of *Die Dämonen*.

Doderer did not make use of the technique in "Die Dämonen der Ostmark." In 1935, when working on a draft of the concluding chapter of Part I, he considered using a "Reifepunkt" as a means of linking Part I to the projected Part II, but when he wrote this chapter, "Der Eintopf," in early 1936 he did not pursue the idea. The fact that he did not is not surprising, given the form and content of this part of the novel. Geyrenhoff's chronicle, which was in fact an eye-witness account of what was taking place, was concerned with a relatively limited number of characters in a spatially and temporally restricted situation. The reader's perspective was bounded by that of the first-person narrator, and his ability to assimilate the content of the novel was not tested by intricacies in the plot, which developed in linear fashion. But when Doderer resumed work on the novel in the 1950s, its changed structure taxed much more severely both the ability of the reader to comprehend the novel in its entirety, and the expertise of the author in dealing with the sheer mass of material involved. Doderer found his "Reifepunkt" technique particularly suited to his need to shape his content to his form.

One instance which is an especially skillful use of the technique is that of the Leonhard insert in chapter six of "Die Dämonen der Ostmark." As has been mentioned, Leonhard was one of the most important additions to the novel in the 1950s. Between 19 April and 4 June 1952 Doderer wrote the chapter "Am anderen Ufer," the second chapter of Part II, concerned with Leonhard during the spring and early summer of 1926. It will be remembered that in this chapter Leonhard achieves self-realization by breaking through the "dialect barrier," a feat which is due in the main to his study of Latin grammar, but also to his relationship with Trix K. and Fella Storch.

Doderer paved the way for "Am anderen Ufer" by the Leonhard insert in "Der große Nebelfleck." No doubt one compelling reason for this interpolation of a Leonhard episode was that it could have been construed as a formal weakness had the introduction of a major character been delayed until almost a third of the way through the novel. This was thus an excellent opportunity to use the "Reifepunkt" technique in preparation for the appearance of Leonhard at a much later point in the novel, over 300 pages later. When the "Reifepunkt" at the end of the insert is reached, the reader is prepared for Leonhard's eventual reappearance: "Leonhard hab' ich mit Bildern dicht umstellt; schon hat er Unterfutter und Aura; das ist eine Folge des Detail-Wachstums rund um ihn. So weit, so gut, vor RP des Abschnittes nach I 6, 150ff."[3] As well as serving an important expository function, this insert also forms an additional link between the two parts of the novel.

The Leonhard insert shows that in 1952 Doderer found the use of the "Reifepunkt" advantageous for the integration of new and disparate material. As he reached the closing stages of the work he made frequent use of the technique as a compositional aid. The happenings of 15 July 1927, which form the climax of the novel in the penultimate chapter, "Das Feuer," are not only of socio-political significance for Viennese and Austrian society, the day also marks a focal point in a series of personal relationships. However, the resolution of the problematic nature of these relationships cannot be effected in this chapter without prior exposition and motivation. In order to prepare the way for the dénouement of all these subplots (Doderer referred to them as "Substrate") he decided to incorporate a series of "Reifepunkte" in the chapter "Kurze Kurven:"

In Sp ["Kurze Kurven"]...müssen noch folgende Substrate zum RP gebracht werden, so daß ihre Finalisierung nach F erfolgen kann:

Leonhard - Alfons Croy - Mary
Quapp - Orkay (Finalisierung schon in F (Cobenzl))
Neuberg - Angelika (Kontrapunkt)
Ballog - Pornberger - Graff[4]

By so doing he was able to cut back on the use of discursive passages in the climactic portions of the narrative. Doderer wanted the tempo of "Das Feuer" to be extremely fast-moving and wished to employ in the chapter only descriptive language and to exclude explicative or analytical passages. On 15 July 1927 the individual caught up in the events is confused and bewildered by the manifestation of irrational forces over which he has no control. Doderer wished the narrative to reflect this confusion and clearly could not afford to slow the tempo with long informative sections. His use of "Reifepunkte" in "Kurze Kurven" allowed him the required economy of narrative in "Das Feuer."

While working on "Kurze Kurven" Doderer conceived the climax of the novel as having a formal structure which paralleled the star-pattern of the finale of *Die Strudlhofstiege*.[5] Here, Mary K.'s catastrophe on the Althanplatz on 21 September 1925 was the "teleological" point on which converged the diverse but interrelated strands of narrative, and in which the problematical relationships of various characters were resolved. Discussing Doderer's sketch for the conclusion of *Die Strudlhofstiege*, Fischer says:

> Das "Detailblatt No 3, IV/Stern" fällt insofern aus dem Rahmen der übrigen Skizzen, als es (im Gegensatz zum sonst praktizierten Horizontal/Vertikal System) im Sinne des Uhrzeigers um ein Zentrum geordnet und auch so zu lesen ist. Diesem Zentrum ist der "teleologische" Punkt des Romans, der "21. Sept. 1925 nachmittags" eingeschrieben.[6]

Doderer intended to base the finale of *Die Dämonen* on a similar pattern, and referred to the concluding sections of the novel as the "Stern auf F:" "*DD-Stern auf F*: Das eigentliche generale Thema liegt in der Schluß-Composition: Coupierung, Überrennung und 'Lösung' (soweit sich das als solche bezeichnen läßt) der individuellen Komplikationen durch das anonyme Geschehen."[7] However, four weeks after starting to write Sp, he adopted a new structural pattern for the concluding sections of the novel:

DD-Finalsatz: Es ist kein Stern, es wird ein Katarakt sein: nicht so sehr

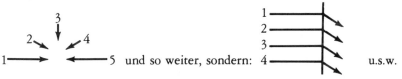

Jede Linie verfolgen, ihren RP für F feststellen: starke Effekte (das breite Blech im Orchester) für F reservieren.[8]

The new structure is much more telling and dramatic. As the image of the cataract suggests, the "Reifepunkte" take the action (and with it the reader) to the edge of the falls, but leave it poised on the brink until the ensuing chapter. The fact that the paths of the individuals pursue a parallel course and do not converge underscores the fact that they are concerned with their own private interests and are not affected as a group by the irruption of the historical event into their everyday existence.

The "Reifepunkt" technique is a narrative device which functions well in conjunction with another device that plays a determining role in the structure of the novel, namely, the "excentrischer Einsatz." This technique involves the introduction into the narrative of an episode which is spatially remote from the events being described. The first illustration of the technique occurs in the chapter "Draußen am Rande." Midway through the description of the day spent by Williams and Drobil in the Haltertal in the summer of 1926, the narrative abruptly switches to Munich and Mary K. Further examples of the technique are to be found in the chapter, "Am anderen Ufer," which begins with the "excentrischer Einsatz Fella Storch," and in the climax of the novel, the chapter, "Das Feuer," which begins with three "excentrische Einsätze." Doderer seemed to think that with the discovery of this narrative device he had found the key to his compositional problems with the novel: "Mit den extrem excentrischen Einschlägen glaube ich jetzt das Compositions-Prinzip von DD überhaupt in der Hand zu haben."[9] As Doderer had discarded the linear narration of "Die Dämonen der Ostmark" in favor of discontinuous prose, this was quite definitely a technique which lent itself to the new style of narration.[10] His intention was also to try to have the novel portray life in its totality and the introduction of seemingly unconnected material was often a means of shifting the focus from the main characters to the minor ones. Doderer discovered in the course of the novel's composition that a peripheral approach to the content of the work was the most fruitful one. Both the "excentrischer Einsatz" and the peripheral approach are closely linked to Doderer's preference for "das Indirekte." This preference also explains why he makes such frequent use of metaphor to illuminate his artistic statement, a procedure that is not commonplace with realist writers.

Both the "Reifepunkt" technique and the "excentrischer Einsatz" played an important role in Doderer's approach to the composition of the novel and he relied heavily on them as key elements in the assembly of the narrative structure. The fact that he did so illustrates the problems that he experienced with the relationship of form and content, and the technical aids required to reconcile the two.

II. "Kontraktionsglieder" and "Fenster"

In *Grundlagen und Funktion des Romans* Doderer writes that he makes use of what he calls a "Kontraktionsglied" "das aber nicht lebens-ungemäß abkürzt, sondern schlichthin bespricht, wo eine Darstellung unerwünscht wird, weil sie eine Überbetonung in die Composition brächte."[11] In other words, just as there are occasions in the novel where analytical language is inappropriate to the author's purpose, there are also occasions where the author may propitiously intervene and explicate a potential difficulty for his reader.[12] A technical device such as the "Kontraktionsglied" allows him to manipulate the content of the novel and to strengthen the form.

His use of "Kontraktionsglieder" is always carefully contrived, and their main purpose is to impart the maximum of information with the minimum of words. Doderer was always careful to distinguish theoretically between what he termed "Leitwerk" and "Kontraktionsglieder," but in practice it is difficult, if not impossible, to distinguish between the two terms. He defines "Leitwerk" as sections of narrative in which "durch geringes kommentierendes Einwinken der Leser vom Begehen mißverständlicher Vorstellungsbahnen abgehalten wird."[13] The author, or one of his intermediary figures,[14] may impart to the reader an item or items of information which simplify the workings of the involved plot, and thus condense the content of the novel, a function which is also discharged by the "Kontraktionsglied."

At the time of the composition of A3, "Der Triumph der Rahel," Doderer decided to make the chapter itself a "Kontraktions-Glied": "*DD-Kontraktionsglieder*: Es erhebt sich jetzt die Möglichkeit, A3 als un-additives, simultan (fast extrem) gebautes Kontraktions-Glied einzusetzen:...A5 jedoch und R III müssen ähnlich konzentrierte Einheiten ineinandergeschmolzen enthalten wie A3."[15] The chapter contains one of the most crucial points in the novel, the first meeting of Leonhard Kakabsa and Mary K., and it also brings together several important narrative strands. Doderer utilizes two "Kontraktionsglieder" to introduce the material in as concentrated a fashion as possible. First, he links Schlaggenberg to an incident which took place on 28 March 1927. On that evening Schlaggenberg made the acquaintance of Grete Siebenschein. Although this meeting was only two months before the party given by Mary K., which forms part of A3, in the novel it was mentioned over 300 pages previously.

Doderer introduces this "reprise" of Schlaggenberg in the form of an authorial intrusion ("Man erinnert sich vielleicht...," p. 663), which is a very pointed guide to the reader. He makes a point of dating exactly Schlaggenberg's conversation with Levielle and his meeting with Grete Siebenschein as 28 March 1927, using this chronological reference to draw together this day and Mary K.'s party on 17 May 1927 and thus tightening the novel's structure. Second, he gives a résumé ("konzentrierte Einheiten") of the affairs of "Die Unsrigen" prior to this time, and a description is given of the breaking-up of the group (p. 663). This interpolation not only clarifies the status of the various characters involved, but also forges another link between the two parts of the novel. In addition, it also points forward to some later developments. It is an excellent illustration of how succinctly the author can impart information in a "Kontraktionsglied" yet without detracting from the authenticity of his portrayal of events, without becoming "lebens-ungemäß."

"Kontraktionsglieder" condense and accelerate the narrative. Doderer on occasion uses "Retardationsglieder" to slow down the pace and also employs a technique, to which he gives the name "Fenster," to expand on the content of the novel. His choice of the term "Fenster" for this narrative device may be partly explicable in terms of the symbolic significance which he attached to windows. As Weber says, for Doderer "das Fenster ist der eigentlich existentielle Ort der Verwirklichung einer Person."[16] When a person steps to a window he perceives, in all its connotations, reality: ego and external surroundings fuse, optimum conditions obtain for the realization of the individual's existential potential.[17] It is not fortuitous that Doderer chose as an expression of his autobiography in *Meine neunzehn Lebensläufe* in 1966 an aphorism he had written six years previously: "Erst bricht man Fenster. Dann wird man selbst eines."[18] The metaphorical breaking of windows onto existence may also render the individual more receptive to happenings which are not translatable into experiential terms: "Die immer gleichen Wände, welche uns da umschließen, in Fenster umzuschaffen, durch die wir hinaus schauen, während die Transzendenz, sei's auch nur metaphorisch, durch den Blick in ein Jenseits im Diesseits, hereinscheint."[19]

Although Doderer projected the incorporation of several "Erweiterungsfenster" into the fabric of *Die Dämonen*,[20] there is in fact only one instance of a "Fenster" in the novel, and that is the Herzka episode. Before examining this "window" it will be helpful to consider Doderer's remarks on the use of the technique with respect to *Die Wasserfälle von Slunj*. There is one significant difference between the Herzka episode and the two "windows" in *Die Wasserfälle von Slunj*.[21] The former was added to the novel in the course of its composition, the latter were added after the novel was substantially complete. However, all three serve the same purpose, to elucidate the novel's contents and to prevent any stringency dictated by plot or theme: "'Handlung,' das ist die Befangnis in welche wir eingemauert sind. Je mehr 'Fenster' wir in sie brechen, um so deutlicher wird auch sie sichtbar."[22]

Doderer was at pains to insist that a "window" is not merely an addition to the novel, but is an animation of the entire work: "Eine Einfügung ist noch lange kein Fenster. Jene nur ein ergänzender Konstruktionsteil, dieses eine Neubelebung des Ganzen."[23] As he reached the conclusior of *Die Wasserfälle von Slunj*,

Doderer was apprehensive that the novel was assuming more the form of a novella than that of a novel. While conceding that what he termed "Das Novellistische" was an integral part of any novel, he did not consider it to be the sole voice: "Das Novellistische ist im Roman als agens unentbehrlich, aber es stellt eine Stimme unter anderen dar, wie das Lyrische, und ist für den Romancier kein Solo-Instrument."[24] For Doderer one of the essentials of novel composition was the freedom enjoyed by the author to improvise on his material, within the confines of a pre-established form. Too great a rigidity in the plot not only curtailed this freedom, but also imposed a certain artificiality on the novelist's portrayal of life, by restricting him to a limited zone of experience and not allowing him to encompass the totality of existence.

One means of avoiding this danger was to introduce into the work a "Roman im Roman:" "Hier weiß ich doch nun schon einiges. Der Roman im Roman bewahrt diesen vor der Novellistik (hält diese als bloßes technisches Mittel!) der eigentlichen steten Gefahr jedes compositorischen Gebildes. Novellistisch werden heißt hier: die Composition nicht frei improvisieren, sondern ihrem dynamischen Sog verfallen."[25] Doderer made use of the "Roman im Roman" in *Die Dämonen* on two occasions: Trix K. and Leonhard Kakabsa on the steps by the Danube in the chapter "Am anderen Ufer," and the chapter "Im Osten." Each serves the purpose of making the novel's contents more universal.[26] Doderer considered that only by exploring the potentialities inherent in any plot adopted by the author "kann überhaupt die Romanschreiberei nach ihrem wahren Rang greifen, als eigentliche Wissenschaft vom Leben, und damit nach ihrer Universalität."[27]

When Doderer decided to make the Herzka episode into a "window" he did not find the process to be without difficulty: "Ich bin jetzt zweifelhaft geworden bezüglich des Herzka, mag er auch ein Fenster aufstoßen und viel Neues hereinlassen."[28] The businessman, Jan Herzka, was only a minor character in "Die Dämonen der Ostmark." He was a participant in a discussion about witch trials with René von Stangeler, but it is not clear whether it was Doderer's intention at that time, 1936, that Herzka should play a more prominent role in Part II, or if, even at this early stage, he was already linking Herzka's sadistic tendencies to the idea of a "second reality." However, when the Herzka "window" was incorporated into the novel in 1953 it was intended that it should serve as an illustration of the novel's new main theme, that of the "second reality." Herzka's sadistic sexual fantasizing distorts his attitude to reality. He wants his sexual experiences to conform to his fantasies and not to be the basis of a relationship in which there is a mutual exchange of emotions. Two days after his discussion of witch trials with Stangeler, he suddenly becomes for the first time physically aware of his secretary, Agnes Gebaur, although she has been employed by him for a year. He is not really conscious of Agnes as a person, but sees her only cast in the role of a flagellant, passively submitting to any degradation which he might choose to inflict on her. This fantasy reminds Herzka of an incident five years before, when in another city he had assaulted his lover, Magda Güllich. At this point Doderer gives a synopsis of his first novel, *Die Bresche*, published in 1924, of which Herzka was the main character. It is rather a strange interpolation, inasmuch as it is stressing the fact that Herzka, like all the other characters in the novel, is not a flesh and blood figure, but is a figment of the author's imagination, and this despite the fact that *Die Dämonen* is supposed to be based on Geyrenhoff's chronicle. However, this insert does illustrate one of the functions of a "window," the expansion of the spatial and temporal horizons of the novel: "Ausweitung in Zeit und Raum (dies auch die Funktion der 'Fenster')."[29] Herzka regrets not having married Magda Güllich: "Er hätte sie zu seinen Wünschen erzogen" (p. 683). He is living in a "second reality" from which only the shock-treatment administered by Anny Gräven and Agnes Gebaur's totally unexpected accident enable him to break free, as both experiences confront him with his actual existential situation.

Dietrich Weber considers the Herzka episode to be "der intensivste Fall zweiter Wirklichkeit."[30] As well as being an illustration of this theme the Herzka "window" opens up new perspectives on the novel.[31] Herzka's "second reality" is sexual in origin, as is Schlaggenberg's, with his "Dicke-Damen-Doktrinär-Sexualität" (p. 851). Achaz von Neudegg, Herzka's fifteenth century ancestor, was also blinded to reality by his sexual aberration. His desire to humiliate respectable women caused him to accuse them of witchcraft and to incarcerate them in the dungeons of Schloß Neudegg. Their supposed witch trial is a tragicomedy, an "Affentheater der Leidenschaften."[32] Stangeler describes Achaz's voyeurism as "Programm-Sexualität. Sexuelle Montagen und Bastel-Stunden. Der Kajetan mit seinen dicken Damen macht im Grund genau das gleiche. Errichtung einer zweiten Sexualität" (p. 1054). Doderer was firmly convinced that totalitarianism and sexual deviancy sprang from the same irrational thinking. To the ordinary reader the connection between the two appears tenuous in the extreme and nowhere does Doderer offer an explanation in convincing philosophical, political or even psychological terms. One is forced to the conclusion that like Doderer's initial attraction to National Socialism it is an emotional response, not a logically argued attempt to explain a political phenomenon. It may owe part of its *raison d'être* to Doderer's admiration for the Viennese philosopher, Otto Weininger, whose book *Geschlecht und Charakter*,[33] an anti-feminist, anti-Semitic diatribe, can be manipulated by radical thinkers into becoming a plaidoyer for fascist theories of race. When one bears in mind the fact that Doderer's first wife, with whom he had a very bitter relationship, was Jewish, a possible source of his somewhat mystifying theory linking sex and ideology starts to emerge.

Doderer's choice of a title for the fictitious sixteenth century manuscript of the happenings in Burg Neudegg is borrowed from Huysmans' *Là-bas*, which is also a fictitious chronicle of the misdeeds of Gilles de Rais, the infamous "Blue-Beard," the difference being that Achaz von Neudegg was a figment of Doderer's imagination whereas Gilles de Rais actually existed. Both authors are drawing a comparison between historical events and contemporary happenings, but Doderer sees the late medieval period as a prefiguration of the twentieth century, especially in the political sphere. Whether he is correct in this assumption is debatable, but by his insistence on it in the "Dort unten" episode he certainly elevates it to a central issue in the novel. As Weber says, in the chronicle of Achaz von Neudegg's witch trials Doderer is concerned with "wie weit ein entscheiden-des Problem des 20. Jahrhunderts, nämlich das Ideologische, bereits an der Wende vom Mittelalter zur Neuzeit sichtbar ist."[34] The problem is stated quite categorically in the novel itself. Stangeler says:

> "Herr Achaz von Neudegg war ein sehr moderner Mensch...Weil bei ihm schon auftritt, was unsere Zeit beherrscht: eine zweite Wirklichkeit. Sie wird neben der ersten, faktischen, errichtet und zwar durch Ideologien. Die des Herrn Achaz war eine sexuelle" (p. 1021).

In Doderer's eyes, sexual deviancy, ideology, and totalitarianism are all manifestations of the same evil, namely, the refusal by the individual to perceive reality as it exists, a phenomenon which results in the individual and the state living in a "second reality." The Herzka "window" offers two illustrations of this thesis, and endeavors to show that this is not a particularly twentieth century failing, but was already discernible in a much earlier period. No doubt Doderer could have uncovered further historical parallels, but he seemed to believe that his fictional creation, Achaz von Neudegg, fitted the bill quite nicely.

The Herzka "window" is also a variation on the recurrent theme of evil lurking in the depths of society. The demons of the title of the novel are the irrational forces which Doderer considers are omni-present, biding their time, awaiting a favorable opportunity to manifest themselves. When they do appear, society will be powerless to control them. It is not by chance that Herzka is fascinated by the dungeons of Schloß Neudegg, the scene of Achaz's witch trials. The physical depths are symptomatic of the moral depths to which the individual, who is prey to his obsession, can sink. Other illustrations of this theme are the octopus lurking in the sewers, waiting to snatch an unwary prey, the criminal Meisgeier's descent to the sewers of Vienna on 15 July 1927 to set a snare for the police who are marching overhead, the fascists "dort unten" in Burgenland, and the suggestion by Doderer that the lower strata of Viennese society, the "Ruass" as he calls them, were responsible for the rioting on 15 July. R.H. Watt sees this "Einbruch von unten" as a common feature in the works of Broch, Musil and Doderer, and makes the point that all three of them clearly separate the criminal and the political: "What is most interesting for the sociologist of literature is that all three writers, although associating the lower or criminal classes with irrational tendencies, take care not to attribute political motives to such characters in their novels."[35] Watt also explains the choice of the criminal as embodiment of these irrational tendencies as being conditioned by the social status of the three writers in question: "It can scarcely be coincidence that they embody the irrational forces in characters drawn from the lower and criminal classes...Can we see the traditional fears and prejudices of their middle-class system of values unconsciously intruding into and determining their choice of literary images?"[36] By using the Herzka "window" as part of this motivational substructure Doderer causes it to be a strong unifying element in the novel.

When he was constructing the "windows" in *Die Wasserfälle von Slunj* Doderer discovered that "Die Fenster-Technik kann schließlich auch in jedem Augenblicke einen neuen Einschlag provozieren."[37] This is certainly true of the Herzka "window" as a study of the genesis of the chapters involved clearly demonstrates. A few weeks before he started writing the chapter "Die Falltür" Doderer was sceptical about introducing Herzka into the novel, despite the opportunities this episode appeared to offer for extending the scope of the work. When the episode was completed it had assumed proportions the author had not anticipated,[38] and had emerged as one of the most significant episodes in the entire novel. It fulfilled all the requirements that Doderer's theory of the "window" technique was to lay down when he elaborated it when working on *Die Wasserfälle von Slunj* six years later. By interrupting the linear development of the novel the Herzka "window" expands the temporal framework and prevents the possible danger that too great stringency of form might hamper the author's attempts to improvise on his material. Despite his initial misgivings about the episode, the "window" more than lives up to Doderer's expectations and is a very successful realization of his wish to experiment with his literary techniques.

4

"Das Feuer"
The Craftsmanship of the Writer

I HAVE SINGLED OUT "Das Feuer" for closer scrutiny because as well as being the climax of the novel it is formally the most complex chapter of the entire work. In addition, it illustrates Doderer's view of the historical process and exemplifies his attitude toward the differing roles of the historian and the novelist. In the previous chapter we examined some of the technical devices adopted by Doderer to shape the raw material of the novel. In "Das Feuer" Doderer relies heavily on his technical expertise to prevent the contents of the chapter from becoming totally diffuse. He is forced to do so because of the nature of these contents. The chronology is fragmented and there is no causal connection between the various episodes. The fire itself is not the focal point of the chapter; the significant events are those which take place on its periphery. Doderer is seeking to convey the atmosphere of the day, which is one of confusion and turmoil. All these factors contribute to an erosion of the form of the chapter. Doderer's problem is how to achieve the contrived formlessness which he considers to be essential to portray the happenings of 15 July 1927 without completely destroying the narrative form. An examination of the genesis of the chapter and an analysis of its content reveal how Doderer resolved this problem and others which he faced during the course of the composition of the chapter.

The development of the chapter indicates that Doderer had no preconceived idea as to its form when he resumed work on the novel in 1951. On the inside cover of Ms I, probably noted in 1952, he listed the embryonic chapter headings for Part II, his intention at this time being to compose a two-part novel:

1. Auf offener Strecke
2. Am anderen Ufer
3. Im Osten
4. Mary...(oder anderer Titel)
5. Dort unten
6. Eine CS
7. Der Sturz vom Steckenpferd
8. Im Haus zum blauen Einhorn
    5 Kapitel
    Feuer I
    Feuer II
    Feuer III
    Schlaggenbergs Wiederkehr[1]

However, "Das Feuer" was already definitively placed and the projected division of the episode, the climax of the novel, into three chapters would seem to suggest that its importance was to be reflected in its length. (It did in fact emerge as the longest chapter, 127 pages long.)

Not only does "Das Feuer" mark the culmination of the events of the novel, it is also an integral part of "Textmasse C," which consists of "Vor verschlossenen Türen," "Auf der Schanze," and the two-part chapter "Kurze Kurven." "Das Feuer" is closely linked to these chapters, one of whose functions is to lead up to the events of 15 July 1927, a day which is not only a "historical moment" but also sees the resolution of a whole series of personal relationships. "Das Feuer" illustrates Doderer's thesis that all "second realities" inevitably collapse when they are forcibly confronted with reality as it actually exists. He also wishes to show that the intrusion of the historical event (the "anonymous happening") into everyday life (the "Alltag") is without significance for the individual. He pre-figures the "anonymous happening" of 15 July by the anonymous letter written to the police by Malva Fiedler, accusing Leonhard Kakabsa of having a suspicious relationship with some young girls. Leonhard has no difficulty in clearing himself of the charge, but he senses a form of irrational threat to his ordered existence. The happenings of 15 July will have a similar outcome for the majority of the characters involved, consciously or unconsciously, in them. Their lives will not be radically affected by the political happenings.

A favorite saying of Doderer, borrowed from Gütersloh, was: "Die Tiefe ist außen." Ideally the self and external reality should exist in a state of equilibrium, and, in this relationship, external reality plays a preponderating role. However, should its demands become too extreme, the result is a loss of balance in the ego/reality relationship and the creation of an unbridgeable gap between the two. The idea of this chasm between internal and external reality occasioned by the "historical moment" of 15 July 1927 caused Doderer to write the chapter "Kurze Kurven," to which he initially referred as "Sp(alt)," to bridge the gap which he saw existing between "Vor verschlossenen Türen" and "Das Feuer." As well as the gap between internal and external reality there was also a chronological gap between the two chapters. Doderer attempted to minimize this gap by having "Vor verschlossenen Türen" anticipate some of the happenings which take place during this time. Sp, in turn, developed certain of the subplots of the novel to their "Reifepunkt" so that they could be expeditiously resolved in "Das Feuer," with the minimum of exposition. All of these subplots developed independently of one another, and the form of the novel began to reflect the nature of its contents. The short, discontinuous segments of narrative depicted the lack of communication between the individuals, each of whom was involved with his or her own personal problems, to the exclusion of the political happenings.

When Doderer completed "Kurze Kurven I" on 1 December 1954 he felt that all the preparations were well under way for "Das Feuer." This was not the case, however, and he spent the next nine months on the planning of the chapter. During this time he also wrote "Auf der Schanze" and "Kurze Kurven II." Strangely enough, it was not the beginning of "Das Feuer" which took up his attention at this period, but the end, as he thought about concluding the chapter with Geyrenhoff's arrival at Friederike Ruthmayr's home in the late afternoon of 15 July.[2] He then turned his attention to the introductory sections of the chapter, which he decided to open with three "excentrische Einsätze." They would involve Quapp, Leonhard and Anny Gräven and would lead up to a "Reifepunkt," thus discharging an expository function. His plan for the chapter was now to begin with three "Vortakte," short introductory passages, intended to create an atmosphere of silence. As such they act as a contrast to the increasing noise and confusion of the rest of the chapter. (Doderer made increasing and effective use of pairs of contrasts as the chapter developed.) Next would come the three "excentrische Einsätze" just mentioned, and then would follow the ten main episodes into which the chapter was to be divided. However, Doderer intended to intersperse throughout this series of episodes what he termed "Leuchtpunkte" or "Partikel," which, because of their antithetical nature, did not require an assigned place in the compositional structure but could be interpolated at random. Generally speaking, each of these "Leuchtpunkte" corresponds to an empty room somewhere in the city—"Still-Räume" is also used to refer to them. Among them are Kajetan's room, which is empty because he has gone off to London, and the room which formerly belonged to Frau Kapsreiter in the "Haus zum blauen Einhorn." Like the three "Vortakte," these "Leuchtpunkte" are intended to serve a contrapuntal purpose. They are isolated from external reality, havens of peace in which everyday reality is undisturbed by the irruption of the "historical moment."

To underscore further the contrast between everyday reality and the "historical moment," Doderer decided to make "Das Feuer" "eine Fuge aus zwei Gerüchen."[3] These two odors are the smell of burning and the aroma of camphor. The burning of the Palace of Justice is the physical manifestation of the anonymous happening; the smell of mothballs characterizes, for the author, summer in Vienna in the early part of the twentieth century, when houses are closed up as their owners go off to the country. Doderer anticipated this metaphorical content of "Das Feuer" in "Kurze Kurven II" and spoke of the period from 25 June until around 15 July as a "Kampfer-Zeit."[4] By so doing he established yet another link between these chapters of the novel. Doderer makes use of metaphor in "Das Feuer" to integrate the historico-political content into the chapter and to create a narrative expression which reproduces the atmosphere of the day. By conveying his interpretation of the situation in such terms he is adopting an indirect approach and it is precisely this indirect approach to the political events which certain critics find unsatisfactory. They would prefer to see him comment upon the happenings of the day, but this would run entirely counter to his view of the role of the novelist as opposed to that of the historian.

Two days before starting to write text for "Das Feuer" Doderer noted as one of the guiding principles of the composition: "Nie direkt auf F: dieses muß stets seitlich in der Aura bleiben."[5] By choosing to have the major political happening, the burning of the Palace of Justice, remain on the periphery of the action of the novel, he freed himself from any obligation to focus attention on it or to have it condition the chronological sequence of the narrative or the order of priority in which certain of the events were to be narrated. He could continue with the compositional pattern which he used in "Kurze Kurven," which was of a highly episodic nature, and make use of narrative techniques to achieve formal unity, despite the lack of causal connections and the simultaneity of the chronological structure.

On 22 September 1955 Doderer wrote the three "Vortakte," the short introductory sections, of "Das Feuer." His original intention was to continue by writing the next three "Vortakte," the three "excentrische Einsätze" concerned with Quapp, Leonhard and Anny Gräven, and thus establish a pattern of narration which involved moving from one character to another at critical moments for each throughout the day. However, he now reached the conclusion that from a compositional point of view it might be preferable to focus his attention successively on each individual character and recount the experiences of the entire day for the individual concerned. Each episode could then be split into subsections and interspersed more or less arbitrarily among the other subsections which would be created:

Text und Composition müssen jetzt gleichzeitig vorschreiten. Jede durchkon-
struierte Reihe—hier bleibt gleichgültig, welche man da zuerst vornimmt—ergibt
implicite schon die ganze Sequenz von den 2 x 3 Vortakten bis zum Nachtakt.
Theoretisch könnte jede Reihe in continuo durchgeführt und dann zerlegt werden.[6]

Thus, after writing the first of the "excentrische Einsätze" (2Qa),[7] that concerned
with Quapp, he went on to write the sections 2Qb and 2Qc of the Quapp sequence,
which described her day from nine o'clock in the morning until the late afternoon.
The same procedure was adopted for the writing of the Geyrenhoff sequence,
which followed Geyrenhoff's actions from six o'clock in the morning until his
arrival at Friederike Ruthmayr's home at five o'clock in the evening. Doderer was
quite clear in his mind as to just how he intended to divide each episode into its
subsections,[8] and was already considering possible juxtapositions for certain of
these subsections. He decided, for example, to have the first subsection of the
Geyrenhoff sequence, 1/11a, lead up to a "Reifepunkt" for 1/11b, in which the
shooting of the old woman, the uprooting of the street-lamp and the death of
Gyurkicz take place. However, it was not his intention to have 1/11a and 1/11b
follow immediately upon each other but to separate them with a less eventful
passage, such as the encounter between Quapp and Orkay on the Mariahilferstraße. In 1/11a Geyrenhoff and Gontard are unaware of what is going on in the
city. After breakfast they hear a noise, but there is nothing to see, there are no
police visible, and Geyrenhoff is unaware that this is because they are defending
the Palace of Justice (pp. 1233-34). It is at this point that 1/11a breaks off, leaving
the reader wondering what is happening. His curiosity will not be satisfied until
1/11b. One reason for the splitting up of the episodes is to achieve suspense, and
the alternating changes in the tempo of the narrative also serve this purpose.

On completion of the Quapp and Geyrenhoff sequences, which merge in the
episode 1/11/2Q at Palais Ruthmayr (pp. 1296-99), Doderer wrote the "Vignette," the concluding section of the Anny Gräven sequence, 13c (pp. 1328-31).
He had now reached what he looked on as the main action of the entire novel, the
episodes involving Leonhard Kakabsa on 15 July 1927. Doderer considered
Kakabsa as an exemplary figure and wanted him to play a major role in the climax
of the novel. He is the working-man who has broken through not only the
"dialect barrier" but social barriers as well and is the epitome of Doderer's anti-
revolutionary thinking. On 15 July Leonhard is faced with a decision; as a member
of the working class should he become involved in the happenings of the day or
should he remain aloof from political events and pursue his own individual
desires? It is on this polarization within Leonhard's being that Doderer constructed the entire Leonhard sequence, which is of a highly antithetical nature.

To express this dichotomy in Leonhard's being Doderer established a series of
contrasts which emerge throughout the sequence. The sequence itself he viewed
in symphonic terms, divided into three movements:

7 TWENTIETH CENTURY ODYSSEY

Jetzt, mit 17, tritt ein der eigentliche symphonische Satz, Orchester im Orchester, dreiteilig, was merkwürdig genug ist, dreiteilig wie das ganze Werk selbst.

a	*b*	*c*
Vortakt	Spontaneität - Stille	Bewegung - und Auslauf[9]

The first movement, 17a, sets up the first pair of contrasts. It is a bright sunny day in mid-July, but Leonhard is conscious of an autumnal feeling. This is no mere freak of the weather; it is explicable only in terms of Leonhard's "biographisches Kerngebiet."[10] The first phase of his existence came to an end with the breaking-through of the "dialect barrier." Leonhard identifies the summer with the second phase of his existence, and this came to an end when he "crossed the Rubicon" (p. 1118), leaving his previous life as a workman behind him and becoming librarian and scholar in the Palais Croix. In 17b the break with his past life is further highlighted by the fact that he, the former workman, spontaneously helps the porter to close the doors of the university against his fellow-workers who are demonstrating in the streets.

Doderer had been thinking of the Leonhard sequence in symphonic terms, and he realized that the third movement, 17c, was of major significance. It was in this movement that he wished the full contrastive structure of the sequence to emerge: "17c muß von Gegensätzen gespannt werden bis zum Zerreißen."[11] The importance which Doderer attached to this section of the narrative may be seen in the fact that before starting to write 17c he drew up a sketch for it, the only part of "Das Feuer" which he treated in such a detailed fashion.[12] At the beginning of 17c Leonhard is in the precincts of the university during the afternoon of 15 July: "Eingeschlossen blieb er zugleich ausgeschlossen von allem, was dort drüben geschah" (p. 1291). Isolated in his own private world, he is cut off from external reality. His only reason for leaving the safety of the university is to keep his appointment with Mary K. The polarization of Leonhard's being is concretized in the choice of direction which he has to make on leaving the university. By turning left Leonhard is following the path of involvement in the political happenings of the day, an involvement which might be related to his working class origins and his socialist thinking. By turning right, he is electing to prefer his desires as a private individual, to place the demands of everyday reality above those of the "historical moment." Paradoxically, Leonhard does turn left on leaving the university, but senses intuitively that this will nonetheless take him to Mary. External reality then intrudes, and in the company of his two former workmates, Niki Zdarsa and Karl Zilchner (the motivational structure is underlined by their taking up their position, one to the left and one to the right of Leonhard), Leonhard finds the body of his friend, the policeman, Karl Zeitler.

When asked by a police-inspector if he is a workman, Leonhard answers in the affirmative. He and his two friends go off, heading toward the right and Mary. In the solidarity of their friendship Leonhard realizes that there need not be an unbridgeable gap between his past existence and his present. This awareness that past and present need not be mutually exclusive causes Leonhard to experience "ein wirkliches Glück" (p. 1311). Doderer expresses the idea of the reconciliation of the opposing claims on Leonhard's loyalties in figurative language, continuing the idea of the paths diverging to right and left: "Und die Wege nach links und nach rechts, sie fielen zusammen jetzt, er hatte sie beide zugleich unter den Sohlen" (p. 1311).

After completing the Leonhard sequence Doderer wrote the concluding section of the René Stangeler sequence, 4b. (He did not write the two introductory segments of this sequence until almost two months later and they were the last text of the chapter to be written.) He considered that the only function of this episode was that it should act as "der Kontrast-Vorraum, die Antecamera der großen Aufwölbung ex 16 (b)."[13] René's professional success, his edition of the Neudegg manuscript, ensured his acceptance as Grete's future husband by the Siebenschein family, and put his relationship with Grete herself on a more stable footing. Their relationship was no longer problematic, a direct contrast to that of Mary and Leonhard, which was described by Doderer as "ausweglos" and "absichtslos."[14] Despite the fact that the Stangeler episode, 4b, was not of major consequence, and Doderer implied that he had merely tacked it on to the main body of the narrative, it nonetheless assumed more significance as it developed: "DD-F-4b: Das ist jetzt eine—Einlage (F 4 b). Aber in den Einlagen, die wir garnicht meinten, wird uns zu Teil, worauf es ankommt—und es erweist sich alles andere nur als mühevoll aufgestelltes Hilfsziel."[15] Doderer here made the same type of discovery as he did when he realized that the seemingly peripheral happening was the one which was most important. The Stangeler episode also illustrated how, despite the claims he made for the priority of form over content, he could become so involved in a minor character or event that it assumed proportions not originally intended in the composition. This is true of the two most significant "Leuchtpunkte" in the chapter, LPM and LPN, those concerning Frau Mayrinker and Dr. Neuberg, especially the former.

When Doderer first mentioned Neuberg's room in his diary during the compositional stages of "Das Feuer," his intention was to use it merely as one of the "Still-Räume," which were to act as a contrast to the chaotic conditions in the city itself. But the fact that from his balcony Neuberg can overlook the entire city gives him a vantage point similar to that of Geyrenhoff on the "Schanze" and thus permits this episode to become part of the contrapuntal situation between Frau Kapsreiter in the cellar and Geyrenhoff on the roof on the novel.[16] Doderer then changed his mind as to the function which this episode could serve. It could still form part of a contrapuntal situation, the entire climax of the novel being established on such contrastive relationships, but this time it would be Neuberg's personal situation which would be contrasted with that of Geyrenhoff. Neuberg's engagement to Angelika Trapp has been broken; Geyrenhoff and Friederike Ruthmayr become engaged: "Es gibt noch eine Kontrapunktierung außer Ka/Br: die Glücklichen und Effektiven contra: LP Neuberg (am Balkon) und Aufwölbung, deshalb: 16/17 LPN 1/11cII."[17] The situation between Leonhard and Mary K. parallels that of Neuberg, inasmuch as the future of their relationship is highly problematic. They do not face the secure prospects, and not only from a financial point of view, of Geyrenhoff and Friederike.

Doderer made one change to the chronology of the chapter which effectively made the Neuberg episode a more successful illustration of a "Leuchtpunkt." In the early stages of writing the chapter Doderer's intention was that Neuberg should witness from his balcony the outbreak of the fire in the city below. However, instead of following this plan, Doderer decided to have Neuberg work in his room for several hours and then fall asleep. When he awakens it is around nine o'clock in the evening and he is completely unaware of the events of the day. He sees the red glow of the fire through the French windows of his balcony, but it has no political significance for him, and suggests only a mythical analogy of his own personal situation. That the Neuberg episode should culminate in metaphor is in keeping with Doderer's "indirect" approach to the novel and to life in general: "mir ahnt' es schon vor längerem, daß hier im Randlichen, in den LP's, die eigentliche Essenz des Werks liegt, wie auch im Leben, dessen nuclei nicht im Gemeinten und Direkten angetroffen werden."[18]

The development of LPN clearly illustrates how freely the author was putting into practice his intention "an allen Ecken und Enden die Composition improvisieren."[19] The development of the second major "Leuchtpunkt," LPM, illustrates even more clearly how in the course of the composition certain situations could steadily gain momentum and assume dimensions not anticipated.

As was the case with LPN, Doderer at first intended that the former home of Frau Kapsreiter in the "Haus zum blauen Einhorn" should simply be a "kleiner Leuchtpunkt in F."[20] On 15 July 1927 it is empty, as its present occupants, the Mayrinkers, are in the country. This is the situation in the Mayrinker episode in the chapter "Kurze Kurven II." However, on 14 August 1955, the day on which Doderer finished writing "Kurze Kurven II," he noted: "Die Mayrinker könnten mir Vergnügen machen,"[21] and it was no doubt as a result of his desire to be able to continue to deal with these characters that he decided that he would have Frau Mayrinker present in Vienna on 15 July, and moreover, would have her succeed in extinguishing a household fire.

As Doderer continued to reflect on the composition of this episode, it became clear that Frau Mayrinker was assuming the role of Frau Kapsreiter. Not only that, Doderer wished her to illustrate how he would wish humanity as a whole to react to the "anonymous happening" which threatened it. When a fire breaks out in her kitchen, Frau Mayrinker acts resolutely to extinguish it, and does so quite independently of outside help (p. 1283). For her, the individual, "nichts war beschädigt, nichts war ruiniert" (p. 1284), in marked contrast to the effect of the political happenings on Viennese society.

In order to portray the conflict between everyday reality and the historical moment, Doderer once more employed the contrast between "Kampferduft" and "Brandgeruch." After she puts out the fire in her kitchen, Frau Mayrinker goes to her bedroom to fetch some clean clothes. She opens the closet and the odor of mothballs wafts toward her: "Und hier erst schwand der Brand vollends, wichen seine letzten Spuren aus der Nase, verwischt, ja, getilgt vom kühlen Kampfer-dufte" (p. 1286). Everyday reality has triumphed over the intrusion of the historical event: the individual has successfully resisted the threat to his ordered existence.

With the completion of LPM Doderer seemed to consider that he had written the essential part of the chapter. Although he decided that he need not work in such sustained fashion on the remaining seven sections of the narrative, when he came to write them in January 1956, after a break of over three weeks in the composition of the chapter, he continued to add to the text on a daily basis. He termed these seven sections of narrative "Improvisationen,"[22] a nomenclature which suggests that their role was to act as variations on the theme of the chapter, in similar fashion to the contrastive function exercised by the "Leuchtpunkte." Some of these "improvisations" were themselves "Leuchtpunkte," and Doderer wished to intersperse them throughout the chapter in order to separate the various subsections into which he intended to divide the main episodes.

Before considering the final stages in the composition of the chapter, which in effect constitute a further fragmentation of its temporal structure, I propose to examine the various techniques used by Doderer to prevent the complete disintegration of the narrative form. To integrate the Quapp sequence into the chapter and into "Textmasse C," Doderer made use of parallel incidents and a motivational link. In the chapter "Kurze Kurven I," after she has failed her audition on 23 May 1927 and has realized that she has no hope of making a career in music, Quapp is picked up by Géza von Orkay in the chauffeur-driven car belonging to the Hungarian Embassy (p. 1008). In "Das Feuer," on 15 July 1927, when she is on her way to meet Géza, she is forced out of her taxi by some members of the Republikanischer Schutzbund, who wish to use it for the transport of wounded. As she is standing helplessly on a traffic-island, the Embassy car pulls up alongside and whisks her away (p. 1263). Doderer strengthened the link between the two incidents by the use of the motif of Quapp's violin-case. In the first incident, Géza gets out of the car to speak to her and to offer her a lift: "Sie gab

Orkay die Hand. Nun war sie erst frei. Richtig wäre gewesen, den Geigenkasten einfach auf dem Pflaster stehen zu lassen. Aber sie nahm ihn doch noch mit in den Wagen. 'Nach Döbling?' fragte Orkay. Sie nickte" (p. 1008). Quapp's violin-case is a symbol of the "second reality" in which she has been living, her ambition to be a professional violinist, even although she lacks the necessary talent. Three things combine to free her from her obsession. First, her inheritance from the estate of Achaz von Neudegg solves her monetary problems, and thus removes the financial incentive to become a successful musician. Second, she fails her audition and realizes that her hopes of success in the world of Viennese music are illusory. Third, she falls in love with Géza von Orkay, and chooses the career of diplomat's wife in preference to that of a professional musician.

At this point in the relationship between the two of them she has not quite broken free of her "second reality." She feels that she should leave her violin-case on the sidewalk in order to make a complete break with the past. She nonetheless takes it with her into the car. Two months later, on the other hand, she is completely free of her obsession with music. Sitting in the Embassy car on the way out of the city: "Immerwährend hatte Quapp gegen jede Vernunft das Gefühl, auf der Verkehrs-Insel dort unten am Beginne der Mariahilferstraße ihren Geigenkasten stehen gelassen zu haben" (p. 1264). This can only be interpreted metaphorically, as, of course, Quapp does not have her violin-case with her when Géza picks her up in the car. It merely emphasizes the fact that her relationship with Géza is the final factor which allows her to break out of her "second reality."

Doderer made similar use of parallel incident to link the Geyrenhoff section 1/11c/I and the Leonhard section 17c. When Geyrenhoff leaves Gontard's residence on the Schmerlingplatz to go to keep his appointment with Friederike Ruthmayr, he is let out of the building by the Hausmeister, Waschler: "Waschler ...kam herab, sperrte rasch auf, ließ mich durch den Spalt, und alsbald hörte ich, wie hinter mir sich zweimal der Schlüssel im Schlosse drehte" (p. 1280). Geyrenhoff's sole reason for leaving his place of safety was to keep an appointment with the woman hè loved; Leonhard has a similar reason for leaving the safety of the university. Doderer underlines the similarity of their situation, and in so doing draws together two threads of the narrative, by using almost identical language to describe their leaving their refuge. When Leonhard leaves the university he is let out by the Gebäudeverwalter, Fessl: "Fessl zog einen Schlüssel, öffnete, sah hinaus, winkte Leonhard und ließ ihn durch den Spalt...Hinter ihm drehte sich zweimal der Schlüssel im Schlosse" (p. 1292).

Doderer performed the vital function of linking up unrelated segments of narrative also by using "Synchronisierungsmittel," a device whereby an occurrence at a precise instant of time is apprehended by certain individuals, who stand in no spatial proximity to one another. When working on the Geyrenhoff sequence Doderer decided to make use of three such means of synchronization: the churchbells ringing at noon, the rain starting at five o'clock, and Leonhard's seeing Stangeler on his way to Grete Siebenschein's at five o'clock.

His use of the "Mittagsläuten" is particularly effective. Geyrenhoff, at the window of Gürtzner-Gontard's apartment, sees Gyurkicz being shot. He experiences a feeling of identity with him, and realizes that his death was caused by the fact that he was living in a "second reality," and was not the outcome of his seeming involvement in the political happenings. Geyrenhoff and Gontard say the "De Profundis" for the dead man, and: "Nicht lange, nachdem wir geendet hatten, begann das Mittagsläuten. Ich verwunderte mich tief über die paradoxe Kälte, welche, unter den gegebenen Umständen, von diesem Malzeichen täglicher Ordnung jetzt ausging" (p. 1249). To Geyrenhoff the everyday sound seems like a death-knell tolling for Gyurkicz, and he feels closer to the latter in his death than he did in his lifetime. The irony of this situation is underlined by the fact that the sound of twelve o'clock striking is also heard by Quapp, who had quite recently been Gyurkicz's lover: "Noch während sie auf dem Balkon stand und in die Rosen hinabblickte, begann es zwölf Uhr zu läuten von den Kirchtürmen der Umgebung" (p. 1261). However, for her the bells have no funereal tone. They start ringing just after she has been thinking of the time she spent in the Eroicagasse, the time when she had the affair with Gyurkicz. This period now seems part of her "Vor-Biographie" (p. 1261), and is buried in the past. She is, of course, unaware of Gyurkicz's death, but the implication is that for her it no longer matters and that she, unlike Geyrenhoff, will be unaffected by his death.

Doderer was forced to discard his plans for using the rain starting at five o'clock as a "Synchronisierungsmittel" when he discovered that this was factually incorrect. He had noted in his diary for 1936: "Schießerei und Blutlachen/5h ca Regen (Gewitter-Regen), dann Ruhe, Ströme an Verwundeten."[23] However, on 16 December 1955 he contacted the Meteorological Institute and, according to their records, which were indisputably more accurate than personal recollection, he found that 15 July was "warn, sonnig, Temp. max 26½°. Abends Eintrübung, Gewitter 22h15-23h15. 21h schon Regenschauer. *Kein Regen 5h nm.*"[24] He had made quite frequent mention in his diaries of this rain at five o'clock. More importantly, he had also included it in the text of 17c/II, and this resulted in three quite substantial deletions from the passage having to be made. Although the rain shower was thus eliminated as a narrative device, the incident does stress the importance which Doderer ascribed to factual accuracy and his scrupulous attention to the *minutiae* of his material.

Doderer made use of devices such as parallel incident, motivational links, and simultaneous happening, to compensate for the lack of causality and linear development. As the chapter stood on 11 January 1956, it consisted of the three major sequences, Quapp, Geyrenhoff and Leonhard, followed by the two main

LPs, Mayrinker and Neuberg, and the seven "improvisations." The three major sequences, of course, each followed a linear pattern. Doderer now subjected the chapter to what he termed an "Exaratio," preparatory to undertaking the "Reihung" of the twenty-eight sections into which he divided the content of the chapter. This was not the first time that Doderer had carried out an "Exaratio," but the process normally involved only a revision of the text, with minor additions and deletions, before handing it over for typing. However, in the closing stages of the novel's composition he came to look on this procedure as an integral part of the creative process: "Die Exaratio ist eine sprachliche Pflicht, Gütersloh erwähnt sie einmal (als 'Verbesserung') verbaliter."[25] With respect to "Das Feuer" Doderer was using the term in its literal meaning, as he really was about to "plough up" the chapter in its existing form. However, he was at pains to stress the constructive as opposed to the destructive nature of this procedure: "Exaratio=Compositio. Dies die Formel."[26] The introductory sections and the conclusion of the chapter caused him no problems, as he had always intended to start with the three "Vortakte" followed by the three "excentrische Einsätze" (2Q/a, 13a and 17a), and to close with the Anny Gräven "Vignette" (13c), which was a form of epilogue to the chapter and took place in January 1928. The "Reihung" involved the reordering of the segments of the main sequences and the interspersing of the LPs and the seven "improvisations." Doderer followed a chronological pattern, with a rough division of the day into morning and afternoon. On the whole he was successful in avoiding an overlapping of morning and afternoon. The first fifteen episodes all take place in the morning, except 13b, which takes place in the afternoon. The remaining thirteen episodes take place after midday. The majority conclude in the early evening, but LPM and LPN are prolonged until around nine o'clock and Geyrenhoff does not leave the Ruthmayr mansion until midnight. The critical times are noon, which is, of course, a "Synchronisierungsmittel," and five o'clock, five-thirty, and six o'clock, which are the times that certain of the main characters must keep important appointments. The two major LPs, LPM and LPN, differ from the other sequences in that their chronology is not fragmented, but runs unbroken from the early morning until about nine o'clock in the evening. Doderer may here be using chronological considerations to show that these two individuals, Frau Mayrinker and Dr. Neuberg, are completely unaffected by the external happenings.

The only problem which Doderer encountered was what he termed the "anachronism" of Zeitler in 17c. He had mentioned the problem during the compositional stages of the chapter, where it seemed that he was interpreting the incident symbolically. Zeitler is linked to Leonhard's past, to his days as a workman; Leonhard's discovery of his body retards him in his progress toward Mary K. and his new life. Doderer did not pursue this idea, however, and the problem became one of the respective chronology of the two sections 1/11c and 17/cII.

Geyrenhoff leaves the Schmerlingplatz shortly before half past four (p. 1280), and almost immediately sees a police-officer firing into the sewers. He then comes across the body of Zeitler. Leonhard and his friends arrive on the scene shortly thereafter, when Geyrenhoff has continued on his way to Friederike Ruthmayr. Geyrenhoff must find Zeitler's body before Leonhard does, as the police-inspector who speaks to Leonhard asks some members of the Republikanischer Schutzbund to remove the body. Thus, in his reordering of the episodes of the chapter Doderer had to ensure that 1/11cII preceded 17/dII in order to avoid any possible conflict in the chronology of the episodes.

Lest the impression should arise that the remodelling of the chapter was an affair of moments, it should be pointed out that Doderer spent two weeks, between 12-25 January 1956, on the "Exaratio" and "Reihung." The latter process, which involved taking the twenty-eight segments of narrative which were the outcome of the "Exaratio" and arranging them in a new sequence, was a completely new compositional method for him. To help him oversee the rather complex problem of ordering which he faced, he drew up a "Composition ex post."[27] He also had to give his typist, Professor Günther, an "Ariadnefaden," so that he could transpose the episodes from their original order in Ms III into their new juxtapositions.[28] When he completed this radical remodelling of the chapter he was still stressing the constructive as opposed to the destructive nature of this process: "Exaratio war hier in der Tat Compositio, und diese wurde auch ex post am Brette noch einmal zur Gänze getan."[29]

While engaged in the writing of "Das Feuer," Doderer stated that what he was seeking to present in the chapter was a "Gesamtbild des Lebens,"[30] and if life itself was turbulent and disorganized, then it was this atmosphere which he had to seek to convey in the novel. It is testimony to his skill that his careful planning of the chapter and use of certain literary stratagems—synchronization, analogy, motifs, parallel incident—enabled him to convey this sense of chaos, without the chapter itself becoming completely formless. Doderer felt able to manipulate the weight of content in the chapter because of his confidence in his mastery of the technical stratagems which he intended to employ: "F hat sich so entwickelt, daß ich nur leise besorge, es könnten meine Augen größer sein als der Magen. Doch ist alles im Technischen beschlossen und also durch dieses erreichbar. Das beruhigt wieder tief."[31] The final form of "Das Feuer" amply justifies his belief in his craftmanship as a writer. Despite the "ploughing up" and the radical reordering of the contents of the chapter, it remains both cohesive and comprehensible, as formal and thematic devices furnish the links between the various episodes, taking the place of the non-existent causal connections.

Our examination of this chapter reveals how Doderer solved certain fundamental compositional problems. "Das Feuer" is undoubtedly the most complex chapter in the entire novel, in respect of both form and content. Stylistically, it marks a new departure for the author, in that he makes sweeping, and seemingly arbitrary changes to the organization of his material so that it corresponds more closely to the capricious nature of the happenings of 15 July 1927. It mediates the author's view of the historical process and his attitude to politics, his Thomist interpretation of reality, and his belief that the "second reality" disintegrates when it is forcibly confronted with true reality. The density and multiplicity of the content of the chapter are most skillfully ordered and canalized by the formal structure and narrative stratagems.

The chapter also shows that those critics who believe that Doderer always followed slavishly a predetermined form for the composition of the novel are mistaken, and that Doderer himself often ascribed too great a significance to his "Skizzen." Apart from the sketch for the Leonhard episode, 17c, there is only an incomplete sketch (the one numbered 3g in the folder of sketches in the *Nachlaß*) and the "ex post" sketch for the chapter, and the "Reihung" indicates that the form of the chapter was far from immutable. "Für den Romancier ist die Form die Entelechie jedes Inhaltes."[32] Our examination of this chapter would seem to give the lie to this assertion of Doderer, and shows that the tension between form and content is not so easily resolved.

5
History and Politics

THE QUESTION OF THE POLITICAL CONTENT of *Die Dämonen* is highly complex, because one is faced with the difficulty of reconciling the seemingly irreconcilable. The long genesis of the novel means that it encompasses Doderer's attraction to National Socialism in the 1930s and his later rejection of all ideologies. Similarly, it reflects the fact that in spite of his years of study at the Institut für Österreichische Geschichtsforschung his conception of the role of history for the novelist was not that of an orthodox historian.

I propose to examine Doderer's historico-political thinking under three headings. First, a consideration of his religious views, in particular of his professed Thomism, as his thinking in this area colors his political outlook; second, a treatment of his political thought, and third, a discussion of his attitude to history and how this influences the historico-political content of *Die Dämonen*.

I. Doderer and Religion

Although Doderer's works are not overtly of a religious nature, a certain religiosity can be detected in his writings in the 1920s. In 1925, for example, he composed the short piece entitled "Seraphica," about the journey of St. Francis to Assisi. To research his material he visited Assisi in September of the same year and the following year he published an article entitled "Franz von Assisi."[1]

Doderer's friendship with Gütersloh undoubtedly was a factor in the shaping of his religious thought. The latter was a devout Catholic and was well-versed in theology, having begun studies for the priesthood before turning to art and literature. His theological training exerted an unmistakable influence on his writings,[2] and Doderer's familiarity with these writings could possibly have paved the way for his conversion to Catholicism in the winter of 1939-40. Doderer was born into a family that had been Protestant for generations and his decision to convert was a complex one, based on several problems which confronted him. In fascist Austria he had just resigned his membership of the Nazi Party, and he seemed to regard his conversion as part of the cathartic process of purging his misconceptions of National Socialism. His failure to complete "Die Dämonen der Ostmark" had caused him to doubt his abilities as a writer and he appeared to be looking for some form of metaphysical underpinning of his faith in his creative talents. His public disavowal of fascist ideology which this proclamation of faith signified was not without possible unpleasant consequences for him. Indeed, he believed that only his conscription into the Luftwaffe spared him from persecution. His conversion was an emotional decision, for whatever reasons, as he did not seem to have much knowledge of the canon of the Catholic church.

In the philosophy of St. Thomas Aquinas, however, with which Doderer became acquainted in 1942, he found a support for his attitude to reality and also a system of belief which adapted itself to his literary practice. He first mentioned Aquinas in his diary in a footnote of 27 May 1942, without indicating what had aroused his interest in this philosopher. It may possibly have been Gütersloh who introduced him to Aquinas. On 29 May Doderer wrote, again in a footnote: "Schon eine erste und bisher nur flüchtige Berührung mit S. Thomas scheint mich stark zu influenzieren und tritt bereits aus Spontaneitäten meines Denkens hervor...'De ente et essentia' ist übrigens das einzige Buch, welches ich bei mir führe."[3] Almost three years later he said that he was carrying *De ente et essentia* with him, in the edition annotated by a former teacher of his, Rudolf Allers.[4]

For Doderer the key concept in the teachings of St. Thomas is that of the *analogia entis*, the belief that creation is the manifestation of the Divine Being. It is thus *ipso facto* good; outside this divinely-ordained pattern lies nothingness. Man's refusal to perceive this goodness and his search for what lies outside divine creation is the source of all his ills. This metaphysical doctrine obviously strikes a chord with Doderer and links with his theory of "Apperzeptions-Verweigerung," the refusal of the individual to perceive, in all its connotations, reality in the world as it is. In the chapter "Auf offener Strecke," Gürtzner-Gontard, who is quite unambiguously acting as the author's *porte-parole*, claims that the proclivity of young people toward revolutionary behavior is due to the fact that they are unwilling to accept reality as it exists: "'Der junge Mensch wehrt sich einfach dagegen, unter den dargebotenen Bedingungen ins Leben einzutreten, er will diese Bedingungen nicht einmal ganz auffassen, er will sich die Augen zuhalten und die Hände vor's Gesicht, was man merkwürdigerweise als Kind im Mutterleibe wirklich tut...'" (p. 487). Doderer added new material to this chapter in 1952 to reinforce his thesis that "Apperzeptions-Verweigerung" is the root cause of all revolutionary behavior, behavior which in his eyes is synonymous with the disintegration of the individual and his value-system.

By the time Doderer wrote the first version of "Sexualität und totaler Staat" in 1948, he was claiming that Thomism was fundamental to his nature: "Daß ich beim Schreiben oder Denken immer nur die Analogia entis mit Variationen umspiele ist mir außer Zweifel; zudem, daß ich sozusagen gebürtiger Thomist bin, ohne Bedürfnis—bis jetzt—dieses mein Fundament kritisch zu prüfen."[5] He explained both the emergence of the Hitler regime and his own political short-comings as the rejection of the *analogia entis*: "Der totale Staat entstand durch die Flucht der Analogia entis und die Etablierung einer zweiten Wirklichkeit neben dieser: und genau so lebte ich."[6] This use of Thomist philosophy, however uncritical, enabled him to come to terms with his political past. It also enabled him to resume work on *Die Dämonen*, for he considered that the novelist is the individual for whom a heightened awareness of the *analogia entis* establishes a firm connection between the self and external reality: "Man könnte den Roman-cier ein Individuum nennen, dem eine ferne Abspiegelung der analogia entis in besonders hervorstechender Weise als persönliche Eigenschaft innewohnt, frei-lich in einem verhobenen und übertragenen Verstande des Begriffs: als fester Konnex zwischen Innen und Außen."[7] By linking his metaphysical thinking to his literary practice Doderer was able to dispel his self-doubts. Thomist philos-ophy allowed him to justify his attraction to National Socialism and to explain his subsequent rejection of it. We must now consider the consequences of both actions for the content of the novel.

II. The Political Content of *"Die Dämonen"*

Undoubtedly the most decisive event in the life of Doderer as a young man, and certainly the one which had the greatest influence on his later development, both as an individual and as a writer, was his military service during World War I. The time spent on active duty was actually rather short, for he was captured by the Russians in July 1916 and spent four years in various P.O.W. camps in Siberia.[8] Several of Doderer's friends claim that he was attracted to National Socialism out of a mistaken identification of Hitler's Reich with the "Reichsidee" nurtured in him as an officer of the Imperial Army.

Doderer was not particularly politically conscious and decided in the 1920s to limit his journalistic activity to feature articles of a non-political nature: "Zu einer journalistischen Betätigung in politischer oder wirtschaftlicher Hinsicht bin ich ja noch garnicht fähig, da mir Kenntnisse, Einblick, Versiertheit—und vor allem, jede irgendwie geartete fachmännische Bildung völlig abgehen! Es bleibt also für mich das Feuilleton jeder Art."[9] Even in the 1930s, when he became attracted to National Socialism, he did not publish any articles of a political nature. Hans Joachim Schröder takes Doderer to task for not adopting a political stance, and for not passing a moral judgment in the articles which he published at this time. Schröder says of the article "Vor dem Schafott. Hinrichtungen aus 5 Jahrhunderten, geschildert von Augenzeugen" (Der Wiener Tag, 23.8.1932): "Aus heutiger Sicht wirkt es mehr als befremdlich, wenn ein Historiker im August 1932 eine umfangreiche Artikelserie über die Scheußlichkeiten öffentlich gebilligter und organisierter Exekutionen drucken läßt—unter anderem beschreibt Doderer auch eine Bücherverbrennung; kaum ein Jahr später finden in Deutschland wieder Bücherverbrennungen statt—, und wenn er dabei kaum irgendwelche moralischen, geschweige denn politischen Überlegungen anstellt."[10] Schröder is expecting rather a lot of Doderer. After all, in 1932 Hitler had not acceded to power, and no one, inside or outside Germany, was fully aware of the atrocities of which he was capable. Moreover, Doderer's reading-public was looking for entertainment, not moralizing.

Doderer's relationship with his first wife inspired in him very strong anti-Semitic feelings, and it is likely that his attraction to National Socialism sprang from such personal grounds rather than from any identification with Hitler's politics. This was certainly the reason that he later gave for his fascist interlude.[11] Another cause of his anti-Semitism was the fact that he felt his lack of success in having his works published was due to the fact that the publishing-world was dominated by Jews: "Was hab' ich in Wien? Kaum eine Redaktion, kaum einen Verleger mehr. Fast alles jüdisch und daher jetzt zergehend wie Eis in der Hand."[12] Doderer seems here to be showing signs of the neurotic irrationality which characterizes the response of many of its adherents to fascist politics.

The year 1934 marked the nadir of his personal misfortunes, as the following diary entry shows:

Im übrigen werde ich mit meinen Mitteln in knapp zwei Monaten zu Ende sein... Vollends arm, im Berufe ohne äußeren Erfolg oder dessen nur kleinstes Anzeichen, .nach zweijähriger, durch die Art ihres Vollzuges nie mehr gutzumachender Trennung von meiner Frau...Es ist hier auch der Ort zu sagen,...daß ich also heute von der Öffentlichkeit völlig abgeschnitten bin, und derzeit nicht einmal die Möglichkeit habe, auch nur eine Zeile gedruckt und dafür Geld zu erhalten: hier in Österreich kommt solches unter den herrschenden Umständen und vom verlegerischen Gesichtspunkte überhaupt nicht in Frage und im Reiche draußen ist mir bisher nicht gelungen, auch nur einen Schritt breit Boden zu gewinnen, eine recht verwunderliche Tatsache, wo man doch glaubte, daß für Schriftsteller meiner Art nun ein Morgenrot angebrochen sei.[13]

If Doderer's personal situation made him particularly susceptible to the appeal of fascist politics, his admiration for Gütersloh was also a contributory factor of considerable importance. Schröder is correct in his assessment of the role played by Gütersloh in Doderer's attraction to fascism: "In einer eingehenden Untersuchung zum Faschismus Doderers müßte die politische Haltung Güterslohs in den dreißiger Jahren mitberücksichtigt werden...Die Tagebucheintragung Doderers vom 25.8.36 und sein Brief an Gütersloh vom 30.10.36 (beides in 'Commentarii 1935/36') beweisen, daß auch Gütersloh Faschist war. Er muß vermutlich als der Hauptvermittler angesehen werden, der Doderer für den Nationalsozialismus aufnahmebereit gemacht hat."[14]

At the beginning of August 1936 Doderer moved to Munich. He did not take up residence in Munich itself, because it was too expensive, but rented a studio in Dachau. Shortly after his arrival there he wrote of experiencing "die Befreiung von jenem entsetzlichen Druck, der vom Politischen her auf meiner bisherigen Heimat lastete, zumindest aber auf allen Menschen meiner Art und Gesinnung."[15] He had found Austrian politics authoritarian and repressive and expected to find in Hitler's Reich a regime more in accord with his political views. However, traces of a certain disenchantment with fascism become discernible from now on. The reasons for this are not clear. It may have been his realization that Hitler's Thousand Year Reich did not correspond in practice to his own ideal vision of a reincarnation of the Holy Roman Empire.[16] In later years he attributed his move away from Nazism to his experiences in Nazi Germany: "'In meinen Idealen enttäuscht' kam ich Ende 1937 wieder nach Wien; das ist sehr milde ausgedrückt; ich kotzte Knochen—und war doch bis dahin ein begeisterter Nazi gewesen."[17]

Another reason for Doderer's disillusionment with Nazism may have been his dislike of bureaucracy. Within the first few weeks of his arrival in Munich he was complaining of the pettifogging of the "Reichsschrifttumskammer," the administrative body which controlled the functions of the entire literary profession:

Heute langten die Vorschreibungen der Schrifttumskammer bei mir ein. Ein ganzer Akt. Ich kann dem freilich tadellos gerecht werden, da ich ja alle Voraussetzungen erfülle: jedoch wird's zeitraubend sein. Und vor Erledigung darf ich nirgends veröffentlichen. Der Anblick solcher riesenhafter bürokratischer Maschinerie wirkte auf mich äußerst niederschlagend.[18]

Anton Reininger believes that it was this conflict between what Doderer regarded as the ethos of the literary artist and the demands of the totalitarian regime that was the prime cause of his rejection of National Socialism: "Der

Konflikt mit dem Nationalsozialismus, der schließlich zur völligen Abwendung Doderers von ihm führte, reifte freilich anfänglich nicht im Feuer einer moralischen Ablehnung. Seine Wurzeln sprossen vielmehr—ähnlich wie im Falle Benns—in dem unsicheren Grund der Beziehungen zwischen den eigenen literarischen Vorstellungen und den kulturpolitischen Ansprüchen des neuen Regimes."[19] As Reininger goes on to say, Doderer's criticism of the bureaucratic machinery of the Third Reich did not mean that he necessarily found fault with the whole fascist system of government: "Deswegen wäre es aber sicher verfehlt, in Doderer damals schon einen Opponenten des Regimes sehen zu wollen. Er identifizierte sich grundsätzlich noch mit ihm, war aber nicht bereit, alles gutzuheißen, was geschah, und dies besonders in dem Bereich, für den er sich kompetent betrachtete."[20]

Although Doderer completed Part I of "Die Dämonen der Ostmark" in 1936 and in the following year signed a contract for it with C.H. Beck, he then refused to allow the work to be published. His ostensible reasons (*post factum*) were that he feared that the political content of the novel would lend itself to polemical misuse and also that in the climate of the times the work would not be a success. Neither reason is entirely convincing and they appear to be mutually contradictory. The anti-Semitic content, the "Wasserscheide" theme, could have been expected to prove popular in the Reich; however, this political content was not so overt that it could have served any useful purpose in the Nazi propaganda machine. His plans for the continuation of the novel as laid down in the "Aidemémoire" and in the letter to Gerhard A. were much more anti-Semitic than the content of "Die Dämonen der Ostmark." I strongly suspect that Doderer's alleged reasons actually played only a small part in his decision not to publish. These seventeen chapters formed the first part of the novel and his plans for its continuation were unrealizable. Had he published at this time, it is likely that he would never have completed the novel. He therefore made the wise decision to defer publication until the novel was complete.[21] One is tempted to wonder why Doderer and his publishers took such pains to stress that it was the political content of the novel which was the reason for its non-publication. Perhaps the anonymous interviewer for Der Spiegel came close to the truth when he suggested that not only Doderer but his publishers had difficulties with a Nazi past at the end of the war: "Nach dem Ende des Zweiten Weltkrieges...bekam der Schriftsteller zunächst Entnazifizierungsschwierigkeiten, ebenso wie sein Münchener Verlag C.H. Beck, der seine Produktion aber bald in dem neu begründeten Biederstein Verlag fortführen konnte."[22]

In April 1940 Doderer was conscripted into the Luftwaffe and was posted to various parts of Europe until his capture in Norway in May 1945. During these years his political thinking underwent considerable modification, and these changes are reflected in the content of the novel. His rejection of National

Socialism was accompanied by a rejection of all ideology, by the taking up of not just an apolitical stance but indeed of an anti-political position. In the chapter "Auf offener Strecke," written in 1940, Doderer attacks the ideology of the revolutionary. He considers revolutionary behavior destructive of the moral fibre of society, and believes that society should not be changed by violent upheaval. Indeed, he sees the revolutionary as an "Apperzeptions-Verweigerer," whom he epitomizes in the novel as the embryo, covering its eyes with its hands. He considers revolution to be a rejection of the *analogia entis*, and therefore onto-logically as well as politically unsound. Society can and should be changed from within the individual. This is the message which he will later spell out quite unequivocally in Leonhard Kakabsa's self-realization. Change is ultimately personal and not political in its essence. Doderer's point of view is essentially conservative: "Jede wirkliche Apperzeption ist konservierend. Was man genau sehen will, wünscht man nicht geändert zu haben. Der Grundzug des Geistes in Bezug auf die Objektswelt ist konservativ."[23]

According to his friend, Hans Flesch-Brunningen, Doderer told the Allied Commission, on his return to Vienna in 1946, that he was a former Party member. As a result he was banned from publishing and suffered great financial hardship for a number of years, until the publication of *Die Strudlhofstiege* in 1951 unlocked the door to a successful career. In the same year Doderer reworked "Sexualität und totaler Staat," a work in which he sought to do two things, each of which is linked to the contents of *Die Dämonen*. First, he wished to give an inter-pretation of the phenomenon of the totalitarian regime in Thomist terms, by considering it as a rejection of the *analogia entis*:

> Denn der totale Staat ist garnichts anderes als der Zusammenfall zahlloser pseudo-logischer Räume und ihre Konsolidierung in einem einzigen ungeheuer dick-wandigen, was die Unansprechbarkeit aller darin Eingeschlossenen zur Folge hat... der totale Staat ist konsolidierte Apperceptions-Verweigerung: somit eine zweite Wirklichkeit.[24]

On 10 September 1951 he noted in his diary: "Es scheint, daß die Vollendung der zweiten Fassung von 'Sexualität und totaler Staat' auch für die 'Dämonen' was zu bedeuten haben wird."[25] As Schmidt-Dengler says:

> Der distanzierte Ausdruck *scheint* verwundert; der Traktat "Sexualität und totaler Staat"...reflektiert ebenso den Versuch, seine Position thomistisch zu festigen und die Ereignisse des Nationalsozialismus in den Bereich dessen zu verbannen, was Phantasmagorie ist, kurz zum Bereich der "zweiten Wirklichkeit" zu schlagen. Ex post erhält dadurch die Besessenheit Schlaggenbergs ("Dicke Damen") ihr ideo-logisches Korrelat.[26]

This leads to the second of Doderer's aims in writing "Sexualität und totaler

Staat." He wanted to prove that political aberrations such as the Hitler regime are closely linked to or foreshadowed by deviant sexual behavior:

> So hat denn der Europäer durch lange Zeit den totalen Staat in sexueller Praxis... vorgeübt, bis in der Mitte des Erdteils der Einbruch erfolgte, welcher nichts abzuwarten hatte, als eine noch durchaus vom Analogischen, von der wirklichen Geschichte herkommende Situation: jener aber setzte er dann alsbald ein pseudo-logisches Ende.[27]

This is certainly not a widely held belief and there is little evidence that Doderer was influenced by any particular individual when he formulated his theory. There is no doubt that he himself was quite convinced of the validity of his thesis, although to the reader it seems to be based on rather dubious premises.

After the completion of "Sexualität und totaler Staat" Doderer was ready to resume work on *Die Dämonen*. At this stage the projected alterations to "Die Dämonen der Ostmark" were minimal. He merely intended to add "Draußen am Rande" and the Leonhard episode in "Der große Nebelfleck" to the existing 700 pages of manuscript to create Part I of the novel. Horst Wiemer confirms this: "Er schrieb mir, er habe in die vorliegenden 700 Seiten nur einhundert Seiten einzufügen, dann sei der Anschluß an die 'Stiege' vollzogen und er könne an die Niederschrift des Zweiten Teils der 'Dämonen' gehen."[28] This statement of Wiemer's would also validate Doderer's assertion in his letter to Paul Elbogen that he did not have to make sweeping changes to the novel in order to eradicate pro-Nazi sentiments, because there was no evidence in his work of his political aberration of the 1930s:

> Man zeige mir eine Zeile in irgendeinem meiner Bücher, oder auch nur in einem Aufsatz, in einer kleinen Erzählung oder in einer kritischen Notiz, die in irgend-einem, sei's kackebraunen, sei's kakerlgrünen "Sinne" verfaßt wäre. Vergebliches, weil unmögliches Bemühen: selbst meine Feinde mußten's aufgeben; und aus ihrem Munde ward mir die Feststellung vor eigenen Ohren, daß ich "als Schriftsteller einen fleckenlosen Schild habe, was jedermann wisse."[29]

Anton Reininger is mistaken in his assertion that Doderer expurgated from the seventeen chapters of "Die Dämonen der Ostmark" all material which might lend itself to a fascist interpretation and he believes, incorrectly, that Doderer remodelled it prior to the composition of the remainder of the novel.[30] The major alterations which were made to Part I were necessitated by the demands of the overall structure of the novel and were not a means of eliminating any embar-rassing political content from the text. When Doderer curtailed Schlaggenberg's role in 1956, he did not change the essential features in his make-up. Schlaggen-berg is still living in a "second reality," a victim of his sexual hang-up, of his neurotic anti-Semitism, with frustrated career prospects, and so on.

Although he is mistaken, Reininger at least offers an interpretation of the facts as he sees them. Schröder on the other hand offers an interpretation of the facts as he would like to see them. He himself has not examined the manuscript of "Die Dämonen der Ostmark." His rather lame disclaimer that it was not his intention to make textual comparisons may excuse his not examining the manuscript, but it does not excuse his passing value-judgments on the work unseen. Schröder cites Schmidt-Dengler's remark that a comparison of "Die Dämonen der Ostmark" with Part I of *Die Dämonen* bears out Doderer's assertion that he did not have to make any sweeping changes to the novel out of political necessity: "Die Änderungen, die am Text selbst vorgenommen wurden [1951], sind im allgemeinen geringfügig."[31] Given the choice between Schmidt-Dengler's interpretation and that of Reininger, Schröder chooses the latter: "Wenn Reininger nichts Falsches mitteilt, dann müssen die Feststellungen Schmidt-Denglers, vorsichtig formuliert, ungenau sein."[32] As Schröder is intent on proving that Doderer is an arch-conservative, which in his eyes is synonymous with fascist, it is clearly grist to his mill if he can say, however erroneously, that "Die Dämonen der Ostmark" was a piece of polemical writing which Doderer had to amend in the 1950s to suit the altered climate of the times. The facts do not support him. The left-wing bias of Schröder's study spoils what is otherwise a penetrating examination, particularly of Doderer's concept of "Apperzeption." I agree with Schröder, however, that a more objective analysis of Doderer's fascist interlude is required than that offered by certain of his friends, who tend to gloss over what was certainly more than a passing phase in his existence. Doderer himself admitted to having been a convinced Nazi, and he was attracted to the movement, for whatever reasons, over a period of several years before disenchantment set in.

The paper which Schröder delivered at a "Doderer-Symposium" sponsored by the Österreichische Gesellschaft für Literatur in Vienna on 17 December 1976 is also rather one-sided. After making a convincing case for the interpretation of Doderer's conception of reality in Freudian terms, he more or less dismisses Doderer's problematic stance as typical of his class:

> Psychoanalytisch gesprochen, wird Doderer zum Sklaven eines allmächtigen Über-Ichs. Die Forderung nach totaler Selbstverwandlung, die ihm durch das Über-Ich, also durch die ihm vertraute bürgerliche Gesellschaft gestellt ist, reißt ihn als Person auseinander, spaltet ihn in zwei Wirklichkeiten. In der ersten Wirklichkeit ist er der, der er sein *will*, der er aber niemals *wird*. In der zweiten Wirklichkeit ist er derjenige, der er tatsächlich ist, der er aber niemals sein will. Das Dilemma der Doppelgesichtigkeit, der Doppelmoral, der Selbstspaltung und Realitätsverleugnung kennzeichnet, so fürchte ich, nicht nur den Schriftsteller Doderer, sondern auch die Schicht, der er angehört.[33]

This is fruitful ground for investigation, as there is undoubtedly a strong element of the irrational and the neurotic in Doderer's character. But part of the conflict in his personality was caused by the feeling of *not* belonging to his middle-class background. He actually cut himself off from his family in the 1920s and associated with a bohemian group, some of whom served as models for "Die Unsrigen." He described himself in an interview as a throw-back, and considered that his rather mongolian features proved that he did not really belong to his social background. He believed that his tendency to depression was inherited from the poet Lenau, who was one of his ancestors, and who committed suicide.[34] He even had contacts with the Viennese underworld, which may perhaps explain his fascination with criminality. Doderer, like Thomas Mann, suffered from the "Bürger-Künstler" conflict, which was exacerbated by his feelings of inferiority vis-à-vis his father. In this respect the figure of René Stangeler is clearly an *alter ego*.

In 1951 Doderer still intended to have anti-Semitism as one of the themes of the novel. He had, of course, dropped the "Wasserscheide" idea, the splitting of Viennese society into Jews and Gentiles, something of which he himself had approved in the 1930s, but he did not wish to disregard the fact that anti-Semitism was a phenomenon of the times. He made two remarks on the subject when he was making his preliminary attempts to resume work on the novel. One of the themes of Part II was to be that "Die antisemitischen Komplexe einer Reihe von Individuen sind Objekt der Darstellung (Relativierung durch den Lebensverlauf selbst)."[35] In Schlaggenberg's case (the autobiographical element is unmistakable) anti-Semitism is seen to be a form of neurosis, caused in part by his disastrous relationship with his Jewish ex-wife and by his failure in the literary field, a failure which he blames on Jewish domination of the publishing-world.

The character who expresses the strongest anti-Semitic feelings is Geyrenhoff's nephew, Dr. Körger. He views the splitting-up of "Die Unsrigen" into two groups on a ski-outing (an implied splitting into Jew and Gentile) as politically desirable:

> "Fassen Sie dieses getrennte Marschieren sinnbildlich auf, dann kommen Sie dem wahren Sachverhalt am nächsten," bemerkte mein Neffe.
> "Wie -?" fragte Stangeler.
> "Von mir aus als die Vision einer besseren Zukunft" (p. 309).

When Grete Siebenschein, a Jewess, asks if she can cross over to the other group, it is Körger who says, "in aller Seelenruhe" (p. 309) that she cannot. It is he who can see advantages in having Schlaggenberg, with his anti-Semitic feelings, infiltrate the Jewish-controlled world of "Die Allianz," a large newspaper concern. Schlaggenberg reports this fact to Geyrenhoff in the following terms: "Er war geradezu begeistert, der Dr. Körger. 'Sie müssen, Herr von Schlaggenberg'—so sagte er—'sich dort oben eine ganz feste Position schaffen. Das kann für uns von der allergrößten Bedeutung werden'" (p. 368).

At this point the political and the historical contents of the novel begin to overlap. Anti-Semitism, the rise of fascism, and the threat of communism in Austria in the late 1920s are temporally and spatially restricted phenomena. However, they are also part of a much larger historical process, and it is in relation to Doderer's view of this process, and its significance for the individual that they must now be assessed. As Schmidt-Dengler says: "Er [Doderer] versucht, die politische Geschichte zu transzendieren, aus den beengenden Grenzen rein nationaler Geschichtsschreibung herauszuführen und eine 'apriorische Geographie' geltend zu machen."[36] It is Doderer's belief that quite aside from the physical geography of any country there exists, as part of the *analogia entis*, a predetermined pattern of events which can take place only in that particular location.[37] This is a rather deterministic view of the historical process, but it might help to explain Doderer's naive political theories.

III. *Die Dämonen* as a Historical Novel

When Doderer returned to Vienna from Siberia in 1920 he embarked on a course of history studies. His prime ambition, however, was to become a writer, and this ambition conditioned not only his choice of history as his main subject but also that of psychology as his subsidiary subject: "Ich denke stark daran als Nebenfach für das Doktorat die Psychologie zu wählen. Geschichte und Psychologie, zwei Wissenschaften, die sich mit dem Leben unmittelbar beschäftigen. Dies wäre eine entsprechende wissenschaftliche Ausbildung für einen Prosa-Erzähler!"[38] In the light of this statement I find it difficult to believe Georg Schmid's hypothesis that Doderer turned to literature as a *métier* only when he was thwarted in his attempt to make a career in history. On completion of his doctoral thesis in 1925 Doderer was accepted, after a rigorous examination, as a student at the prestigious Institut für Österreichische Geschichtsforschung. Schmid claims that Doderer's subsequent rejection by the Institut forced him to accept a career in literature as second-best to one in the historical field: "Wohl kann man vermuten, daß ihn seine Eliminierung aus dem Institut für Österreichische Geschichtsforschung in den Zwanzigerjahren mehr oder weniger dazu gezwungen hat, die Geschichte beiseite zu lassen und sich der Literatur zuzuwenden, doch erscheint es immerhin ebenso denkbar, daß sein literarisches Oeuvre quasi als Kompensation zumindest in seinen initialen Stadien zu verstehen wäre."[39] I am more inclined to accept Schmidt-Dengler's thesis that Doderer turned away from history when he realized that the work of the trained historian was not compatible with his aspirations in the field of literature: "Schon während der Arbeit an ihr [the "Hausarbeit" for the Institute] distanziert sich Doderer zusehends von seinen Kollegen am 'Institut für Österreichische Geschichtsforschung,'...das er nach einer peinlichen Auseinandersetzung hatte verlassen müssen. Aber nicht nur solche äußerlichen Unannehmlichkeiten waren es, die den Schriftsteller zu einer Abkehr von der Wissenschaft zwangen. Es war die Einsicht, daß die Arbeit des Gelehrten unvereinbar sei mit der des Schriftstellers."[40]

The interrelationship of history and psychology was of great significance for the subsequent development of Doderer's creative writings. The psychological implications of the historical situation, its relevance for the individual, interested him more than the significance of the historical event as part of the historical process. Doderer did not see the task of the novelist as being to present a catalogue of facts. This is the task of the historian. The writer is not concerned with history in the abstract but with its relevance to everyday life. In *Die Dämonen* Neuberg echoes the sentiments of the author when he says: "Dies sei auch der einzige Sinn historischer Studien: daß sie der Gegenwart eine noch höhere Wirklichkeit verliehen" (p. 108).

In 1930 Doderer wrote the novel *Das Geheimnis des Reichs*, based on his experiences as a P.O.W. in Siberia. Although in later life he distanced himself from this work (in accordance with his wishes it was never republished during his lifetime), the novel is nonetheless interesting to the critic of *Die Dämonen* from the methodological point of view, that is, how the author sought to incorporate historical fact into a work of fiction. Doderer originally conceived the work as a "Divertimento" but it "degenerated" into a novel,[41] and this falling between two stools helps explain the significant number of blemishes in the work. The contents are too dense for the form; the historical content, which accounts for almost one-fifth of the total narrative, is not successfully integrated into the novel;[42] there is a mass of banal and often unassimilated imagery. Doderer was later to call the novel a "chronologisch ablaufenden Bericht,"[43] and it is interesting to note that it was precisely this narrative form which he discarded in *Die Dämonen* in favor of discontinuous authorial prose.[44]

Two works of Doderer were set in the past. In the first of these, *Das letzte Abenteuer*, the main function of the historical background appears to be to supply local color. Doderer considered the tale as a piece of escapism, inviting the reader "zum Ritt ins romantische Land."[45] He was concerned not with the events of history, but with the self-realization of his hero, Ruy de Fanez. The historical details are factually correct, but were probably not as closely researched as those of the later works.

The second of the two works set in the past is the novel, *Ein Umweg*. The material for the story was taken "aus dem Zeitstoffe des österreichischen Barocks,"[46] but the work itself was chiefly concerned with two of Doderer's major interests, self-realization and fate. The figure of the dragon appears, as it did in *Das letzte Abenteuer*. In that novel it was a symbol of Fanez's triumph over life. In *Ein Umweg* in symbolizes Manuel Cuendias's inability to escape from the "fatological web" which has been spun around him. This novel does not merely offer the reader a form of escapism, but provides an illustration of Doderer's view that it is the individual who is important and not the impersonal forces of history. The novel opens two years after the Thirty Years' War ends, but Doderer is concerned with this cataclysm only in its consequences for the individual. World War I is treated in similar fashion in *Die Strudlhofstiege*. There are only peripheral references to the political happenings of the times; what is important to Doderer is the attempt by Melzer to come to terms with the effect of these happenings on his private life. Franz Sulke remarks on this fact:

> Obwohl "Die Strudlhofstiege" zweifellos ein historischer Roman par excellence ist (sie ist so breit angelegt, daß sie eine ganze Epoche total zu spiegeln vermag), fehlt in diesem farbigen Buch—bis auf geringfügige allgemeine Anspielungen—jedwede Verknüpfung mit den äußeren geschichtlichen Vorgängen.[47]

Sulke seems to miss the point that Doderer was *not* writing a historical novel. He always disclaimed any desire to write one and accepted the definition of his works as historical novels only in a very limited sense, as in this conversation with Adolf Holzinger:

> AH: Sie gestalten also aus dem Erinnerungsvermögen?
> HvD: Nur.
> AH: Ihre Romane sind in erster Linie historische Romane—in einem besonderen Sinn. Historische Romane als Darstellung von Vergangenem?
> HvD: Nein, nicht Vergangenheit dem Inhalte nach, sondern die unendliche Vergangenheit, die jeder Mensch in sich trägt.[48]

Doderer was always at great pains to distinguish between the function of the novelist and that of the historian. In the draft of his letter of 21 July 1936 to Gerhard A., he considered the relationship of the writer to history, and the view he expresses did not alter over the next thirty years:

> In diesem Zusammenhang und erst jetzt gewannen auch die früher absolvierten historischen Universitäts-Studien ihren eigentlichen Sinn. Denn ich erkannte den Romanschriftsteller (der wirkliche Roman ist *immer* Gesellschaftsroman!) *als den eigentlichen contemporänen Geschichts-Schreiber seiner Zeit,* deren Geschehen er aber nicht, wie der Historiker das einer vergangenen Epoche, nur in den großen Zügen und den Mitteln der bloß begrifflichen ("wissenschaftlichen") Sprache vorführt, sondern aus der Nähe und gleichsam unter der Zeitlupe und mit der Anschaulichkeit erzählender Prosa: auf solche Weise unserem Zeitalter, dessen

größte Gefahr in der immer mehr zunehmenden Mittelbarkeit seines Lebens liegt, auf recht eindringliche Art in Erinnerung bringend, daß alles, was wir so "Geschichte" zu nennen pflegen, sich ja letzten Endes in den Hirnen, Herzen, Nerven der *einzelnen Menschen* abspielte und abspielt, *daß die Geschichte im Menschen geschieht und geschah,* und nicht auf irgendeinem Podium, wohin sie uns vielfach von der Wissenschaft mit ihren Abstraktionen projiziert wurde.[49]

In his introductory remarks to readings from *Die Strudlhofstiege* given in C.H. Beck's publishing-house in Munich on 6 April 1951 Doderer said: "Der große Roman als solcher müßte ja ohneweiteres in jedem einzelnen Teilchen die Forderung Benedetto Croces erfüllen, daß jede Spezialgeschichte implicite die Universalgeschichte zu enthalten habe."[50] Doderer sees the task of the novelist as being the search for reality, a reality which has been imperfectly perceived by the individual and inadequately reproduced by the writer, who has not succeeded in presenting in his work the totality of human existence. He will later formulate the goal of novel-writing as the "eigentliche Wissenschaft vom Leben,"[51] a knowledge that includes an awareness of the universality of the human condition, translatable by the author into a composition which is all-encompassing, both in respect of content and formal techniques.

Die Dämonen culminates in the events of 15 July 1927 and Doderer's portrayal of these events is regarded by critics such as C.E. Williams as highly suspect, and even factually incorrect: "It is Doderer's account of the events of 15 July which raises the gravest doubts as to his impartiality...The selective nature of Doderer's account exceeds the limits of fictional licence—it amounts to a covert *apologia* for the police and the Seipel government which endorsed their actions."[52] At the root of Williams' criticism of Doderer lies the fact that he does not accept the fact that the writer may seek only to convey the atmosphere of the historical situation, and not present a carefully documented catalogue of facts. The reader who is interested in this type of presentation should resort to contemporary newspaper accounts or to later assessments by competent historians. It is interesting to note that Julius Deutsch, the leader of the Republikanischer Schutzbund in 1927, wrote in a letter to Doderer two years after the publication of *Die Dämonen* that this was the most accurate description of the events of the day that he had ever read.[53]

Although there is no mention of police brutality in the novel, Doderer was aware of the excesses of several members of the force. He ascribed much of the blame for this to Polizeipräsident Schober, whom he described as a "widrige Figur."[54] But he felt that the demands of the demonstrators for class-justice undermined the democratic process.[55] The real victims of the happenings of 15 July 1927 were the Austrian people. As a counter-measure to the threat seemingly posed by the parties of the Left the government greatly increased the powers of the Heimwehr. This made the struggle between the Left and the Right even more one-sided and eventually led to the annihilation of the Socialists as a political force within Austria. This effectively removed from the scene the one political faction that could have offered opposition to Hitler at the time of the Anschluß, and condemned Austria to becoming a fascist regime.

The behavior of Geyrenhoff's nephew, Dr. Körger, on 15 July illustrates how political ideology contributes to a rapid breakdown of society. Körger, a rabid anti-Semite, is committed to the introduction of a fascist government to Austria. It suits his purpose for the Socialists to confront the Government forces. He is quite in accord with Eulenfeld's remark, "mögen sie einander die Köppe einschlagen. Um so besser für uns" (p. 1323), and is utterly ruthless. He considers his friend, Eulenfeld, who also has fascist leanings, as politically unreliable, useful only for his military expertise and thereafter expendable:

"Altes Schwein," dachte er,..."solche Leute, wie der da, sind natürlich erledigt und unbrauchbar für uns. Aber, man muß ihnen einiges noch abknöpfen, denn Front-Erfahrung und militärisches Wissen, von der Ausbildung und diesem ganzen Zeug, das haben sie eben, da mag man sagen, was man will. Uns fehlt das. Sollen sie ausbilden, wenn's so weit einmal ist. Dann fort mit ihnen. Verstehen können sie uns nie" (p. 1325).

In the chapter "Das Feuer" Doderer is attempting to portray the reaction of the individual to the events of the day. In the main these people are completely unaffected by what is going on around them. They are going about their own business, totally uninvolved in political happenings. No one appears to realize the significance of what is taking place: "Es geht alles rasch vorbei, niemand ist sich des 'historischen Augenblicks' bewußt, manche sind zerstreut und ver-heddert."[56] Quapp is so oblivious to what is happening that Géza has to explain it all to her at a later date (p. 1295). The younger members of society, Schlaggen-berg's "Bande," are completely uninterested in the political events: "Sylvia wußte sogar ganz Genaues: daß man Arbeiter-Demonstrationen befürchte (sie sagte auch warum, aber das beachtete niemand)" (p. 1221). Geyrenhoff sums up the events of the day by saying: "So endete für uns dieser Tag, der ganz nebenhin das Cannae der österreichischen Freiheit bedeutete. Aber das wußte damals niemand und wir am allerwenigsten" (p. 1328). Geyrenhoff himself was an eye-witness of the burning of the Palace of Justice and the fighting around it, but even he was not aware of everything that took place and had to depend on later information to fill the gaps in his knowledge.

Only two of the characters in the novel become actively involved in the happenings of the day, and each for a personal reason which is totally divorced from a political motive. The criminal, Meisgeier, is shot by the police while he is trying to impede them in the execution of their duty. In fact, he causes the death of one of their number, Karl Zeitler, the friend of Leonhard Kakabsa. But

Meisgeier is acting out of maliciousness and not out of any desire to help the workers and the Socialists. He despises the latter almost as much as he does the police: "Die Sozi—das sind die größten Feinde von unsereinem, die's gibt und überhaupt von jedem, der kein Haderwachl oder Lamperl ist. Die Roten, die kommen bei mir gleich nach der Höh' (Polizei)!" (p. 954). Doderer put the blame for the day's disturbances on the criminal element in Viennese society, the "Ruass," as he called them. The validity of this interpretation is open to question but certainly this was the information released by the government. The Vice-Chancellor said that of the civilian dead thirty-two had police records.

Imre von Gyurkicz, an Austrian commoner, who pretends to be a member of the Hungarian nobility, is shot by the police because he points a revolver in their direction, after standing on a soapbox and haranguing the crowd, inspiring them to further action. But Gyurkicz's sympathies actually lay with the right-wing movements. He was involved with the "Erwachende Ungarn," a fascist group that was active in Burgenland. Geyrenhoff, who observes the death of Gyurkicz from the window of Gürtzner-Gontard's home, realizes: "Was ihn getötet hatte, war für mich, in diesen hellsichtigen Sekunden, nicht die Kugel, sondern der Starkstrom des Lebens selbst, von Imre zum Kurzschluß gebracht" (p. 1248). His death is the culmination of his "anabasis," and Doderer intended the reader to see it as the ineluctable outcome of the predetermined pattern of Gyurkicz's existence. The decisive factor in bringing about his death is his jealousy of Géza von Orkay. Orkay is all that Gyurkicz has pretensions to be, but is not; he is a successful diplomat, belongs to the Hungarian nobility, and has *entrée* to circles whose doors are closed to Gyurkicz. Doderer implies that Gyurkicz's behavior on 15 July is caused by his desire to achieve notoriety, to outdo Géza's achievements. At a meeting with Pinta, who is also involved with the Hungarian Fascists in Burgenland, the latter advises Gyurkicz to turn to Géza von Orkay should he need any assistance in Vienna. Doderer says of this encounter:

> Imre spürt wirklich eine profunde Hemmung seines Lebens, das zunächst ohne Ausgang scheint: Pinta, der ihn—freilich ganz ahnungslos—an Orkay weist, veranlaßt damit jenen ressentimentalen Umschwung in Imre, der ihn zu seiner Wirksamkeit vor dem brennenden Justizpalast bringt...und führt so indirekt dessen Ende herbei. Die Begegnung mit Pinta bedeutet also für Gyurkicz garnichts Geringeres als den Tod: und sie erhält erst unter diesem Gesichts-Winkel ihr volles Gewicht.[57]

Thus Gyurkicz dies, in the last analysis, not because of his revolutionary aspirations, but because he has not come to terms with reality and has created a role for himself, a role which he is unable to sustain.

When Doderer started work on the novel at the beginning of the 1930s he saw communism as a serious threat to Austrian society. In his letter to Gerhard A. he spoke of the collapse of the Bodencreditanstalt and "jene marxistischen Gärungen."[58] How tenable this opinion is remains open to question, although it seems to have been the view promulgated by the Seipel government. Subsequent events would seem to prove that fascism posed a much greater threat to the fabric of Austrian society than did the nascent communist party. When Doderer recommenced work on the novel in the 1950s, he had altered his interpretation of the happenings of the late 1920s and early 1930s and saw, in hindsight, the slide into fascism as the major hazard faced by Austrian society in these years.

Doderer's choice of title for a work which was to deal with the disintegration of the Austrian social structure was taken from Dostoevsky's novel, *The Possessed*, whose German title is *Die Dämonen*. Apart from the superficial resemblances between the two works which leap to the eye, there are two main points of comparison: 1.) Both novels deal with revolutionary behavior. 2.) Both climax in a fire, Dostoevsky's a fictitious one, Doderer's factual. However, Doderer's treatment of the two topics is quite different from that of Dostoevsky. Although Doderer was essentially a Realist and made great use of factual accuracy to authenticate his presentation, he was also strongly influenced by two beliefs which worked together and tended to counteract this realism. The first of these was his conviction that the indirect approach was the most efficacious: "Das Indirekte erweist sich mir als bedingender Grundmechanismus jeder Aktion des Geistes und als Fundament aller seiner Haltungen, von welchen solchermaßen der tierische Ernst und die Formlosigkeit ausgeschlossen bleiben."[59] Thus we can expect that in the novel there will be no direct confrontation with the political situation. This may sometimes appear ambivalent and not to the satisfaction of the left-wing critic. The indirect is best illustrated, in Doderer's view, by the use of metaphor: "Die Metapher ist Platzhalter des Indirekten in der Sprache, stellt also deren Grundbedingung dar."[60] This thesis helps to explain the creation of a vast metaphorical substructure in *Die Dämonen*, which not only clarifies the everyday action of the novel but extends the range of its significance.

It should not surprise the reader to find this transposition of political reality to the metaphorical plane.[61] The construction of a symbolic substructure not only offers fruitful ground for literary creation, but also reinforces Doderer's belief that problematical situations can be resolved only when they are approached from a new perspective:

> Wozu auch sonst brauchte ich als Naturalist Hunderte von Seiten einer erzählenden Darstellung, die als Ganzes eine einzige Metapher ist? Und liegt nicht der Sinn aller Metaphorie vielleicht schon in einem Gesetz begründet, das da etwa sagen möchte: kein Gegenstand kann auf der Ebene dargestellt werden, auf welcher er erfahren wird—so wie kein Problem auf jener Ebene lösbar ist, auf der es sich stellt?[62]

Although Doderer was always punctilious in the matter of factual accuracy, on occasion discarding pieces of narrative when he discovered that they were factually incorrect, there is a strong symbolic admixture to the historical and political content of the novel. Indeed, some critics see as the main theme of the work not that of the struggle between conflicting ideologies, but the fundamental issue of the conflict between good and evil: "Kein Zeitgemälde haben wir in den 'Dämonen' vor uns, sondern den mythischen Kampf zwischen Gut und Böse, Hell und Dunkel, Wirklichkeit und Nichtwirklichkeit, der am Ende...die zeitge-mäßen Namen des Antagonismus von Politik und privater Existenz erhält."[63]

Claudio Magris suggests an interesting interpretation of the aims which Doderer was setting himself in the novel. In the paper presented at the Doderer Symposium in Vienna in 1976, titled "Doderers erste Wirklichkeit," he does not judge Doderer as negatively as he did in his book *Der habsburgische Mythos in der österreichischen Literatur*, where he speaks of the "Naivität der geschicht-lich-politischen Ideen des Autors," and says that "vor allem fehlt Doderer...der Sinn für die Geschichte."[64] He now considers that Doderer's chief goal in his novels is "die Gesellschaft, die entfremdete Gesellschaft des entfremdeten modernen Romans wieder in Natur zurückzuverwandeln."[65] In Magris's view, *Die Dämonen* expresses most felicitously this search for harmony when the author makes use of metaphor; when he endeavors to incorporate content with an overtly political character, Magris considers this to be a "peinlich unverar-beitetes Material:" "Die Wahrheit des konservativen und apolitischen Schrift-stellers liegt im Verzicht auf die Politik, in der bewußten Zurückhaltung vor der Politik, nicht in der unbesonnenen politischen Stellungnahme."[66] I agree with Magris's view. Doderer succeeds admirably in capturing both the social climate of Vienna in the 1920s and the atmosphere of the events of 15 July 1927. Where he propounds his "anti-ideological" viewpoint, in Gontard's attack on revolutionary behavior, for example, he is much less convincing. His thesis of the attack on established values by anonymous demonic forces, the "Einbruch von unten," is tenable in the metaphorical substructure, in the dungeons of Neudegg, and in the sewers of Vienna. However, he offers too facile an explanation for the political happenings by attributing the blame for the events of 15 July 1927 to the criminal element in the lower strata of Viennese society.

Despite the many variations in both form and content of the novel, one factor remained constant during its twenty-five year genesis. The novel is an intensely personal expression of the author's world-view and mediates the attitude to reality of an individual who has actually lived through the period of time in which the novel is set. *Die Dämonen* is Doderer's attempt to explain his, and by implication his contemporaries' attraction to National Socialism, a phenomenon which was peculiar not merely to German-speaking society but to Europe as a whole. Doderer's views have been judged variously by his critics to be idio-syncratic, simplistic, fascist (despite his rejection of fascist ideology), ultraconservative, or politically naive. The spectrum of interpretations of the novel is as wide as that of the political biases of the critics concerned.

Our examination of Doderer's historico-political system of belief has revealed that it is indissolubly linked to his Thomist interpretation of reality and has its roots in a fundamentally conservative attitude of mind. In the novel Doderer is seeking to express a view of reality which has evolved over a period of a quarter of a century and which, like the novel itself, has experienced the vagaries of fate. One may find Doderer's political views distasteful, one may have serious reservations about his perhaps simplistic conception of the historical process. But these shortcomings, if such they be, do not detract from the literary stature of the novel. Doderer has written a social novel of impressive dimensions, indeed a masterpiece, and one that captures more vividly than any other account the climate of a specific historical situation.

Appendix I

Rodolphe H. Lévièlle, *(Conseiller)* [Membre] de la chambre agraire *(et indus-trielle)*x

Dr. Trapp, Rechtsanwalt

Frau Trapp, seine Gattin, genannt: "der zerlassene Eidamerkäse"
(Angelika Trapp, beider Tochter, Braut Neuberg's)[6]

    Direktor Dulnik, Leiter einer großen Papierfabrik

x [der Titel etwa so; jedenfalls prunkvoll]

3. Gruppe

Camy (Kamilla) von Schlaggenberg, (geboren Schedik)
(Sanitäts)[Obermedizinal]rat Schedik, ihr Vater

Dr. Ferry Siebenschein, Rechtsanwalt

Frau Irma Siebenschein, seine Gattin

Grete Siebenschein, beider Tochter

Titi Lasch, geboren Siebenschein, Grete's Schwester

Cornel Lasch, ihr Gatte

Siegfried Markbreiter, Inhaber eines Bändergeschäftes am Franz Josefskai,
    Onkel Grete Siebenschein's

Frau Clarisse Markbreiter, seine Gattin

Lily Kries, geboren Markbreiter, beider Tochter

Frau Glaser, chef de réception in einem vornehmen Wiener Cottage-Hotel,
    Schwester der Frau Clarisse Markbreiter

Frau Thea Rosen

Frau Lea Wolf

Eduard Altschul, Bankdirektor

Rosi Altschul, seine Gattin

Dr. Mährischl, Rechtsanwalt

Frau Martha Mährischl, seine Gattin

[Dr.] Beppo *(D)*[T]raxler, *(Bankbeamter)* [Rechtsanwalt], hat die Eigenschaft
    in ganz virtuoser Weise die Guitarre zu beherrschen

[Selma Steuermann (Witwe)][7]

4. Gruppe: "Allianz"

Oplatek, Administrationsdirektor der "Allianz, Allgemeine Zeitungs A.G."

Cobler, Chefredakteur bei einem der führenden Allianzblätter
    Leopoldine Kienbauer, Redaktionssekretärin

Zepler, Präsident der "Organisation Héctor"

Dr. Trembloner, Redakteur, Volkswirtschaftlicher Teil

Holder, Feuilletonredakteur

Wangstein, Redakteur

Rosi Malik, "Dichterin"

5. Gruppe: Stemmklub "Eisen" und "Schenke"

(Imre von Gyurkicz, jedoch hier unter seinem richtigen Namen...)[8]
"der Pfarrer," versoffener Theologe
"der Mesner," versoffener Kirchendiener
Didi, Schnapsausschenkerin
([Fiala])[9]

Außerhalb aller Gruppen

Lehrer Kajetan's (in Südfrankreich) [Albert Scolander]
Unbekanntes Mädchen (im Haus "zum Einhorn")
*([Julius Zihal], wirklicher Amtsrat beim Zentral-Tax-und-Gebühren-(Ver)[Be]
     messungsamt)*[10]

[Dr. Hartog, Tropen-Arzt]
[Sektionschef Gürtzner-Gontard][11]
[Gruppe der Zwischenfiguren:]
[Pianistin Wiesinger]
[Illegible name], deleted in blue [Beppo D.], deleted in blue
[Zwischenfiguren, welche an der "Wasserscheide" zu Decision gebracht werden,
     sind natürlich außerdem noch:
Gyurkicz
Neuberg
Angelika
Ruthmayr
Altschul u.a.][12]

Appendix II

"Aide-mémoire zu 'Die Dämonen der Ostmark'"

This document is to be found in the *Nachlaß* in the folder Ser.n. 14.188,
"Materialsammlung R 7 und DD." It consists of twenty-five typescript pages and
is undated. However, it was probably composed in the fall of 1934, and certainly

before the introduction of the "Ouvertüre" and of Geyrenhoff as the first-person narrator.

The "Aide-mémoire" is important for the light it sheds on the development of both the form and the content of *Die Dämonen*. In tone it is unmistakably anti-Semitic, much more discernibly so than the novel itself, and the extreme right-wing bias of Doderer's political thinking at this time is also clearly evident.[1] The significance of the "Aide-mémoire" lies in the fact that, as well as outlining his plans for the projected development of the novel, Doderer also gives a résumé of its contents at this time. As there is extant no manuscript of the novel prior to 1935, when Doderer remodelled the chapters already written to make them conform to the changed narrative mode of the novel, the "Aide-mémoire" is a valuable source of information on the period immediately preceding that radical alteration in the form of the work, and supplements the material concerning the genesis of the novel to be found in his diaries.

It seems likely that, by analyzing the content of the novel in this fashion, Doderer became dissatisfied with its formal structure and inclined to the idea of changing the narrative mode to that of the first-person narrator. The novel was at this time at a critical stage in its evolution and one function of the "Aide-mémoire" was to enable Doderer to clarify his ideas about its potential development. For this reason the document must be taken into account in any genetic study of the novel, and it was this consideration which prompted me to include the manuscript in the book.

The document consists of three letters written by Doderer to his friend Fritz Höpfner, who appears in the novel as Robert Höpfner. Doderer wanted to draw on Höpfner's knowledge of the business-world to help him create an authentic background for the machinations of Levielle and Cornel Lasch. In 1935 he enlisted Höpfner's aid with factual details for the chapter "Der Eintopf."

Certain emendations have been made to the manuscript, mainly in pencil, some in colored pencil. It is impossible to date them with any degree of accuracy. Some were probably made in March 1939, when Doderer carried out a review of both the "Aide-mémoire" and "Dämonen I." Notes on this review are to be found at the back of "Commentarii 1935/36." Other changes were probably made after Doderer resumed work on the novel in 1951. Additions to the manuscript will be given inside square brackets, deletions inside italicized brackets. Immediate corrections have not been taken up, and minor oversights have been corrected. Illegible words or phrases are indicated by (illegible). It is interesting to note that the top right-hand corner of pages 1 and 14 has been removed, presumably by Doderer himself, in order to delete "der Ostmark" from the title of the novel.

I²

[1]³ Lieber Fritz!

Wenn ich Dir zu unserer Arbeit eine Reihe von Anhaltspunkten geben soll, so kann dies vor allem einmal nicht reihenweise geschehen in einer additiven Folge, eins nach dem anderen, sondern ich muß voll in medias res hüpfen—so wird die Sache am lebendigsten. Ich muß alles so erzählen, wie ich es erlebt habe, und da beim schreibenden Menschen leben und schreiben ein und dasselbe ist, bin ich der Pflicht überhoben auseinanderzuhalten, was mir von Außen zustieß und was aus der Komposition wuchs. Dieses als gleichgültig betrachtet, erinnere ich mich vor allem einmal eines unvergeßlichen Frühjahrstages, den ich in der Wiener inneren Stadt zubrachte. Ich war den ganzen Tag in der Stadt. Und das bedeutete damals einen sozusagen außergewöhnlichen Zustand für mich. Als ich um den Stock-im-Eisen bog, sah ich gerade vor der Konditorei Gerstner Frau Friederike Ruthmayr aus ihrem Auto steigen. Es war ein so seltsamer Zufall, gewissermaßen ein symbolischer Zufall. Ich begrüßte sie und durfte ihr Gesellschaft leisten; wir saßen in der Konditorei beisammen. Während der ganzen Zeit als ich mit dieser entzückendsten Frau sprach, die ich je gesehen habe—Du erinnerst Dich, daß sie gegen 80 Kilo wiegt—empfand ich Mitleid mit ihr, denn ich fand es ungeheuerlich, ein so vornehmes Geschöpf von einem Menschen wie Levièlle⁴ sozusagen überschattet zu wissen. Du weißt, daß Levièlle Ruthmayr's nachgelassenes Vermögen verwaltete, Du weißt auch, was ich damals noch nicht wußte, daß von diesem Vermögen ein Teil eigentlich Quapp, der Schwester Kajetans gehörte. Von all dem aber später—.⁵

[2] Als ich mich von Frau Ruthmayr empfohlen hatte—veranlaßt dadurch, daß die Frau des Rechtsanwaltes Trapp an Gerstners süßem Horizont erschien— ging ich die Kärntnerstraße gegen den Ring zu und diesen entlang bis in die Gegend der Burg. Und hier stoßen wir auf einen Punkt, der—wie der später geführte große Strafprozeß klar herausstellte—der eigentliche Angelpunkt meiner "Dämonen" ist. Ich möchte beiläufig erwähnen, daß sich [die Darstellung] jene[r] hier *(geschilderten)*[berührten] Vorgänge am Schluße *(meines)*[des] ersten Teiles meines Buches befinde*(n)*[t], am Schluße des *(11.)*[14.] Kap.⁶

Ich treffe dort—wie gesagt ungefähr in der Gegend der alten Burg—den mir wohlbekannten Direktor Altschul von der Creditanstalt. Altschul ist, wie Du Dich vielleicht erinnern kannst, ein Frankfurter Jude, ein naturalisierter Oesterreicher und ein ausgezeichnet aussehender und anständiger Mann. Wir begrüßten einander, ich ging ein Stück mit ihm und trotz seines stets beherrschten und korrekten Benehmens konnte mir die bleierne Niedergeschlagenheit des Mannes einfach nicht entgehen. Wir waren kaum bis zur Universität gekommen, als uns jenes Ehepaar begegnete, das hier in unserem Roman eine so gottverdammte Rolle spielt: de*(m)*[r] Herr*(n)* Dr. Mährischl in ganzer Person, samt seiner Frau,

Martha. Jetzt muß ich aber schon etwas deutlicher reden. Es hat sich nämlich später im Verlaufe des Prozeßes gezeigt, *daß um jene Zeit, als mir Altschul damals auf dem Ring begegnete, Levièlle und Cornel Lasch zweifelsohne schon entschlossen gewesen sein müssen ihn fallen zu lassen und seine Existenz zu vernichten.* Levièlle ist auf dem Rücken des Ruthmayr'schen Vermögens hochgekommen. Ruthmayr, der Gutsbesitzer und Reserve-Rittmeister war, ist, wie Du Dich wahrscheinlich erinnerst, in einer der wenigen [3] großen Reiterschlachten, die es im Kriege in Galizien gab, erschlagen worden.[7] Wie kam nun Levièlle dazu, das ganze große Real- und Effektenvermögen in die Hände zu bekommen?

Dieses hängt merkwürdigerweise mit der Familie Schlaggenberg zusammen. Ruthmayr war mit Friederike schon verheiratet gewesen, als er—gut zehn Jahre vor dem Kriege—eine junge Aristokratin schwängerte. Ich drücke das sehr gemein aus, weil es mir um den Tatbestand geht, merke aber dazu an, daß es sich hier um eine wirkliche Liebe handelte. Die junge Dame—eine verwitwete Frau[8]—entdeckte diesen Umstand viel zu spät, wußte sich auch, wie es in diesen Kreisen zu sein pflegt, nicht praktisch zu helfen. In dieser Lage hat sich Ruthmayr an seine*(n)* allerbesten Freund[e] gewandt, nämlich den *(alten)*[9] Herrn von Schlaggenberg und seine Gemahlin, die Eltern Kajetans, welche damals so wie heute[10] auf ihrem Gut in Südsteiermark saßen. Der alte Schlaggenberg hatte—was zu jener Zeit in großen Häusern garnicht selten war—eine Art Haus-Juden, der alles machte und finanziellen Rat gab. Dieser eben war Levièlle (hieß damals wohl anders). Woher dieser Mann eigentlich kommt ist mir bis heute unbekannt geblieben. Levièlle arrangierte alles. Die junge Frau verschwand in die Schweiz, auch Schlaggenbergs zogen sich von der Gesellschaft zurück, verreisten unbekannten Aufenthaltes (die Details sind hier nicht anzuführen, obwohl sie sehr unterhaltend sind). In irgendeine[r] ebenso einsamen wie gesunde[n] Hochgebirgsgegend irgendwo in der Schweiz kam Ruthmayr's Geliebte nieder (starb bei der Geburt)[11] und nachdem man von Seiten des Ehepaares Schlaggenberg in geschickter Weise Gerüchte über einen noch bevorstehenden Nachwuchs in der Gesellschaft zu lancieren gewußt hatte, wurde eines Tages unter [4] großem Gepränge Charlotte von Schlaggenberg, Kajetans Schwester (die mit ihm auch nicht einen einzigen Tropfen Blutes gemeinsam hat) aus der Taufe gehoben. Ruthmayr's Ehe blieb ungestört und, siehe da, Schlaggenberg[s] hatten eine Tochter bekommen, beziehungsweise Kajetan, der damals noch ein Junge war, eine Schwester.

Solche Agenden Levièlles also bildeten den Enterhacken mit dem er sich an Ruthmayr und späterhin an dessen Witwe und Vermögen anhackte. Woher indessen die Verbindung Levièlles mit Cornel Lasch, dem Schwager des Frl. Grete Siebenschein (Geliebte Stangelers) stammt, weiß ich selbst nicht. Genug, sie arbeiteten zusammen und mit Altschul, wobei letzterem zum angegebenen

Zeitpunkt sozusagen schon das lange Messer winkte.

Es handelt sich bei alledem nicht um reine Börsengeschäfte. Wie Du dies vielleicht bemerken wirst, hat Levièlle wahrscheinlich mit Ruthmayr'schem Geld auch seine Machtposition bei der "Allianz"[12] fundiert. Ich möchte bei dieser Gelegenheit nicht unerwähnt lassen, daß ich ihn eigentlich nicht für einen Defraudanten halten kann, der ein ihm anvertrautes Vermögen verludert. Denn der Prozeß hat gezeigt, daß das Ruthmayr'sche Vermögen sogar gut verwaltet war und so ziemlich unvermindert aus der ganzen Schlamassel herauskam.[13] Direkt unterschlagen aber hat er jenes bedeutende Vermögen, das Ruthmayr seiner unehelichen Tochter Charlotte v. Schlaggenberg testierte. Dieses Testament oder der betreffende Teil desselben ist von Levièlle beiseite geschafft worden.[14] Der später so bekannt gewordene Einbruch in der Wohnung des Kammerrates, den Schlaggenberg zusammen mit Stangeler verübte (welch letzterer ohne [5] zu wissen, um was es sich eigentlich handelte mehr aus Romantik mittat) hängt mit dem Versuche zusammen, dieses Schriftstück in die Hände zu bekommen. Ein Versuch, der übrigens mißlang.

Nun zu Schlaggenberg selbst. Als er aus dem endgültigen Zusammenbruch seiner Ehe mit Camy, geb. Sch(ä)[e]dik,[15] sozusagen allmählich wieder auftauchte, ist ihm nicht lange nachher Stangeler gewissermaßen über den Weg gestolpert. Stangeler, der sich damals in irgendwelchen unbeschreiblichen inneren Zerwürfnissen herumtrieb (im übrigen ist ja die Art des Burschen meinen Lesern aus dem "Geheimnis des Reichs" bekannt), Stangeler war damals der Geliebte der Grete Siebenschein, der Tochter des Rechtsanwaltes Siebenschein und Schwägerin des Cornel Lasch. Schlaggenberg, den Wert des jungen Mannes erkennend und zugleich in einer viel gründlicheren Weise als die meisten anderen Menschen (ihn) über die [derartige] Aussichtslosigkeit je(n)[d]er Verbindung be(lehrend)[lehrt], welche auf dem dissonierenden Akkorde grundverschiedener Rassen- und Geistesart aufgebaut war (Aussichtslosigkeit zumindest für Menschen von Format—Durchschnitt und Pöbel vertragen sich, auch wenn sie von den verschiedensten Enden der Welt in einen Haufen zusammengeweht werden) Schlaggenberg also, durch seinen Beruf und auch die Art des Zusammenbruches seiner eigenen Ehe aufs härteste darüber belehrt, daß sich hier bereits ein die ganze europäische Welt erschütternder Riß öffnete, um zwei ineinander verfilzte Lager reinlich zu trennen und durch diese Distanz einen Menschen- und Christen würdigen Frieden wieder herzustellen.[16] Schlaggenberg also schien eine Zeit lang gewillt, Quertreibereien zu unternehmen, um die Beziehung zwischen Grete Siebenschein und seinem neuen Schüler René Stangeler zu sprengen. Ein zu jener Zeit, nebenbei bemerkt, völlig aussichtsloses [Unternehmen] [6]. Es hatte dies zunächst den einzigen Erfolg, daß Schlaggenberg sich ein nicht gering zu schätzendes Uebel auf den Hals hetzte, nämlich Levièlle. "Ja, wieso denn das?"—wirst Du, lieber Fritz mich fragen. Und: "Was hat denn dieser alte Schieber mit des Fähnrichs Liebessachen zu tun?" Wie sich zeigt, doch, wenn auch auf einem seltsamen Umweg.

René, ein damals noch recht ungehobelter Bursche, hatte sich aus einer Reihe von Jahren, die er in russischer Kriegsgefangenschaft zubringen mußte, etwelche seltsame Sitten bewahrt. So zum Beispiel: sich irgendwo, wenn es ihm gerade paßte und er müde war, hinzulegen und zu schlafen. Dieses praktizierte er auch in dem jüdisch-kleinbürgerlichen Milieu der Siebenschein[s] und es war das nicht die einzige Art in welcher sich dieser junge Mann mißliebig machte. Genug, dieses Schlafen ist sehr wichtig! Es geschah z.b. einmal, daß René gerade im Musikzimmer schlief, als er Grete nicht zuhause antraf. Der Divan stand hinter dem großen Flügel, der kleine Fähnrich hatte gesunde Atmungsorgane und schnarchte nicht im mindesten, sondern er schlief auf gut Russisch einen gesunden Schlaf. Aus welchem Grund nun eigentlich Levièlle und Cornel Lasch ihre Konferenzen gerne bei Siebenscheins abhielten, darüber lassen sich verschiedne Vermutungen aufstellen. Die Gegend liegt gut, Levielle kann sich abseits und unbeobachtet fühlen. Oder anderes dieser Art mehr. Genug, sie kamen ins Musikzimmer, alle beide, heftig mauschelnd und ohne überhaupt ein Licht einzuschalten, es war ja noch verhältnismäßig hell. Dieses Gespräch ist von außerordentlicher Wichtigkeit. Levièlle plädierte aufs Heftigste dafür, Altschul fallen zu lassen, sich zumindest grundsätzlich dazu zu entschließen, sich sozusagen innerlich in dieser [7] Richtung festzulegen. Beachte, lieber Fritz, den Kreuzweg des Lebens,[17] der sich hier im Siebenschein'schen Musikzimmer bei schon einbrechender Dämmerung zeigt. Levièlle mit seiner hohen Fistelstimme wiederholte ein um das andere Mal: "Mag er fallen, für nichts mehr gut, soll ihn der Teufel holen!" Dieses aber drang in den Traum unseres unglückseligen Fähnrichs, er bezog es im Traum sozusagen auf sich, hatte einen rauhen Angsttraum, der ein merkwürdiges Gemisch aus raßischem Unglück und geistiger Gefährdung darstellte und fuhr schließlich, da Levielles spitze Stimme immer drängender in seinen Angsttraum eindrang und sich dort verkörperte, mit einem Schrei in die Höhe.

Nun muß ich aber sagen, daß dieser Szene, über welche sich der Schwiegersohn Lasch bei den Schwiegereltern aufs bitterste beschwerte, schon andre von der gleichen Art vorangegangen waren (n.b. den Traum Stangelers erzählt er selbst im 11. Kap., ohne natürlich eine Ahnung zu haben, welches der eigentliche Grund dieses Gespräches war, denn er erlebte es ja nur vom Boden seiner Entwicklungsnöte aus.)

Wir können nicht annehmen, daß Levièlle einen Menschen wie den jungen Baron Stangeler, der in seinen Augen zweifellos ein völliger Idiot war,[18] für irgendwie gefährlich gehalten hat, an und für sich. Wenn wir aber dazunehmen, daß Stangelers Verhältnis zu Grete Siebenschein sich seit der Bekanntschaft des Fähnrichs mit Schlaggenberg aus den oben erwähnten Gründen ganz wesentlich verschlechtert hat, wobei es nicht wenig Tränen und Schmerzen von Seiten des guten Mädchens gab, so werden wir es verstehen, daß Levielle den humanitären Vorwand der armen Grete Siebenschein zu helfen, Schlaggenberg ins Gewissen zu [8] reden und Frieden zu stiften nicht ungern benützte, um eines Tages Kajetan auf die Bude zu rücken (nebenbei bemerkt zeigt sich jedoch, daß der *(Kamerad)* [Kammerrat] mit all seiner Intelligenz an einer Erscheinung wie Stangeler insoferne scheitern mußte, als er außerstande war, sich von der Naivität, Indolenz und Uninteressiertheit dieses Burschen auch nur im Entferntesten eine Vorstellung zu machen; (er hat ihn ja, wie ich glaube, doch beim zweiten oder dritten Mal für einen Schlaggenberg'schen Spion gehalten) er rückte also bei Kajetan an, traf ihn nicht zuhause, hinterließ seine Karte (diese wurde übrigens vom Rittmeister Eulenfeld, der am gleichen Nachmittag vorsprechen wollte, entdeckt und gab im Kreise der unsrigen zu den wildesten Vermutungen Anlaß), kam 4 Wochen später wieder, stieß auf den, wie wir wissen, in Not befindlichen Schlaggenberg in seinem Arbeitszimmer und es gelang ihm weiterhin, Kajetan auf eine sehr nachdrückliche Weise unschädlich zu machen. Er bot ihm einen passablen Vertrag mit der Allianz A.G. an, den Kajetan, wenn auch unter Leibschmerzen annahm, um sich von seiner Familie, beispielsweise von seiner Mutter, unabhängig zu machen. Auch Stangeler, der gelegentlich historische Aufsätze in Zeitungen schrieb, sollte hier zu einem Verdienst kommen und beide in eine Verpflichtung dem Kammerrat gegenüber hineingeraten.

Es darf hier nicht unerwähnt bleiben, daß Levièlle ganz in den Mantel einer—beinahe möchte ich sagen—christlichen Nächstenliebe gehüllt erschien, "nur um dem armen Kind Grete zu helfen" und daß er auch beruflich für Schlaggenberg und auch für den jungen Historiker Stangeler noch viel weiter gehende Perspektiven durchblicken ließ (Buchverlag, Lektorat, etc.).

Wir befinden uns hier so ziemlich am Ende des 1. Teiles [9] und halten fest, daß Lasch und der Kammerrat sich entschlossen haben, *Altschul fallen zu lassen.*

Lieber Fritz!

Die Aktion Levièlle—Lasch—Altschul, das ist Dein Arbeitsfeld; diese Gaunereien hast Du Dir auszudenken, bis in den letzten Punkt. Sie müssen konkret, anschaulich und überzeugend vor den Leser hintreten, er muß sogar alle Einzelheiten verstehen können. Wir haben eben den ersten Teil meines Buches ("Die roten Lichter") verlassen und treten in den zweiten Teil ein, welcher den anmutigen Titel führt: "Dicke Damen" oder "die große chronique scandaleuse."[19] Bevor wir das kurz zusammenfassend eintreten, muß ich doch noch Einiges sagen, was im ersten Teil bereits dargestellt erscheint, ich muß also noch einmal einen Auszug aus gewissen Kapiteln dieses 1. Teiles geben.

In einem dieser Kapitel, welches den hübschen Titel trägt: "Rückblick auf eine große Liebe und auf die Mondsucht" wird gezeigt, welch ungeheure Gefahr ein junges, vor den Toren des Lebens stehendes—und natürlich heiratslustiges— Mädchen als Geliebte für einen in Entwicklung begriffenen, spirituellen Jüngling bedeuten kann, der infolge seiner äußeren und, wohlgemerkt, auch inneren Lage zu einer festen Bindung nicht befähigt ist. Oder zumindest nicht anders als auf einem organischen Entwicklungsweg zu ihr gelangen kann, nicht jedoch durch Versprechen oder Vorsatz. Schlaggenberg, der diese Sache bis zur Weißglut durchgemacht hat (von der Rassenkluft dabei ganz zu schweigen) um schließlich [10] in einer kurzen und von vornherein verfehlten Ehe zu landen (Camy Sch(ä)[e]dik) überspitzt seine Erfahrungen und macht daraus eine auf allgemeine Giltigkeit Anspruch erhebende Ideologie. Er meint, daß die Geschichte unserer Zeit getragen wird von der jüngsten Kriegsgeneration, die also noch im Feld stand und noch den Uebergang vom Alten zum Neuen persönlich mitmachte. Die "Nachkriegsjugend" hält er für geschichtslos, für eine Spreu, die zwischen den Maschen des Siebes durchfällt—höchstens als physisch fortzeugend von Belang. Diese junge Kriegsgeneration aber findet, wie er behauptet, unter der ungefähr gleichzeitigen Mädchengeneration kein Korrelat. Die schmale Existenzbasis der Zeit erlaubt nicht so wie früher dem spirituellen Menschen in seiner Entwicklungszeit auch noch ohne besondere Mühe die generative Aufgabe mit zu erfüllen,[20] da sehr unnatürlicher Weise und bezeichnend genug für die Verschrobenheit unseres Zeitalters, Weib und Kind zum unüberwindlichen Hindernis werden können, ja, denjenigen, der solches mit sich schleppe, an den Rand der Entgleisung zu bringen imstande sind. Aus dieser etwas krampfhaften Anschauungsweise mündet Schlaggenberg in eine hymnische Verherrlichung der "reifen Frau," die, die weiblichen Aufgaben schon erfüllt habend, nicht nach dem Traualtar schnappt, wie der Student nach der Doktor-Promotion. Er geht (in einigen Sätzen des Kapitels im 1. Teil "Die Entstehung einer Kolonie") so weit zu behaupten man müsse—um es hier psychoanalytisch auszudrücken—in sich einen Regress auf die Pubertätserotik provozieren,[21] diese sozusagen wieder hervorholen und auf diesem Vehikel die Fahrt ins gelobte Land der reifen Frauen antreten, der reifen, starken, üppigen Weiber, d(ie)[er] "dicken Damen."

Nun aber stellt dem guten Schlaggenberg dabei die merkwürdige [11] Neigung vieler Arier für das jüdische Weib ein belustigendes Bein. Um mich kurz zu fassen, sage ich: er gerät im zweiten Teil ins Judentum, dort, wo es am dicksten, und—wortwörtlich genommen,—am feistesten ist und siehe da, am Ende auf einem weiten Umwege und unversehens mitten in die Siebenschein'sche Verwandtschaft.[22] Es ist hier nicht der Ort und der Raum, um die Fülle von Skandalen aufzurollen oder aufzuzählen, die sich aus alledem entwickeln (daher: Chronique scandaleuse). Wichtig für unsere Handlung ist folgendes: Jener Dr.

Mährischl, den ich damals an jenem Frühjahrstage mit Altschul auf der Ring-
straße gehend mit samt seiner Frau Martha traf, ist ein Agent Levièlles. Der
Mann ist Rechtsanwalt und Levielle und Lasch haben es verstanden, ihm
Direktor Altschul als Klienten zuzuschieben. Frau Martha Mährischl aber,
welche der Leser schon aus dem 1. Teile kennt (ein entzückendes Konzil) hat sich
schleunigst mit der Gattin des Direktors, der nicht gerade mit großen Geistes-
gaben ausgestatteten Frau Rosi Altschul angefreundet und überwacht vermittelst
der *(eigenen)* dummen Frau [Altschuls] und ihres Plaudermundes das einge-
kreiste Opfer von der anderen Seite. Schlaggenberg, der in diese Kreise des Café
Siller insoferne eingedrungen ist, als er in einige üppige orientalische Betten fand
und im untersten Grund der Schweinerei, sozusagen in der Dreckhölle selbst,
angelangt ist, stößt hier auf seinen wesentlichen Gegner Levièlle;[23] damit lass'
ichs gut sein.

Ich teile Dir nur noch mit, daß es Schlaggenberg gelingt Frau Mährischl einen
Brief zu stehlen, der zwar nicht gerade als Waffe gegen Levièlle verwendet
werden kann, jedoch im weiteren Verlauf Anlaß zu dem bereits früher erwähnten
Einbruch Schlaggenbergs und Stangelers gibt.[24] So weit sind die Dinge gekommen, als mit dem 15. Juli 1927 die Flammen aus dem Justizpalast schlagen
[12] und Schlaggenberg's heitere erotische Intermezzi zunächst ein Ende finden.[25]

Ganz kurz will ich noch den dritten Teil streifen, da Du ja vom endlichen
Ausgang *(ja)* auch wissen mußt, wenn wir auch in diesem ersten Teil, vorweg-
nehmend, nur die gröbsten Umrisse der von Dir zu bearbeitenden Aktion
vorbringen wollen (am Schluß des 1. Teiles, dort, wo ich jetzt mit der Niederschrift halte.) Das wesentliche Thema dieses Buches,[26] bisher nur andeutungsweise in diesem Brief gestreift, in Wahrheit aber schon im ersten Teile ("die
roten Lichter") ausführlich behandelt, ist und bleibt ja auch weiterhin die
Zerlegung der Gesellschaft[27] durch die Entscheidung jenes—fälschlich ein
"Problem" genannten—Komplexes, den man gemeinhin mit dem Worte Judenfrage zu bezeichnen pflegt, obgleich [es] sich da, weiß Gott, [auch] um eine Reihe
von Menschen handelt, bei denen sich *(auch)* nicht ein einziger Tropfen jüdischen
Blutes nachweisen liesse. Diese Zerlegung wird im 1. Teile zunächst schon
andeutungsweise vorgreifend dargestellt, an einem Menschenkreis, den ich kurz
und ein für alle Male—darin übrigens dem Beispiel Dostojewskis folgend—[28]
den Namen "Die Unsrigen" ("naschi") gab (1. Teil, "Die roten Lichter," 8. Kap.
"Die Entstehung einer Kolonie"). Die Handlung des dritten Teiles in ihrer
dramatischen Zuspitzung zeigt, in welcher Weise sich diese chemische Zerfällung[29] der Gesellschaft vollzieht und wie weitgehend sie ist, wenn nur ein
kräftiges Ereignis die Menschen auf die Probe stellt: da findet jeder dorthin, wo
er hingehört, und am Schluß stehen zwei völlig wesensfremde Fronten geschlossen einander gegenüber—wobei allerdings das Judentum sich dem Ariertum
im Punkte der Dezidiertheit turmhoch überlegen erweist. In diesem letzten

Umstand liegt, nebenbei bemerkt, meines [13] Erachtens eine wirkliche und furchtbare Möglichkeit zu dem, was man allen Ernstes den "Untergang des Abendlandes" nennen könnte.[30] Dieser dritte Teil meines Romanes *endet* fast ein Jahr noch *vor* der deutschen Revolution, welche jene von jedem *(einsichtigen)* Wissenden bereits damals[31] empfundene Scheidung zu einer ganz allgemeinen und legalen Tatsache gemacht hat, sie mit ihren politischen Mitteln bis zum Aeußersten verflachend, so daß wir im Reiche bald wieder so weit sein werden, jene Cretins bekämpfen zu müssen, welche aus dem Umstande einer arischen Abkunft, bei völliger Abwesenheit jeder Intelligenz, meinen, eine Qualification machen zu können.

[14] Aide mémoire zu: die Dämonen[32]

Lieber Fritz!

Hier folgt die Fortsetzung unserer Handlung.

3 Menschen gibt es, drei lebende Menschen, welche von Quapps wahrer Abkunft wissen: die Mama Schlaggenberg in Südsteiermark, Kajetan, und Levièlle in Wien. Sonst niemand, nicht einmal Quapp selbst. Levièlle hat sowohl dem verstorbenen alten Herrn von Schlaggenberg auf dem Sterbebette, als auch Ruthmayr noch einmal, bevor dieser ins Feld zog, ein "heiliges" Versprechen gegeben, niemals diesen Schleier zu lüften und die Beheimatung dieses Kindes in der Familie Schlaggenberg in garkeiner Weise problematisch werden zu lassen.

Die Fülle von Skandalen der "Chronique Scandaleuse" durch die blutigen Ereignisse des Juli 1927 und den einbrechenden Sommer bis zu einem gewissen Grade zum Stillstand gebracht, nimmt gleichwohl im folgenden Herbst munter plätschernd ihren Fortgang und wir sehen unseren Kajetan in den Kapiteln "Fleisch mit Augen" und "Die Idiotenhölle,"[33] immer von seiner tollen Ideologie geführt, bis in den untersten Bauch der Sauerei steigen. Nur manchmal klingen hier noch zwei Motive aus dem ersten Teil nach, deren erstes dem Lebens-und Liebeskreise seiner Frau angehört, deren zweites zart andeutend eine auch im ersten Teil schon auftauchende Mädchengestalt betrifft. Nicht ohne Humor bleibt es, daß Schlaggenberg durch seine Verwicklung in skandalöse Händel (die Organisation "Negria")[34] letzten Endes sogar in seiner literarischen Laufbahn im äußer(*st*)en Sinn gefördert, nämlich gewissermaßen populär wird. Die ganze Fülle der hier sich eröffnenden geistigen Abstiegsmöglichkeiten mag hier nur hindeutungsweise erwähnt werden.

[15] Inzwischen sind am untersten Grunde dieses Sumpfes die beiden Gegner einander nähergekommen. Frau Lea Wolf, gegen Rosi Altschul schon von vornherein nicht sympathisch eingestellt (1. Teil, 9. Kap: "Ein entzückendes Konzil") wird zum Werkzeug Schlaggenbergs bei dessen Operationen gegen Martha Mährischl und somit gegen Levièlle. Hierin liegt eine gewisse Paradoxie. Denn letzten Endes wird damit den Altschuls genützt, jedoch unsere schöne Lea

hat vor allem an der etwas aufdringlichen Freundschaft Marthas und Rosis *(Ge)*[Miß]fallen gefunden. Dies alles nur nebenbei. Es genügt, hier zu sagen— ich muß, lieber Fritz natürlich Sprünge machen, da dieses aide mémoire sonst uferlos wird—daß dies alles bei Kajetan am Ende in eine ungeheu're Lawine von Ekel zusammenrinnt, die mit elementarer Kraft abrollt, und träge, und mit unermeßlicher Melancholie durch ihre Masse sein Leben für einige Zeit verschüttet.

Jedoch nur eben für einige Zeit (da sind wir im Spätherbst 1928).[35] Kajetan, der sich durch einige*(r)* Veröffentlichungen neuerlich Beachtung verschafft hat, erhält eines Tages die Einladung zu einem großen Fest bei Friederike Ruthmayr, die er bisher persönlich garnicht gekannt hat.

Für diese Einladung zeichne *ich* verantwortlich. Wenn ich auch längst wußte, daß die Ruthmayr'sche ja die eigentliche Realisierung aller Träume Schlaggenbergs bedeuten mußte, so habe ich hier ebensowenig Schicksal gespielt, wie im ersten Teil zwischen ihm und Stangeler, mich aber auch nicht dagegen gesträubt, als es schließlich zum Klappen kam. Sie fragt mich eines Tages, ob ich von Schlaggenberg etwas gelesen habe oder ihn gar persönlich kenne, sie sei von manchen seiner Sachen so entzückt. Und nun freilich hielt ich nicht hinter [16] den Berg mit der Tatsache, daß er mein alter Freund sei.

So kam es zu jenem denkwürdigen großen Empfang im Palais Ruthmayr. Ich muß hier noch etwas sagen, was mir wichtig erscheint. Ich will offen zugestehen, daß es meine grenzenlose Antipathie gegen das schweinische Treiben Kajetans war, welche mich verhindert hat, auf eine so wunderbare Frau wie Friederike Ruthmayr hinzuweisen. Genug davon. Es kam zu jenem Empfang: wenn ich mich recht erinnere war es etwa im April des Jahres 1929,[36] und ich sehe heute noch vor meinem inneren Auge Schlaggenberg die breite Freitreppe emporsteigen zum oberen Absatz, wo die Hausfrau empfing und wo auch ein wunderbares, kleines Orchester aufgestellt war, welches, daran erinnere ich mich auch genau, gerade jene Stelle aus dem Rosenkavalier spielte, welche die Ueberreichung der silbernen Rose durch Quinquin illustriert.[37]—Aber, keine Rose ohne Dornen, heißt es—diese Sache hat einen gewaltigen Dorn. Hier hatschte das Schicksal mit einem ungeheueren Hühnerauge und dieser Leichdorn hieß Levièlle. Er stand neben dem Sessel Friederikes und spielte hier sozusagen den Hausherrn. Ich fand das unerhört.

Zwischen der Ruthmayr'schen und Schlaggenberg entschied sich zunächst alles in den Sekundenbruchteilen ihrer ersten Bekanntschaft. Er sagte mir, er hätte die Empfindung gehabt, sein Leben wie ein zugeschnürtes, fertiges Paket ihr einfach in den Schoß legen zu sollen. "Ich habe oft gedacht," sagte er, "man müsse sozusagen die "dicken Damen*(")* mit dem Herzen ["] suchen—[38] aber das habe ich natürlich nicht getan, und deshalb fuhr es mir gleichzeitig beim ersten Zusammentreffen mit Friederike wie ein Stilett durch die Rippen: 'zu spät!'."

Nichts im Leben, lieber Fritz, steht oder geschieht allein [17] und isoliert und wenn wir Schreibenden gelegentlich in der Novelle tun, als ob es so wäre—weil die Gesetze dieser Kunstgattung es so verlangen—so gestattet der Roman nicht solche edle Beschränkung. Er ist röher, breiter, ein vielarmiges Umgetüm und alle seine Arme müssen sich ständig bewegen. Diese kleine Bemerkung soll dazu überleiten um Dir zu sagen, daß noch während des Ablaufes von Schlaggenberg's endlosem Schmutzstrom in der "Chronique Scandaleuse," die Dinge zwischen der kleinen Grete Siebenschein und Stangeler auf einen unheilbaren Punkt gekommen sind, wobei das Mädchen, letzten Endes eben doch aus dem härteren Stoff gemacht, die Oberhand behalten hat und, sagen wir es frei heraus, ihre jahrelange Unterdrücktheit und wohl auch ein wenig ihr rassisches Minderwertigkeitsgefühl in einer Kette von garnicht unbedeutenden *(kleinen)* Grausamkeiten an René austobt.

Damit aber befinden wir uns an einem Punkt, der Schlaggenberg endlich Gelegenheit gibt in einer reineren Form seine Ideologien zu verwirklichen, wenn auch nicht an sich selbst. Er will eingreifen,[39] Stangeler nunmehr endgültig von Grete trennen und diesen Knaben niemand anderem bringen, als Friederike[n].[40]

Es ist ja fast selbstverständlich, daß bei alledem die ungeheuerlichsten Täuschungen obwalten müssen. Levièlle sieht allein in Kajetan nicht nur den wesentlichen Gegner, sondern auch denjenigen, der ihn von seinem Platz bei Friederike Ruthmayr verdrängen will. Levièlle ahnt freilich nichts von dem, was man mit Stangeler vorhat. Levièlles Eifersucht konzentriert sich auf Schlaggenberg.[41] Einer zweiten Illusion erliegt zunächst Friederike selbst. Sie ist es, die eine Werbung Kajetans zweifellos zu spüren glaubt, welcher aber nur seinen Fähnrich vorschieben [18] will. Ich muß hier aber ganz nebenbei anmerken, daß wir uns hier bereits jenem Zeitpunkt nähern, da die Katastrophe an der Oesterreichischen Creditanstalt beginnt.[42]

Das Schicksal eines dritten Paares noch spielt hier hinein: das sind Quapp und Gyurkicz.[43] Die Liebesgeschichte dieser beiden hat sich in eine Reihe unfruchtbarer Einzelkämpfe aufgelöst. Gyurkicz, von einer unheilbaren Eifersucht auf alles was Quapp irgendwie nahesteht, gehetzt, muß seit Jahr und Tag freilich mit seiner Eifersucht vor der legalen Geschwisterschaft Quapps und Kajetans Halt machen, obwohl er in Schlaggenberg das eigentliche große Hindernis seines Glückes sieht. Von ihm und dem Rittmeister, weiterhin aber auch besonders von einem gewissen Dr. Körger und einem bei den ["]*(u)*[U]nsrigen["] oft erscheinenden jungen ungarischen Aristokraten, der als Attaché der Wiener Gesandtschaft zugeteilt ist *(Name steht noch nicht fest)*[44] gehen ja vorwiegend jene Einflüsse aus, die sich in der oben angedeuteten Richtung bewegen, nämlich der Ausscheidung aller wesensfremden Elemente aus jenem Kreis, den ich mit dem Worte die "Unsrigen" gerne bezeichne. Diesen Druck hat neben Grete Siebenschein, dem Studenten Neuberg, einer gewissen Frau Glöckner (sämtlich Juden) in mehr indirekter Form auch ein Element wie Gyurkicz zu spüren, dessen schlecht verhüllte Abkunft jeder kennt (ebenso wie seinen wahren Namen);[45] nur läßt man ihn vorläufig unter der Marke laufen, die er sich selbst umgehängt hat, wie so ziemlich nur Quapp zuliebe geschieht. Wir haben in ihm auch einen *wesentlichen* Vertreter der "Allianz" zu erblicken, worin uns seine gern und oft geführten antisemitischen Reden in keiner Weise beirren dürfen. Quapp gegenüber ist sein Streben jedenfalls auf Unterjochung, Zerfaserung und Zersplitterung ihrer ihm im Grunde ganz [19] fremden Persönlichkeit gerichtet, wobei er die Sache im Allgemeinen geschickt anpackt, seiner Partnerin von vornherein durch tiefere Wesenskälte überlegen. Ihm nun, ebenso wie Levièlle, ist es freilich bekannt, in welcher engverbundenen Weise unser Geschwisterpaar in Zeiten der Not immer wieder beisammen gelebt hat, oftmals sogar in einem Zimmer, ja, in einer Bettstatt.

Von dem Augenblick an, da Schlaggenberg im Umkreis der Friederike Ruthmayr aufgetaucht ist, fühlt sich Levièlle im höchsten Grade beunruhigt. Er bleibt in der Tat hartnäckig bei der Anschauungsweise, in Schlaggenberg einen Rivalen zu erblicken und legt so seinem wesentlichen Feind auch noch das Attribut des erotischen Nebenbuhlers bei. Kajetan indessen hat längst auf Friederike verzichtet und sich bereit gemacht, Stangeler an seiner Statt vorzuschieben. Dieses letztere nun wird über den Sommer (   ) akut.[46] Wir erwähnten schon, daß Stangeler im Begriffe war, Grete Siebenschein gegenüber grundsätzlich ins Unterwasser zu geraten, welche die sich bietenden taktischen Möglichkeiten vielfach in einer den Methoden Gyurkicz seltsam verwandten Art ausnützte.[47]

Hier befinden wir uns nun schon in der Entscheidung; Altschul soll fallen, Levielle die Höhe seiner Macht und schließlich auch Friederike erringen, Schlaggenberg soll bei Friederike unmöglich gemacht werden—an Stangeler denkt der Kammer-Rat in seiner Kombination noch nicht. Hier liegt sein Fehler.[48] Als er Schlaggenberg das Messer an den Hals setzen will, weiß er erstens nicht, daß es diesem garnicht mehr um Friederike zu tun ist; er haut dadurch an seinem neuen, inzwischen schon durch Kajetan bei Friederike eingeführten Gegner René vorbei. Es gelingt in dieser Phase des Gefechtes tatsächlich den heftigen Bemühungen [20] und Interventionen Kajetans mit äußerster Kraftanstrengung den Fähnrich aus der Siebenschein'schen Verstrickung heraus zu reißen und ihn, treu seiner alten Ideologie, die er hier *(nicht)* nur [nicht] mehr an sich [selbst] anwendet, sondern an einem anderen,[49] der schönen Friederike sozusagen in die Arme zu legen. Zur selben Zeit setzt ihm Levièlle das Messer an den Hals und droht mit dem Verrat seines Geheimnisses. An diesem Punkt aber befinden sich *(ihre)* [seine] Interessen sozusagen in der gleichen Stoßrichtung mit denen Gyurkicz's. Die beiden werden vorübergehend Verbündete (und hier siehst Du schon, wie sich zwei Fronten teilen). Als der Kammerrat unter vier Augen Schlaggenberg endlich offen droht, findet sich Schlaggenberg in einer sehr merkwürdigen und zwiespältigen Lage; denn inzwischen hat sich, nach jenem ersten und erfolglosen Einbruche *(nach jenem)* [auf Grund des] durch Frau Lea Wolf Kajetan in die Hände gespielten Brief[es], endlich eine wirkliche Waffe gegen Levièlle gefunden, dadurch nämlich, daß Friederike Ruthmayr, endlich die Front wechselnd, Kajetan zu denjenigen Papieren verhilft, die er braucht und deren Inhalt sie selbst garnicht kennt.[50] In einer ungeheueren Skandalszene, welche sich abspielt zu einer Zeit, da das Gebälk des Triumvirats Levièlle-Lasch-Altschul bereits in allen Fugen kracht, wirft der Kammerrat in Gegenwart der Ruthmayr Schlaggenberg die Wahrheit über ihn und Quapp*(auf)*[an] den Kopf und nun zieht Kajetan seine geladenen Geschütze ab. Seine Kenntnis von Levièlles Machinationen vor allem aber von der Unterschlagung von Quapp's Erbschaft.[51] Hier erst erfährt Friederike, wessen[52] Tochter Quapp ist (Schlaggenberg hat es erst aus den aufgefundenen Papieren erfahren).[53] Friederike aber wird durch die auf Quapp und Schlaggenberg als Paar sich beziehenden fast direkt geschlechtlichen Verdächtigungen [21] Levièlles (nebenbei ist auch Gyurkicz bei dieser Szene anwesend, die sich im Palais Ruthmayr abspielt) in keiner Weise mehr getroffen,[54] wenn auch Friederike selbst unter dem Drucke dieser Argumentation diesen Verdächtigungen beinahe Glauben schenken möchte. x)[55] Jedoch auch sie ist *(in dem)* [beim] Sprengpunkte der Handlung hieran ja nicht mehr zuinnerst beteiligt, denn um diese Zeit ist zwischen ihr und dem kleinen Fähnrich schon ein festes Band geknüpft.[56] Gyurkicz, zu jener Zeit in die Affaire der ["] Dichterin ["] Rosi Malik verwickelt,[57] welche im weiteren Verlaufe dem Chefredakteur der "Allianz," Kobler, den Untergang bringt, entlarvt sich selbst Quapp gegenüber so weitgehend, daß die Verbindung zu ihm ganz abreißt. Gegen Levièlle aber schlägt man nicht vernichtend los, welches sich damals auch erübrigte, da der Zusammenbruch der Credit-Anstalt seiner Laufbahn auf jeden Fall ein Ende zu machen im Begriffe war.[58] Man stellte ihm nur die Bedingung, daß Altschul gerettet werden müsse.[59] Mit dieser Bedingung machen sich unsere Leute dem Judentum gegenüber wieder einmal gründlich lächerlich, denn Direktor Altschul ist inzwischen aus freien Stücken aus der Credit-Anstalt ausgeschieden und befindet sich überraschender Weise jetzt mit Levielle im Bündnis.[60]— Diese Vorgänge nun, das Ausscheiden Grete Siebenscheins aus dem Kreise der Unsrigen, ebenso das Ausscheiden Gyurkicz'—wobei zu bemerken ist, daß Grete Siebenschein im entscheidenden Moment auch zur Partei Levielle hinübergezogen wird, umsomehr, als ihre Trennung von Stangeler nunmehr als perfekt zu erachten ist,[61] *(D)*[d]as Ausscheiden jener andersartigen die sich nun, am wendenden Punkte angekommen, alle um Levielle—, Lasch, Altschul, den Zeitungskonzern "Allianz," um die Familie Siebenschein, ja, letzten Endes [22] sogar um Schlaggenbergs geschiedene Frau gruppieren, leitet jenes Sichtbarwerden der beiden wesensfremden, getrennten Fronten ein, von denen jede nur mehr aus Art- und Sinnesverwandten besteht, nebenbei bemerkt auch über die rein blutmäßige Tatsache hinausgehend, denn wir finden in der Levièlle-Front eine ganz bestimmte Art von *(lebenden)* [abendländischen] Menschen, die keinen Tropfen semitischen Blutes haben: Münzen sozusagen, die auf beiden Seiten eine einzige Prägung zeigen, nämlich die des Defektes, da mag man nun die Sache von der jüdischen oder von der "gotischen" Seite aus betrachten. Auch diese Qualitätslosen werden in der Stunde der Entscheidung restlos vom anderen Pole aufgesaugt. Rasch vollzieht sich nun die Umgruppierung. Jenes zweite große Ereignis Oesterreichischer Geschichte dieser Jahre, der Zusammenbruch der schon oft genannten Großbank,[62] reißt am Ende doch Figuren wie Levièlle, Lasch und Altschul mit in seinen Sturz. *(Altschul)* [Stangeler] hat, wie schon erwähnt, endgültig zur Ruthmayr'schen gefunden. Grete Siebenschein—eine der sympathischsten Figuren des ganzen Kreises—findet in Neuberg ihren Gefährten, der sich von der ihm wesensfremden Angelika Trapp endlich trennt (sehr bezeichnend, daß ihr Vater, der Rechtsanwalt, in der Aktion [gegen] Levièlle[63] eine bedeutende Rolle spielt). Gyurkicz findet, in die Affaire Malik verwickelt, den Tod. Dulnik, jener geniale Mann, der erstmalig das Closettpapier als Reklamefläche entdeckt hat, bekommt seine Angelika,[64] welche damit deutlich zeigt, daß sie eine solide Versorgung innerhalb der eigenen Kreise dem romantischen und anstrengenden Ueberhüpfen einer gottgewollten Rassenkluft, gut bürgerlich, vorzieht.

Das Schönste ist, daß während dieser ganzen Umgruppierung[,] während der Reinigung *beider* Fronten von Fremdkörpern[,] [23] während jenes merkwürdigen, durch alle Fugen der Gesellschaft knisternden Dezidierens,[65] welches schon jahrelang der deutschen Revolution vorauslief—daß während alledem der Ideologe, Interventionist, Schicksalsverbesserer und Gesellschaftsreiniger Kajetan mit einem ungeheuren Kopfsprung aus dem Kreise der Unsrigen entschwindet und tief hinten in der anderen Front landet, ich möchte fast sagen, dort, wo sie am dicksten ist. Denn er allein bleibt sozusagen unversorgt zurück, steht am Schluß mit leeren Händen da, weil er sich allzusehr in die Angelegenheiten anderer mischte. Er steht da, voll Ekel nach den Erlebnissen der Chronique Scandaleuse, welche ihm diejenigen Organe, mit denen er eine Friederike Ruthmayr hätte erfassen können,[66] verschmutzt hat. Er, der Sexualiker, hat von der Sexualität genug. Camy kommt aus England zurück. In einer unendlich mühevollen und ungeheu're Energien verschlingenden Campagne gelingt es ihm die ehemalige Gattin wiederzugewinnen,[67] trotz der heftigsten Gegeneinflüsse ihrer Freundin Grete Siebenschein, welche das wesentlich Unsinnige dieser Wiederherstellung klar erkennt: sie muß es ja wissen nach ihren Erlebnissen mit Stangeler. Diese Ehe, kaum zum Stehen gekommen, bricht alsbald wieder in einer geradezu beispiellosen und deshalb auch endgültigen Form zusammen. Es ist bezeichnend, daß jene Mädchenfigur, die dann und wann einmal durch den ersten und zweiten Teil geistert[,] nicht[68] auftritt (etwa warnend oder beschützend), während Schlaggenberg in seinen letzten, wesentlichen Irrtum stürzte, sondern erst[69] ganz am Schluß wieder sichtbar wird, da er (für die Unsrigen war er durch Monate verschollen)[70] wieder seine Auferstehung feiert. (letztes Kapitel des Buches: Schlaggenbergs Wiederkehr).

[24] Hier habe ich, lieber Fritz, *(vor allem)* noch einen kleinen Nachtrag zu geben. Er mag Dir dazu dienen, unsere gute Quapp zu charakterisieren, und jene Art von Wirkung, welche sie gelegentlich hervorzubringen imstande war.—Als in Gegenwart von Gyurkicz, Schlaggenberg, Stangeler, Levielle und Friederike Ruthmayr in eben dem großen, letzten, unermeßlichen Skandal im Palais Ruthmayr durch Levielles Verrat die Wahrheit über Quapp's und Kajetans [nicht] bestehende Blutverwandtschaft aufflog, rief man Quapp telephonisch herbei. Levielle wagte es, ihr die Wahrheit ins Gesicht zu schleudern. Der Ausdruck ihres Gesichtes in diesem Augenblick hatte die Kraft, Schlaggenberg zu rechtfertigen und hatte die Kraft, jenen früher erwähnten Glauben Friederikes an den Wahrheitsgehalt von Levielles Verdächtigungen völlig zu zerschmettern. Quapp sagte nichts anderes als: ["] ich halte das für unwichtig; damit ändert sich doch garnichts!" Im nächsten Augenblick hatte Friederike die Tochter ihres gewesenen Mannes umarmt und in diesen wenigen Sekunden sie gleichsam als ihre eigene adoptiert.

Auch zum Kapitel "Schlaggenbergs Wiederkehr" noch ein Wort: hier erscheint denn der Kreis der Unsrigen, in den Kajetan, nun wieder Junggeselle, neuerlich eintritt, wirklich geschlossen und frei von allen wesensfremden Elementen. Die Zentrierung[71] dieses Kreises erfolgt zum Gutteil während der Periode von Kajetans Verschwundensein, also während *(seines)* [des] Wiederherstellungsversuches seiner [25] Ehe, rund um eine Persönlichkeit, welche inzwischen nach langer Abwesenheit in Wien wieder auftaucht: das ist Kajetans Lehrer,[72] der im Roman nur gelegentlich genannt wird, und zwar im Zusammenhang mit einem Buche Kajetans, das die Biographie dieses Lehrers darstellt.[73] Dieser Mann bildet sozusagen den sinnbildlichen Mittelpunkt für den jetzt neuen, gereinigten Kreis, dessen spirituelle Stellungnahme sich eben in diesem einen Mann am stärksten verkörpert hat. Um Dir nun, lieber Fritz, auch über dieses Letzte ein klares Wort zu sagen, füge ich an das Ende unseres Aide mémoire eine Kopie[74] jener Rede (ihr Titel ist: "das neue Reich")[75] welche bei einer vollen Zusammenkunft der "Unsrigen," im letzten Ausklang des Romanes von Schlaggenberg gehalten wird.

Appendix III

Chronological Table of the
Genesis of *Die Dämonen* (1951-1956)

My dating of this material is based on the manuscript of the novel as found in Ms

I-III, Ser.n. 14.051-53, "Die Entstehung einer Kolonie," and "CS," Ser.n. 14.054, and "Schlaggenberg's Wiederkehr," Ser.n. 14.102. Doderer wrote text for the novel on an almost daily basis, and he was always punctilious about dating each portion of the narrative. In addition, he often noted in the *Commentarii* or "Notizhefte" when he commenced or finished a chapter.

21.10.1951 - 12.12.1951	—Draußen am Rande (as "Probetexte" in "Commentarii VI")
21.1.1952	—"Probetext" for the last part of Auf offener Strecke. Between 28.1.1952 and 14.1.1953 Doderer reworked the original version of this chapter, written 15.2.1940-24.4.1940.
19.4.1952 - 4.6.1952	—Am anderen Ufer
10.6.1952 - 8.9.1952	—"Leonhard-Einschub," DD, 116-63
8.4.1953 - 26.4.1953	—Die Falltür
26.4.1953 - 12.6.1953	—Die Kavernen von Neudegg
12.6.1953 - 20.8.1953	—Dort unten
21.8.1953 - 28.8.1953	—Am Strom, DD, 807-14, 1. 26
31.8.1953 - 12.9.1953	—Der Sturz vom Steckenpferd
29.8.1953 - 13.10.1953	—Im Osten, DD, 540-67
22.9.1953 - 9.12.1953	—Im Haus "Zum blauen Einhorn"
10.12.1953 - 2.2. 1954	—Die Anabasis
19.2.1954	—Die Anabasis (Nachtakt), DD, 953-55
21.2.1954	—Das Nachtbuch der Kaps I
3.2.1954 - 12.4.1954	—Im Osten, DD, 567-634
23.4.1954 - 15.5.1954	—Der Triumph der Rahel
17.5.1954 - 20.5.1954	—Am Strom, DD, 814, 1.27 - 824
22.5.1954 - 30.5.1954	—Überm Berg
21.7.1954 - 20.8.1954	—Vor verschlossenen Türen
21.8.1954 - 1.12.1954	—Kurze Kurven I
12.12.1954 - 14.1.1955	—Auf der Schanze, DD, 1057-80
22.3.1955 - 28.4.1955	—Auf der Schanze, DD, 1080-1103
5.4.1955	—"Vignette" zu Strom, DD, 824-27
29.4.1955 - 7.9.1955	—Kurze Kurven II
14.9.1955 - 20.9.1955	—Das Nachtbuch der Kaps II
22.9.1955 - 10.1.1956	—Das Feuer
14.2.1956 - 3.3.1956	—Die Entstehung einer Kolonie I
6.3.1956 - 24.3.1956	—Die Entstehung einer Kolonie II
1.4.1956 - 7.4.1956	—Dicke Damen
21.4.1956 - 11.6.1956	—remodelling of "Die Dämonen der Ostmark"
25.7.1956 - 26.7.1956	—Schlaggenberg's Wiederkehr

Appendix IV

The Composition of "Das Feuer"

The following is a chronological survey of the genesis of the chapter. The page-references are to Ms III; those in parentheses situate the segment in *Die Dämonen*. Also included are the symbols by which Doderer referred to the individual segments in the *Commentarii* and the "Skizzen." In the "Ariadne-faden," which forms the second part of this Appendix, Doderer refers to each segment of the chapter by the page on which it begins in Ms III. The chapter was written between 22 September 1955 and 11 January 1956.

22.9.	—3 "Vortakte" 164-65	(1206-07)
24.9	—"1. excentrischer Einsatz" (Quapp) 166-69	(1207-11)
25.9.-28.9.	—Quapp (2Qb) 169-74	(1260-65)
	(2Qc) 175-78	(1292-96)
29.9.-13.10.	—Geyrenhoff (1/11a) 179-83	(1229-34)
	(1/11b) 184-92	(1242-49)
	(1/11c) 192-201	(1270-80)
	(1/11c II) 201-04	(1296-99)
13.10.	—Geyrenhoff/Quapp (1/11 2Q) 204-05	(1326-28)
15.10.-17.10.	—Anny Gräven (13c) 206-10	(1328-31)
18.10.-21.10.	—"2. excentrischer Einsatz" (Leonhard) (17a) 211-17	(1213-20)
24.10-11.11.	—Leonhard (17b) 217-21	(1224-29)
	(17c/I) 221-26	(1287-92)
	(17c/II) 226-34	(1306-13)
12.11.-17.11.	—René (4b) 234-41	(1313-21)
17.11.-18.11.	—Mary K. (16b/I) 242-43	(1249-51)
18.11.-19.11.	—Mary K./Leonhard (16b/II) 243-44	(1321-22)
20.11.-24.11.	—Neuberg (LPN) 245-50	(1299-1306)
25.11.-28.11.	—Rittmeister/Körger (14) 251-54	(1322-26)
29.11.-5.12.	—Frau Mayrinker (LPM) 254-61	(1280-87)
5.12.-27.12.	—No text	
28.12.-31.12.	—Trix/Hubert (16k) 261a-65	(1252-57)
31.12.-1.1.	—Mary/Küffer (16a) 266-70	(1238-42)

1.1.-2.1.	—"3. excentrischer Einsatz"	(1211-13)
	(Anny Gräven) (13a) 270-73	
3.1.-4.1.	—Anny Gräven (13b) 273-75	(1257-59)
4.1.-5.1.	—Didi/Meisgeier (12) 275-81	(1265-70)
6.1.-7.1.	—Kajetan's "Bande" (5/10)	(1220-24)
	282-86	
9.1.-11.1.	—René (4a/I) 291	(1234-38)
	(4a/II) 293	(1251-52)

When Doderer completed the "Exaratio" and "Reihung" of "Das Feuer" he obviously felt that Dr. Otto Günther, who was typing the manuscript for him, would need a short explanation of how to transcribe the text from Ms III. Accordingly, in Ms III he numbered each of the twenty-eight segments in the order in which they were to appear in the typescript. (In the "Ariadnefaden" these are the numbers which are circled in red.) In addition, he attached to Ms III, p. 164, the following information, written in red ink, with the correction "11" made in green ink:

Ariadnefaden für die Copia des *(10.)* [11.] Kapitel ("Das Feuer")

Die 28 Unterabschnitte (Einheiten) sind nicht in jener Reihenfolge niederge-schrieben, in welcher sie in der Reinschrift stehen zu haben. Maßgebend für die Reihenfolge in der Copia sind die am Beginn jedes Unterabschnittes in rotem Ring stehenden roten Ziffern. Die Reihenfolge ist diese:

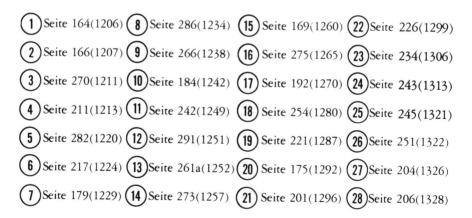

① Seite 164(1206)	⑧ Seite 286(1234)	⑮ Seite 169(1260)	㉒ Seite 226(1299)
② Seite 166(1207)	⑨ Seite 266(1238)	⑯ Seite 275(1265)	㉓ Seite 234(1306)
③ Seite 270(1211)	⑩ Seite 184(1242)	⑰ Seite 192(1270)	㉔ Seite 243(1313)
④ Seite 211(1213)	⑪ Seite 242(1249)	⑱ Seite 254(1280)	㉕ Seite 245(1321)
⑤ Seite 282(1220)	⑫ Seite 291(1251)	⑲ Seite 221(1287)	㉖ Seite 251(1322)
⑥ Seite 217(1224)	⑬ Seite 261a(1252)	⑳ Seite 175(1292)	㉗ Seite 204(1326)
⑦ Seite 179(1229)	⑭ Seite 273(1257)	㉑ Seite 201(1296)	㉘ Seite 206(1328)

Underneath the table is added in green ink:

Alle sonstige Vermerke in Buntschrift (so weit nicht Verbesserungen) sind auf die Composition am Reißbrett verweisende Buchstaben und Ziffern und für die Copia gegenstandlos.

A note is added in pencil in the left-hand margin:

In der Copia selbstverständlich *keine* Nummern!

On 2 February 1956, after a few last corrections to the contents of Ms III, he gives the volume to Günther to be typed. He receives the typescript on 27 March 1956 and immediately starts a "Durchsicht" and "Exaratio," in which no substantive changes to "Das Feuer" are made.

Notes

Introduction

[1] *Die Dämonen. Nach der Chronik des Sektionsrates Geyrenhoff. Roman* (Munich: Biederstein Verlag, 1956). Further references to this work are given in parentheses after quotations in the text and the abbreviation DD will be used in notes.

[2] "On the Posthumous Papers of Heimito von Doderer," *Books Abroad*, 42, no. 3 (1968), 368-71 (p. 371).

[3] Reininger, *Die Erlösung des Bürgers. Eine ideologiekritische Studie zum Werk Heimito von Doderers* (Bonn: Bouvier Verlag, 1975); Schröder, *Apperzeption und Vorurteil. Untersuchungen zur Reflexion Heimito von Doderers* (Heidelberg: Carl Winter Universitätsverlag, 1976); Weber, *Heimito von Doderer. Studien zu seinem Romanwerk* (Munich: C.H. Beck, 1963); Wolff, *Wiedereroberte Außenwelt. Studien zur Erzählweise Heimito von Doderers am Beispiel des "Romans No 7"* (Göppingen: Kümmerle Verlag, 1969), p. 11; Haberl, "Theme and Structure in the Novels of Heimito von Doderer" (unpublished dissertation, Cornell University, 1964); Stengel, "Die Entwicklung von Heimito von Doderers Sprachstil in seinen Romanen" (unpublished dissertation, University of Vienna, 1963).

[4] He claimed that he published his diaries for the years 1940 to 1950, "Nur um für Interessenten den Quellgrund zu zeigen, aus welchem alles kam, was Form gewann und inzwischen publik geworden ist," "Vornotiz" to *Tangenten. Tagebuch eines Schriftstellers 1940-1950* (Munich: Biederstein Verlag, 1964), p. 5.

[5] *Commentarii 1951 bis 1956. Tagebücher aus dem Nachlaß*, edited by Wendelin Schmidt-Dengler (Munich: Biederstein Verlag, 1976). As Schmidt-Dengler explains in the "Nachwort des Herausgebers," *Commentarii*, p. 590, the published version of the *Commentarii* is a selection from the manuscripts, comprising just under half of the original. Some of the material which Schmidt-Dengler has not taken up is relevant to the genesis of DD. Where I quote from such unpublished material, or from the as yet unpublished diaries for 1957 to 1966, I shall follow the guidelines laid down by Schmidt-

Dengler in the "Nachwort," pp. 592-93, for transposing Doderer's sometimes idiosyncratic orthography.

⁶ *Die Strudlhofstiege oder Melzer und die Tiefe der Jahre* (Munich: Biederstein Verlag, 1951); Roswitha Fischer, *Studien zur Entstehungsgeschichte der "Strudlhofstiege" Heimito von Doderers* (Vienna: Wilhelm Braumüller Verlag, 1975), p. 1.

⁷ From 1951 onwards Doderer often wrote the first tentative version of a segment of the novel in his diary and then transposed it, usually with minimal alterations, into the manuscript of the novel.

⁸ I was reluctant to omit this material from the study, but decided against including it because of the technical difficulties involved.

Chapter 1

¹ *Meine neunzehn Lebensläufe und neun andere Geschichten* (Munich: Biederstein Verlag, 1966).

² *Heimito von Doderer*, pp. 295-96.

³ 3.2.1921, "Journal 1. Heft (ab Herbst 1920)," Ser.n. 14.061.

⁴ *Gassen und Landschaft. Gedichte* (Vienna: Haybach Verlag, 1923); *Die Bresche. Ein Vorgang in vierundzwanzig Stunden* (Vienna: Haybach Verlag, 1924).

⁵ "Divertimento No. V," *Merkur* 8 (1954), pp. 647-59. All six "Divertimenti" are now in *Die Erzählungen*, edited by Wendelin Schmidt-Dengler (Munich: Biederstein Verlag, 1972) pp. 9-153.

⁶ Albert Paris von Gütersloh, *Die tanzende Törin. Ein Roman des Märchens* (Berlin: Baumhauer, 1911). Gütersloh was the pseudonym of Albert Conrad Kiehtreiber (1887-1973).

⁷ *Jutta Bamberger*, fragment, unpublished; *Das Geheimnis des Reichs. Roman aus dem russischen Bürgerkrieg* (Vienna: Saturn Verlag, 1930). Both works, along with *Die Bresche*, are now in *Frühe Prosa*, edited by Hans Flesch-Brunningen (Munich: Biederstein Verlag, 1968).

⁸ Albert Paris von Gütersloh, *Die Bekenntnisse eines modernen Malers* (Vienna and Leipzig: Zahn und Diamant, 1926).

⁹ Albert Paris von Gütersloh, *Sonne und Mond. Ein historischer Roman aus der Gegenwart* (Munich: Piper Verlag, 1962). Gütersloh pilloried Doderer as a Nazi, conveniently forgetting the fact that he himself had also been a Nazi sympathizer, and caricatured him in the figure of Ariovist von Wissendrum.

¹⁰ *Der Fall Gütersloh. Ein Schicksal und seine Deutung* (Vienna: Haybach Verlag,

1930). Now in *Die Wiederkehr der Drachen. Aufsätze, Traktate, Reden*, edited by Wendelin Schmidt-Dengler (Munich: Biederstein Verlag, 1970), pp. 39-109.

[11] *Der Grenzwald. Fragment. Roman No. 7, zweiter Teil*, edited by Dietrich Weber (Munich: Biederstein Verlag, 1967).

[12] Austria also had concentration camps, for example, Wöllersdorf, where many Social Democrats were imprisoned after the civil war of 1934.

[13] *Ein Mord den jeder begeht* (Munich and Berlin: C.H. Beck, 1938); *Ein Umweg. Roman aus dem österreichischen Barock* (Munich and Berlin: C.H. Beck, 1940).

[14] "DD Roman-Studien I-III, 'Die Dämonen der Ostmark'," Ser.n. 14.238/40.

[15] "Von der Unschuld im Indirekten. Zum 60. Geburtstag Albert P. Güterslohs," *Plan* 2 (1947/48), pp. 2-14; "Offener Brief an Baron Kirill Ostrog," ibid., pp. 398-402. Both are now in *Die Wiederkehr der Drachen*, pp. 111-32.

[16] *Die erleuchteten Fenster oder Die Menschwerdung des Amtsrates Julius Zihal. Roman* (Munich: Biederstein Verlag, 1951).

[17] "Sexualität und totaler Staat," first version 1948, second version 1951. Unpublished in Doderer's lifetime; now in *Die Wiederkehr der Drachen*, pp. 275-98.

[18] "Die Posaunen von Jericho", *Merkur* 9 (1955), pp. 1039-68. Now in *Die Erzählungen*, pp. 154-89.

[19] *Die Merowinger oder Die totale Familie. Roman* (Munich: Biederstein Verlag, 1962).

[20] *Grundlagen und Funktion des Romans* (Nuremberg: Glock und Lutz, 1959). Now in *Die Wiederkehr der Drachen*, pp. 149-75.

[21] *Die Wasserfälle von Slunj. Roman No. 7, erster Teil* (Munich: Biederstein Verlag, 1963).

[22] On 3 July 1936 Doderer noted in his diary: "Die Toten hießen Mathias Csmarits, hatte ein Glasauge (er war Invalider)...und Josef Grössing (ein kleiner Junge)," "Commentarii 1935/36," Ser.n. 14.073.

[23] Joseph Frank, *The Widening Gyre. Crisis and Mastery in Modern Literature* (New Brunswick, N.J.: Rutgers University Press, 1963), p. 19.

[24] Alfred Doppler, "Historische Ereignisse im österreichischen Roman," *Österreich in Geschichte und Literatur*, 13 (1969), 503-16 (p. 509).

[25] C. Earl Edmondson, *The Heimwehr and Austrian Politics* (Athens, Georgia: University of Georgia Press, 1978), p. 9.

Chapter 2

[1] José A. Palma Caetano, "Ein Interview," in *Erinnerungen an Heimito von Doderer*, edited by Xaver Schaffgotsch (Munich: Biederstein Verlag, 1972), 33-38 (p. 33).

[2] Over thirty years later Doderer described DD in the following terms: "Auf dem Haubenbiglweg. Hier begannen 'Die Dämonen.' Dieses Werk ist nicht so sehr gearbeitet worden, sondern es sind, in Schüben und Stauchungen, schließlich die verschiedensten Teile meines Lebens hier überein gekommen," 21.5.1962, "Commentarii XVII," Ser.n. 14.094/95.

[3] 9.12.1965, "Commentarii XX," Ser.n. 14.100.

[4] *Neue Freie Presse*, 17.11.1929. The clipping is stuck into "Studien Va," Ser.n. 14.177.

[5] Doderer inserted another advertisement in the *Neue Freie Presse* on 26.5.1930: "Junger Doktor, 33 Jahre, aus guter Familie, finanziell unabhängig und desinteressiert, gepflegte, trainierte Erscheinung, sucht ehrbare Bekanntschaft mit distinguierter ca. 45 jähriger israelitischer Dame (Wienerin) von *nur* außergewöhnlich starker, korpulenter, üppiger und überaus mächtiger, breiter Statur, schwarzem, respektive graumeliertem Haar und weißem Teint und von größerer, wirklich imposanter Erscheinung. Strengste Diskretion. Unter 'Restlos dieser Typ 25895' an das Ankündigungs-Büro des Blattes. 25895," "Studien Va." It is interesting to note that the "Annoncen-Campagne" was continued (no doubt to Doderer's great annoyance!) by his nephew, Dr. Kurt Mayer, the son of his sister Ilse and the model for Dr. Kurt Körger in the novel. The following notice appeared in the *Neue Freie Presse* of 5.11.1931: "Junger Herr aus guter arischer Familie, unabhängig, finanziell desinteressiert, tadellose Erscheinung, sucht die ehrbare Bekanntschaft einer gebildeten, wirklich distinguierten israelitischen Dame über 40, von nur sehr starker Figur. Strengste Diskretion. Unter 'Reife Frau 43132' an unser Stadtbüro. 43132." The clipping is also in "Studien Va," with the note added by Doderer, "gestartet von Dr. Kurt Mayer."

[6] "Studien Va."

[7] "Doderer. Der Spätzünder," *Der Spiegel*, 5 June 1957, 53-58 (p. 58).

[8] Meret Riedtmann, "Heimito von Doderer und die Wissenschaft vom Leben," *Wort in der Zeit*, 2 (1956), 607-14 (p. 610).

[9] "Journal TB-TBS 1930/31," Ser.n. 14.067. TBS is the abbreviation for "Tagebuch eines Schriftstellers," a title borrowed from Dostoevsky.

[10] 31.12.1930, ibid.

[11] Ibid., undated entry.

[12] 16.10.1931, "Journal TB-TBS, 12.9.1931-3.3.1932," Ser.n. 14.068.

[13] Ibid. Some thirty years afterward Doderer claimed that the chapter "Topfenkuchen," which he composed at this time, remained relatively unchanged in its 1956 form: "Wo ist Döbling? Die Fäden ziehen sich continuierlich von dort: so etwa ist 'Topfenkuchen' (aus DD) 1931 in der Pfarrwiesengasse geschrieben worden und dem gegenüber nicht viel verändert in seiner heutigen Form," 9.2.1961, "Commentarii XVI," Ser.n.14.092/93.

[14] 18.10.1931, "Journal TB-TBS, 12.9.1931-3.3.1932." Part I of the novel, completed in 1936, has seventeen chapters.

[15] "Journal TB-TBS (Übungen ab 4.3.1932)," Ser.n. 14.069.

[16] Ibid.

[17] 29.9.1932, "Journal TB-TBS (Übungen ab 22.8.1932)," Ser.n. 14.070.

[18] "Mir geht's dreckig. 1933 veröffentlichte ich 12 Novellen; voilà tout. Jedoch absorbiert mich glücklicherweise noch immer mein großer Roman et cetera mihi farcimenta," undated letter of 1934 to Ernst Alker, unpublished.

[19] "Journal TB-TBS (Übungen ab 22.8.1932)."

[20] "Journal TB-TBS (Übungen ab 22.3.1933)," Ser.n. 14.071.

[21] 8.8.1933, ibid.

[22] 9.7.1953, *Commentarii*, p. 224.

[23] "Commentarii 1934, II/III," Ser.n. 14.072.

[24] In "Materialsammlung R VII und DD," Ser.n. 14.188.

[25] 25.1.1953, "Notizheft 1953," Ser.n. 14.209.

[26] "Aide-mémoire," p. 12.

[27] Ibid., p. 22.

[28] 18.1.1936, "Commentarii 1935/36."

[29] November 1930, "Journal TB-TBS 1930/31."

[30] Unlike the majority of critics Dietrich Weber considers that Geyrenhoff, far from being an *alter ego* of the author, as are Schlaggenberg and Stangeler, was introduced by Doderer to exercise a self-critical role. Weber initially identified author and creation and "bemerkte erst später,...daß Doderer den Sektionsrat (der gar keine autobiographische Figur ist) nur vorgeschaltet,...um einen auch nur einigermaßen objektiven Blick auf sich selbst werfen zu können," "Zwei oder drei Dinge, die ich von ihm weiß," *Erinnerungen*, pp. 179-85 (p. 180).

[31] In "Materialsammlung R VII und DD." See Appendix I.

32 "Journal TB-TBS (Übungen ab 22.8.1932)."

33 29.5.1935, "Commentarii 1935/36."

34 Ibid.

35 15.7.1935, ibid. In the typescript of DDO Chapter 8 ends on p. 236.

36 "Commentarii 1935/36."

37 18.1.1936, ibid.

38 Ibid.

39 In 1946 Doderer speaks of the "fruchtbaren Gedächtnis-Distanz, aus der allein irgendwas gesehen, das heißt in den goldnen Schnitt zwischen Nähe und Entfernung gerückt werden kann," 17.7.1946, *Tangenten*, p. 490.

40 "Commentarii 1935/36."

41 Ibid. I have not been able to discover the surname of this person or how close a friendship existed between him and Doderer. Doderer uses the "Du"-form in this letter.

42 Ibid.

43 Ibid. Although Doderer later rejected the "Wasserscheide" as a central theme in the novel, he did not change his view that the events of July 1927 were the result of a communist conspiracy to overthrow democratic institutions in Austria. According to G.E.R. Gedye, who was the correspondent of the London *Times* in Vienna in 1927, the official government line was that the rioting was part of an attempted communist coup: "The Government press published the wildest and most distorted stories of a dangerous and well-planned Communist revolution, which had aimed at the creation of a Soviet Austria, suppressed after violent fighting," *Fallen Bastions. The Central European Tragedy* (London: Victor Gollancz, 1939), p. 38.

44 Doderer later emphatically rejected the historical novel as a literary genre, for much the same reasons as he differentiated between the task of the historian and that of the writer: "Der Historiker ist mit dem bloßen Was beschäftigt, also mit den allgemein gegebenen Zeitumständen und Verhältnissen, unter welchen und gegen welche sich das Wie des individuellen Lebens und Schicksals trotzdem durchzusetzen hat. Deshalb ist der historische Roman widersinnig, denn er nimmt sich eben das zum Gegenstande, dessen Unerheblichkeit letzten Endes zu erweisen ja die Arbeit des Romanschriftstellers ausmacht," 4.8.1944, *Tangenten*, p. 229.

45 He was also disappointed at his failure to achieve a breakthrough in Hitler's Germany, despite his political sympathies: "Und im Reiche draußen ist mir bisher nicht gelungen, auch nur einen Schritt breit Boden zu gewinnen, eine recht verwunderliche Tatsache, wo man doch glaubte, daß für Schriftsteller meiner Art nun ein Morgenrot angebrochen sei," November 1934, "Commentarii 1934, II/III." A more objective assessment of Doderer's

lack of success might ascribe it to the slimness of his literary production, apart from journalistic work, and to the lack of wide public appeal in works such as *Der Fall Gütersloh.*

[46] "Nach Deutschland war ich gekommen, um dort einen Verleger zu finden," *Meine neunzehn Lebensläufe,* pp. 29-30.

[47] "Commentarii 1935/36." He finished *Das letzte Abenteuer* on 7 November 1936, but it was not published until 1953: *Das letzte Abenteuer. Erzählung. Mit einem autobiographischen Nachwort* (Stuttgart: Reclam, 1953). Now in *Die Erzählungen,* pp. 386-449, but without the "Nachwort."

[48] Although the manuscript of DDO was destroyed in 1944, Horst Wiemer, who was until his retirement in 1977 reader for C.H. Beck and Biederstein Verlag and was also a close friend of Doderer, remembers receiving the manuscript: "Ich weiß aber noch sehr genau, daß es aus zweierlei Papier und zweierlei Papierformaten bestand, die von Doderer selbst für den Druck zusammengestellt waren," letter of 12 November 1977 to ECH.

[49] "Commentarii 1935/36."

[50] 16.11.1936, ibid. How thin a dividing-line exists for Doderer between the factual data of his real-life situation and the fictional content of his novel is illustrated by the fact that this scene between Camy and Schlaggenberg is an externalization of Doderer's love-hate relationship with his ex-wife, Gusti: "Das Vorstehende, wohl meine wichtigste Tagebuchnotiz, bewegt sich in der erzählenden Form, was ich für bezeichnend halte," 28.11.1936, ibid.

[51] Ibid.

[52] 17.2.1939, "Commentarii 1939/40/41," Ser.n. 14.075.

[53] These remarks, which are dated March 1939 and headed "Bemerkungen zur Durchsicht des ersten Textbandes und des Aide mémoire von D," are to be found at the back of "Commentarii 1935/36."

[54] He writes later of one theme "swallowing up" another: "Ich erkenne jetzt, rückblickend bis 1930, wie ein 'Thema' das andere verschlang: DD wurde von 'Wasserscheide' verschlungen...Diese selbst ward von 'Genf' verschluckt," 31.1.1940, *Tangenten,* p. 39.

[55] "Commentarii 1939/40/41."

[56] Although the concept of an impaired reality is only now emerging in connection with his attack on ideology, Doderer first made use of the term in 1936: "Heute mit Gütersloh ...Mit dem Meister sprach ich (in extenso) das heuristische Prinzip der 'geminderten Wirklichkeit' durch," 15.7.1936, "Commentarii 1935/36."

[57] 14.7.1939, "Commentarii 1939/40/41." He later describes the projected second part of the novel as "das universale Journal seines Autors," 14.2.1940, *Tangenten,* p. 47.

[58] 30.1.1940, ibid., p. 38.

59 31.1.1940, ibid., p. 39.

60 1.2.1940, ibid., p. 41.

61 12.2.1940, ibid., p. 45.

62 Cf. "Ich hörte in dieser Woche Gütersloh lesen, aus 'Sonne und Mond'," 14.5.1939, "Commentarii 1939/40/41."

63 5.9.1945, *Tangenten*, p. 370.

64 29.6.1946, ibid., p. 481.

65 Ibid., p. 482.

66 7.11.1950, ibid., p. 831.

67 Weber, *Studien*, p. 180.

68 "Daß ein Roman in ein Tagebuch hineinverschwinden kann, habe ich 1940 als Folge meiner Einrückung zum deutschen Militär erlebt: er fand sogar genügend Platz darin, und wurde in seinem neuen Raume einem vernichtenden Verfahren ausgesetzt, das ihn für den Autor gerettet hat," 25.10.1957, *Tangenten*, p. 102. When he later decided to publish his diaries covering the years of the war he had grave reservations about their reception by a reading public, because of the nature of their content: "Heuer erscheinen meine Tagebücher von 1940-50, 900 Seiten, das wird *die größte Pleite*, die mein Verlag mit mir jemals gemacht hat, denn es sind durchwegs denkerische (analytische) Texte," unpublished letter of 25.1.1964 to H.G. Adler.

69 7.6.1939, "Commentarii 1939/40/41."

70 In addition to the problems posed by the novel itself, Doderer was also assailed by doubts as to the insidious effects exerted by external happenings on his ability to create a literary work: "Ich habe in den letzten Wochen...unter einer unbeschreiblichen Depression gelitten, die wohl auch mit Schwierigkeiten in meiner literarischen Arbeit zusammenhing; es tritt, nach so vielen Jahren des Militärs, noch dazu in meinem Alter, die Frage auf, ob nicht hier irreparable Versäumnisse eingetreten sind...Ich rede von geistigen Schäden," unpublished letter to his mother, undated, possibly July 1944, 525/25-121.

71 The "Epiloge" were published in *Tangenten*, titled "Epilog auf den Sektionsrat Geyrenhoff. Diversion aus 'Die Dämonen,' 1940/44," *Tangenten*, pp. 49-100. The two cycles of poems, "Biarritz 1941. Fünf Improvisationen," and "Auf den Wällen von Kursk. Sieben Improvisationen (1942)," were published in *Ein Weg im Dunkeln. Gedichte und epigrammatische Verse* (Munich: Biederstein Verlag, 1957), pp. 65-77. The passages on the theory of the novel were taken up almost verbatim in *Grundlagen und Funktion des Romans*.

72 *Tangenten*, p. 56.

73 Ibid., p. 99.

74 Ibid., p. 86.

75 "Roman-Studien IV ('Dämonen') 1940," Ser.n. 14.184, p. 17.

76 "Ich möchte in den 'Dämonen' von Etelka ausgehen und den Punkt ihrer Katastrophe mit der Peripetie Stangelers koinzidieren lassen. Dieser selbst bleibe anfangs am Rande," 24.8.1945, *Tangenten*, p. 368.

77 Doderer stressed the autonomy of each novel vis-à-vis the other. Cf. "Die Autarkie der DD gegenüber der 'Strudelhofstiege' aufrecht zu erhalten, ist ohne besondere Schwierigkeit möglich, da ja die DD—als das ältere Manuscript—von vornherein nie als 'Fortsetzung' veranlagt waren," 16.12.1951, *Commentarii*, pp. 88-89. However, in a letter to C.H. Hager he referred to Part II of *Die Dämonen*, on which he was then working, as "die Fortsetzung der 'Strudlhofstiege'," unpublished letter of 26.10.1953. Horst Wiemer sees the relationship between the two works in terms of Doderer's attitude to the historico-political content of *Die Dämonen*: "Als dann der Krieg aus war und ich wußte, daß Doderer ihn lebend überstanden hatte, hoffte ich auf die Weiterführung der 'Dämonen.' Das geschah nicht, da Doderer bewußt wurde, er brauche eine längere 'geschichtliche' Vorbereitung der Ereignisse zur Zeit des Justizpalast-Brandes. Aus dieser 'Vorgeschichte' ist dann 'Die Strudlhofstiege' entstanden, von der zuvor nie die Rede gewesen war. Weniger äußerlich zeigen die 'Tangenten' diese Entwicklung," letter of 12.11.1977 to ECH.

78 Unpublished letter of 3.11.1948.

79 Unpublished letter of 3.11.1949 to Astri von Stummer.

80 This list of corrections, titled "D I Noten," is to be found in the folder Ser.n. 14.185. For convenience, in this study of the genesis of the novel between 1951 and 1956 the *sigla* used by Doderer in the *Commentarii* to refer to the various sections of the novel have been retained. A list of the *sigla* and their meaning precedes the Introduction.

81 I disagree with Politzer when he says: "Die 'Dämonen' beginnen mit einer so genannten 'Ouvertüre,' in der sich gleichsam leitmotivisch das Material der folgenden drei Hauptstücke ankündigt," Heinz Politzer, "Zeit, Wirklichkeit und Musik im Werk Heimito von Doderers," in *Das Schweigen der Sirenen. Studien zur deutschen und österreichischen Literatur* (Stuttgart: J.B. Metzlersche Verlagsbuchhandlung, 1968), 70-78 (p. 75).

82 Cf. "Der totale Roman ist—streng genommen—ein Roman ohne Thema. Das heißt: ein Thema oder Themen haben wohl in ihm Platz, doch bestimmen sie nicht seine Struktur. Der totale Roman läßt sich nicht auf ein thematisches Substrat reduzieren," Weber, *Studien*, p. 181. I think that it is true to say that the theme of the "second reality" did determine the formal structure of the novel. It certainly accounted for the introduction of the Herzka/Neudegg sequence to the novel as an illustration of the "second reality."

83 6.7.1951, *Commentarii*, p. 56.

84 25.11.1951, ibid., p. 84.

85 "Leonhard Kakabsa, den Bruder Ludmilla's nach I 6, 150, ganzes Kapitel einschieben, als Vorhalt zu II 2 ["Am anderen Ufer"] (excentrisch—objektiver Einsatz der Sturz-komposition...)," ibid., p. 118.

86 17.8.1952, ibid., p. 142. Alfred Barthofer is one of the very few critics (two others are H.M. Waidson and Martin Swales) who do not see the figure of Leonhard Kakabsa in a positive light. It is certainly possible to use the text of the novel to support such an inter-pretation, particularly if one considers that remarks such as "Der Autor erhebt sich hier, als Ehrenbezeigung vor seiner Figur, für einen Augenblick vom Schreibtische," DD, p. 1112, is an instance of "blatantly ironic self-distancing," Alfred Barthofer, "Leonhard Kakabsa: Success or Failure? Marginalia to a Key Character in Doderer's Novel *Die Dämonen*," *Forum for Modern Language Studies*, 14 (1978), 304-15 (p. 305), and is not a genuine expression of Doderer's admiration for his literary creation. Barthofer considers that certain other remarks pertaining to Kakabsa in the novel are "tinged with benevolent irony," ibid. However, Doderer's diaries quite unambiguously demonstrate that he had no reservations about Leonhard and considered him to be an exemplary character. I suspect that if Barthofer had been familiar with the *Commentarii* he might have reached a far less negative assessment of Doderer's attitude toward his character and his role in the novel.

87 12.10.1952, *Commentarii*, p. 153.

88 18.3.1953, ibid., p. 200.

89 3.12.1955, ibid., p. 476. "LPM-fin" refers to the conclusion of the Mayrinker episode, DD, p. 1287.

90 Apart from two mentions in the *Commentarii*, 17.2.1954, p. 274, and 16.8.1954, p. 332, "Textmasse C" occurs in "Skizzenblatt 1," a sketch drawn up by Doderer in 1952. (The original of this sketch is in the possession of Ivar Ivask.) It is also to be found in the sketch numbered 3g in the folder Ser.n. 14.188.

91 He had stated his intention of writing new material on a daily basis on 30.10.1952, *Commentarii*, p. 156. He did not realize his aims until he commenced work on "Dort unten" on 8 April 1953. Doderer dated each section of text in the margin of the three volumes of manuscript composed between 1952 and 1956, "Die Dämonen. Probetexte und Entwürfe," Ms I-III, Ser.n. 14.051/53. These volumes are bound, blank copies of books which Doderer was given by his publisher. Although his writing is extremely small, it is easily legible, apart from some parts which were written in pencil and which have become smudged.

92 14.4.1953, *Commentarii*, pp. 204-05.

93 28.4.1953 and 29.4.1953, ibid., p. 208.

94 "Dort unten" was not adopted as the title of the chapter until a later date. At the time of its composition Doderer referred to it as "Achaz." He borrowed its final title from

Huysmans: "'Dort unten' ist bewußt nach jenem gleichnamigen Roman von Joris Charles [*sic*] Huysmans ('Là-bas') benannt. Sie wissen, daß ich in der Wahl von Titeln mitunter auf Originalität keinerlei Wert lege," unpublished letter of 19.3.1961 to Dietrich Weber, 525/25-192. Whether or not the title is original is of lesser importance than the fact that it summarizes Doderer's thesis of the evil lurking in the depths of society.

[95] 15.6.1953, *Commentarii*, p. 217.

[96] 7.7.1953, ibid., p. 223.

[97] Ibid., p. 231.

[98] The "Einhorn" sequence was originally one chapter, consisting of the two parts B1(E), the later chapter "Im Haus 'Zum blauen Einhorn'" and E/E/G, the later chapter "Die Anabasis." In Ms I there is no chapter-division on p. 252.

[99] 17.2.1954, *Commentarii*, p. 274.

[100] Reininger describes this section of narrative (DD, pp. 620-26) as a "kurzes chronik-artiges Referat," and says that without this "Orientierungshilfe" the events in Burgenland would be incomprehensible to the reader, *Studie*, p. 161.

[101] 8.4.1954, *Commentarii*, p. 285.

[102] 29.6.1954, ibid., p. 309.

[103] The intrusion of external reality into the life of the individual is foreshadowed in Malva Fiedler's denunciation of Leonhard Kakabsa to the police. She accuses him of having a sexual relationship with minors: "Zum ersten Mal erlebt es Leonhard, daß irgendeine ihm bisher ganz unbekannte Macht neben ihm aufsteht und sich über seinen Weg werfen will," 3.9.1954, ibid., p. 341.

[104] 6.7.1954, ibid., p. 313.

[105] 26.7.1954, ibid., p. 326.

[106] The significance of the title is explained in the novel itself. Neuberg claims to feel a sense of awareness of the increasing tempo of life and an anticipation of an impending traumatic happening, DD, p. 1025. Stangeler draws the parallel of little pond-creatures coming to rest momentarily on the surface of the water and sending out ripples in concentric circles ("Kurze Kurven"). The reason for the frenzied activity of these creatures is that they are aware of the presence of a crab at the bottom of the pond, and although they are in no danger from it, "Sie zeigten ein Kommendes und ihnen Unbekanntes unten in der Tiefe an," ibid., p. 1026. Thus, society may be sending out ripples because it is aware of the evil lurking in its own depths.

[107] "Der ganze Schluß des Finalsatzes hat im Grunde ein einziges—völlig ungenanntes und unberührtes—General-Thema: das Zurückweichen der zweiten Wirklichkeit," 4.6.1955, *Commentarii*, p. 426.

[108] "Was Herzka appliziert bekommt, ist Choc-Therapie," 9.11.1954, ibid., p. 364.

[109] "14 (Kurven), eventuelle Einschübe," 3.12.1954, ibid., p. 373. It would perhaps be appropriate at this point to consider the problem of the numbering of the chapters of Part II of the novel. Although Schmidt-Dengler says: "Die Kapitelfolge war auch durchnumeriert worden von dem ersten Kapitel des zweiten Teiles an," "Nachwort," *Commentarii*, p. 583, he does not explain how, for example, "Vor verschlossenen Türen" is referred to by Doderer as II/13, whereas in the published version of the novel it is the fifteenth chapter of the original Part II. In September 1954 the first thirteen chapters of Part II are as follows: 1. Strecke 2. A1 (Ufer) 3. A2 (Osten) 4. A3 (Rahel) 5. A4 (Cavernen) (includes "Die Falltür") 6. A4 (Dort unten) 7. Am Strom 8. A5 (CS) 9. R II 10. Be 11. Einhorn (not split into two chapters) 12. Nachtbuch 13. R III ("Türen"). Doderer experienced some difficulty when placing R IIIb ("Auf der Schanze"). He considered interpolating it, as a separate chapter, into Sp, which would result in the following sequence of chapters: Sp 1-4 (14), R IIIb (15), Sp 5-7 (16), F (17). Alternatively, he could simply interpolate R IIIb into Sp as one chapter, which would result in the following sequence of chapters: Sp 1-4 - R IIIb - Sp 5-7 (14), F1 (15), F2 oder Reserve-Kapitel (16), W (17). Sp 1-7 becomes the single chapter "Kurze Kurven" and is followed by R IIIb, but so many additions are made to "Kurze Kurven" that the chapter "Kurze Kurven II" is added and the eventual sequence of chapters is: KK I (14), R IIIb (15), KK II (16), F (17), W (18).

[110] II/15 itself offers an excellent illustration of how these chapters are expanding beyond the dimensions originally set for them. Doderer intended II/15 to be relatively short: "Damit schließt 15 (höchstens etwa zwanzig Seiten)," 19.12.1954, *Commentarii*, p. 378. It eventually consisted of fifty-two pages of manuscript in Ms III, pp. 1-52.

[111] "Sicher ist, daß ich ab jetzt in symphonischen Einheiten mit abgesetztem Tempo bis zum Schlusse gehen werde," 19.7.1954, *Commentarii*, p. 323.

[112] 20.1.1955, ibid., p. 391.

[113] 27.1.1955, ibid., p. 392. Doderer started going through DD I on 17 January 1955, and although he was doing this primarily for thematic reasons, he was also giving thought to the condensation of DD I. The entry for 27.1.1955 continues: "Die Durchkürzung von I schneidig und en bloc." He was contemplating a reduction of over 50% in the contents of "Die Dämonen der Ostmark."

[114] 17.2.1955, "Commentarii X," Ser.n. 14.084.

[115] From the point of view of the symmetry of the narrative framework it should be noted that Part II begins and ends with a Geyrenhoff chapter.

[116] One wonders why this decision should have been such a traumatic experience for Doderer One also wonders why he should say of DD, three years after its completion, that its "Dreiteiligkeit samt dem dynamischen Konzept übrigens ganz ebenso als apriorische Form gegeben waren," *Grundlagen und Funktion des Romans*, p. 164, and how Horst Wiemer can claim that the decision to split the novel into three as opposed to two parts

was taken in the summer of 1952: "In jener Nacht ist die Neugliederung des großen Werkes in drei Teile beschlossen worden," *Erinnerungen*, p. 190. Doderer himself later suggested that it was his inability to come to terms with Part I of the novel which resulted in his adopting the tripartite form for the work: "Vielleicht war's nach jener schlimmen Krisenzeit, welche auch für 'Dämonen' die Entscheidung bildete, als ich DD I zum ersten Mal bearbeitete, dies noch gar nicht vermochte, und endlich die Lösung der 3-Satz-Form fand," 6.5.1958, "Commentarii XIII," Ser.n. 14.088.

[117] Doderer is not forgetful of the political situation and has Grete Siebenschein and Stangeler meet at 9 p.m.: "Grete und René müssen so früh einander treffen, daß noch kein Urteil im Schattendorfer Prozeß erfolgt oder eigentlich von den paar hundert Leuten, die in den Anlagen vor der Nationalbank gewartet haben, promulgiert sein kann," 25.8.1955, *Commentarii*, p. 449.

[118] 19.5.1955, ibid., p. 421.

[119] See *Commentarii*, p. 414.

[120] 4.2.1956, *Commentarii*, p. 499. The "Notizen-Sammlung zur Bearbeitung von DD I" is to be found at the back of "Commentarii Xb," Ser.n. 14.085. The notes concern fairly minor interpolations to DD I, e.g.: "*ab ovo* in den Texten G-ff's als Vorhalt" and "Eintopf - Herzka: Großmutter Neudegg."

[121] 5.2.1956, *Commentarii*, p. 500.

[122] The "Ausscheidung" of 6.2.1956 and the "Substratverzeichnis der Ausscheidung" drawn up between 7.2.1956 and 11.2.1956 are in the possession of Ivar Ivask and Schmidt-Dengler has photocopies of them.

[123] "1. Graphicon zu DD I (kleines Reißbrett)," "Notizheft 1956," Ser.n. 14.212. This sketch is now in the folder Ser.n. 14.188.

[124] 2.4.1956, "Commentarii XI," Ser.n. 14.086. Some of this material goes right back to the very first beginnings of the novel: "CS Text (mit Benutzung von Texten ex 'chronique totale' 1929/1930)," 6.4.1956, "Notizheft 1956."

[125] 6.4.1956, *Commentarii*, p. 515.

[126] 24.6.1956, ibid., p. 536.

[127] 7.7.1956, ibid., p. 538. Cf. "Nur ein Strom apperceptiver Vorgänge kann...fünfund-dreißig Jahre der Deperception aufwiegen," 20.6.1956, ibid., p. 535.

[128] The short delay between the completion of the writing of the novel and its publication on 10 October 1956 is due to the fact that while still engaged in writing the last chapters of the novel Doderer has been carefully revising his earlier chapters. He terms this procedure an "Exaratio," but the process does not involve a radical alteration of the formal structure of the chapters but consists rather in stylistic changes, interpolations and modifications, greater precision in factual detail and other changes of this nature. The

manuscript was typed by his friend, Professor Otto Günther, from 15.11.1954 onwards and the typescript also underwent an "Exaratio" before being sent off to the publisher. On 11.7.1956 Doderer finished proof-reading Part I of the novel, and on 24.7.1956 he completed proof-reading the entire novel, with the exception of "Schlaggenberg's Wiederkehr," which he was just about to write.

[129] 12.8.1956, *Commentarii,* p. 548.

[130] Unpublished letter of 17.8.1957 to Ernst Alker.

[131] 26.9.1956, *Commentarii,* p. 554.

[132] 26.5.1957, "Commentarii XII," Ser.n. 14.087.

[133] 7.7.1954, *Commentarii,* p. 315.

[134] *Grundlagen und Funktion des Romans,* p. 164.

[135] Cf. "Ich habe bis jetzt etwas über 1200 Seiten von mir bereits accceptierten Text liegen," unpublished letter of 14.3.1954 to Armin Mohler. This number of pages assumes the inclusion of "Die Dämonen der Ostmark," uncondensed.

[136] *Der Spiegel,* 5 June 1957, p. 57.

[137] "Nachwort," *Commentarii,* p. 579.

Chapter 3

[1] 30.10.1952, *Commentarii,* p. 156.

[2] *Grundlagen und Funktion des Romans,* p. 171.

[3] 5.9.1952, *Commentarii,* p. 148.

[4] 5.7.1954, ibid., p. 313.

[5] It had been his intention for some time that the concluding portions of the novel should follow this pattern: "'Textmasse C' 'Sturz und Stern' (ca. 100 Seiten)," "Skizzenblatt 1," dated "Sa. 25. Oct. 52."

[6] Fischer, pp. 282-83. Fischer reproduces the sketch at the end of her book and analyzes it on pp. 282-86.

[7] 1.6.1954, *Commentarii,* p. 304.

[8] 18.9.1954, ibid., p. 345. The sketch is unpublished, "Commentarii IX," Ser.n. 14.083.

[9] 16.4.1954, *Commentarii,* p. 288.

[10] When Doderer was reviewing the manuscript of *Die Wasserfälle von Slunj* he noted: "Wieder zeigt sich—, wie durch das excentrische Ansetzen der Nebensätze die räumliche Weitung entsteht. Ein ähnliches Phänomen wie bei DD I ('Draußen am Rande') nur hier weit ausgebauter und distincter," 24.1.1961, "Commentarii XVI."

[11] *Grundlagen und Funktion des Romans*, p. 171.

[12] Doderer considered that mastery of both types of language, discursive and analytical, was the hallmark of the true novelist: "Beide Anwendungsarten der Sprache erst machen zusammen einen Schriftsteller aus, und schon gar den Romancier," ibid., p. 168.

[13] Ibid., p. 171.

[14] This is one of the functions of the conversations between Geyrenhoff and Schlaggenberg: "Vieles (zum Verständnis von Seiten des Lesers—bezüglich der Leitmechanik)—kann diskursiv gegeben werden in Gesprächen zwischen Kajetan und G-ff," 9.7.1954, *Commentarii*, p. 317.

[15] 3.5.1954, ibid., p. 294.

[16] Weber, *Studien*, p. 42.

[17] Cf. "René blieb vor den großen Fenstern und der Fernsicht stehen...Die Situation war sein, im höchsten Grade; es war die seine. Innen und Außen fügten sich ineinander zu einem festen Gelenk," DD, p. 721.

[18] 25.11.1960, "Commentarii XV," Ser.n. 14.091.

[19] "Innsbrucker Rede. Zum Thema Epik," *Akzente*, 2 (1955), 522-25 (p. 525).

[20] Cf. "So etwa, wie ich im 'Mord' mit Contraktionsgliedern arbeitete, werde ich in DD 'Erweiterungs-Fenster' einbauen," 12.1.1953, "Commentarii VIII," Ser.n. 14.082.

[21] These two "windows" are F 222, the Ergoletti episode (*Die Wasserfälle von Slunj*, pp. 154-73), and F 311, Chwostik's return to the Adamsgasse (ibid., pp. 263-74).

[22] 29.11.1960, "Commentarii XV."

[23] 21.12.1960, ibid.

[24] 19.7.1964, "Commentarii XIX," Ser.n. 14.098/99. Published in the "Anhang" to *Der Grenzwald*, p. 255.

[25] 27.12.1960, "Commentarii XV."

[26] Cf. 29.5.1952, *Commentarii*, p. 132, 17.8.1953, ibid., p. 230, and 18.8.1953, ibid.

[27] 17.8.1953, ibid., p. 229.

[28] 7.2.1953, ibid., p. 193.

[29] 13.2.1961, "Commentarii XVI."

[30] "Der intensivste Fall zweiter Wirklichkeit nämlich—der Fall Herzka und das durch ihn vermittelte spätmittelalterliche Manuskript 'Dort unten'—ist genau in der Mitte des Buches plaziert. Einzig der ästhetische Ort ist es ja, der die Wichtigkeit eines Phänomens im Roman statuiert," Weber, *Studien*, p. 182.

[31] Cf. "Wo immer man einbaut—öffnet man," 24.11.1960, "Commentarii XV."

[32] 23.6.1953, *Commentarii*, p. 219.

[33] *Geschlecht und Charakter: Eine prinzipielle Untersuchung* (Vienna: Otto Braumüller Verlag, 1903).

[34] Weber, *Studien*, p. 205.

[35] " 'Der Einbruch von unten': an Austrian Syndrome of the Inter-War Years?," *German Life and Letters*, 27, no. 4 (July 1974), 315-24 (p. 315).

[36] Ibid., p. 323.

[37] 1.12.1960, "Commentarii XV."

[38] The Herzka episode eventually came to represent almost one-eighth of the narrative. "Dort unten," a literary *tour de force*, also developed from very obscure beginnings: "Mir beweist eine Notiz..., daß ich am 16. März von dem Abschnitt 'Achaz'...noch kaum einen Dunst hatte, ja, in bezug auf dieses Segment geradezu in 'blühendem Unsinn' schwamm," 21.7.1953, "Commentarii VIII."

Chapter 4

[1] These projected seventeen chapters correspond to Doderer's note of 4.5.1952: "I: Ouvertüre und 1-17. II: 18-34," "Notizheft 1952," Ser.n. 14.208. The only time that Doderer consistently refers to "Das Feuer" as comprising three chapters is in his diary for 1954. See *Commentarii*, pp. 274, 280, 284, 285, 294, 298.

[2] Cf. 21.3.1955, *Commentarii*, p. 407.

[3] 21.8.1955, ibid., p. 446.

[4] 17.7.1955, ibid., p. 434.

[5] 20.9.1955, ibid., p. 454.

[6] 24.9.1955, ibid., pp. 455-56. The "Nachtakt" is the Anny Gräven "Vignette," which takes place in January 1928.

[7] See Appendix IV for the meaning of the symbols used by Doderer.

[8] Cf. "Da ich die Ab-schnitte bereits im einzelnen kenne, kann ich jede Sequenz durch-schreiben und so einrichten, daß sie durch Zäsuren teilbar, und zur Einfügung in die Gesamt-Composition von F praktikabel wird," 29.9.1955, *Commentarii*, p. 457.

[9] 19.10.1955, ibid., p. 464.

[10] 21.10.1955, ibid., p. 465.

[11] 31.10.1955, ibid., p. 469.

[12] Two other sketches relate to "Das Feuer." The first of these, that numbered 3k in the folder Ser.n. 14.189, deals in a fairly detailed manner with the three main sequences 1/11, 2Q and 17, and the second, the sketch reproduced in *Kindlers Literatur Lexikon*, edited by Gert Woerner (Zurich: Kindler Verlag, 1965) is a "Composition ex post," which was drawn up after the chapter was completed in January 1956.

[13] 12.11.1955, *Commentarii*, p. 471.

[14] Cf. ibid., pp. 428 and 464.

[15] 13.11.1955, ibid., p. 471.

[16] Cf. "N ist der Keller, 'die Schanze' das Dach des Buchs," 12.12.1954, ibid., p. 376.

[17] 22.10.1955, ibid., p. 465.

[18] 3.12.1955, ibid., p. 476.

[19] 4.10.1955, ibid., p. 460.

[20] 6.7.1955, ibid., p. 431.

[21] Ibid., p. 443.

[22] Cf. 24.12.1955, ibid., p. 483.

[23] 8.7.1936, "Commentarii 1935/36."

[24] 16.12.1955, "Commentarii Xb."

[25] 7.12.1955, *Commentarii*, p. 478.

[26] 17.1.1956, ibid., p. 495.

[27] As mentioned, this is the sketch which is reproduced in *Kindlers Literatur Lexikon*. It is unfortunate that the sketch had to be reduced in scale and is almost illegible.

[28] See Appendix IV.

[29] 26.1.1956, *Commentarii*, p. 498.

[30] 2.10.1955, ibid., p. 459.

[31] 8.10.1955, ibid., p. 461.

[32] *Grundlagen und Funktion des Romans*, p. 172.

Chapter 5

[1] "Franz von Assisi," *Illustrierte Zeitung*, no. 4244 (Leipzig, 1926).

[2] Cf. "Seine [Güterslohs] Aussagen, vor allem im 'Innozenz' und in der 'Rede über Blei,' sind deutlich vom biblisch-theologischen Begriffsarsenal gespeist," Frank Trommler, "Doderer und Gütersloh," in *Roman und Wirklichkeit. Eine Ortsbestimmung am Beispiel von Musil, Broch, Roth, Doderer und Gütersloh* (Stuttgart: Kohlhammer Verlag, 1966), 133-67 (p. 156).

[3] *Tangenten*, p. 124.

[4] 18.1.1945, ibid., p. 280.

[5] 4.8.1948, ibid., p. 616. I agree with Else Buddeberg that Doderer accepted Thomist teaching quite uncritically and never succeeded in establishing any epistemological evidence for the *analogia entis*: "Die analogia entis ist von Doderer wohl nicht systematisch rezipiert, so oft er sich auch auf Thomas von Aquin beruft, und schließlich den Schriftsteller—und das heißt wiederum in erster Linie sich selbst—so etwas wie einen geborenen Thomisten nennt. Er hat sie gewissermaßen psychologisch-psychisch adaptiert. Nicht eine exakt begriffliche Übertragung, sondern Aneignung durch imitatio fand statt, die aus vorbewußter Affinität aufsteigt. Sie ist Vorrecht des Dichters und entspricht wohl im allgemeinen der selektiv-eklektizistischen Übernahme geistiger Gehalte in einem späten Zeitalter," "Schreibe, als ob du allein im Universum wärest," *Deutsche Beiträge zur geistigen Überlieferung*, 7 (Heidelberg, 1972), 160-239 (p. 168) Trommler makes a similar point: "Wenn sich Doderer verschiedentlich als Thomist bezeichnet und auf die Analogia entis beruft, so sucht er damit Wirksamkeit und Gültigkeit dieses Anspruchs aus der Tradition zu legitimieren," "Doderers Moral der Sprache," *Colloquia Germanica* (1971), 283-98 (p. 286).

[6] 10.7.1950, *Tangenten*, p. 762.

[7] *Grundlagen und Funktion des Romans*, p. 167.

[8] Cf. "Ich glaube, die vier Jahre in Rußland haben über mich entschieden. Ob jenes Resultat aus ihnen seine Giltigkeit behaupten wird—davon kann ich jetzt nichts wissen," 12.11.1920, "Journal 1. Heft (ab Herbst 1920)," published in *Frühe Prosa*, p. 361, and: "Es ist mein Schicksal gewesen, ein Schriftsteller zu werden—ich wurde es in Rußland, September 1916, und aus durchaus wichtigen Gründen und Anlässen—...," 29.12.1961, "Commentarii XVI."

[9] 18.11.1920, "Journal 1. Heft (ab Herbst 1920)."

[10] *Untersuchungen*, p. 182, fn. 165.

[11] See 5.5.1946, *Tangenten*, pp. 442-43.

[12] 29.9.1932, "Journal TB-TBS (Übungen ab 22.8.1932)."

[13] November 1934, "Commentarii 1934/III."

[14] *Untersuchungen*, p. 395, fn. 86.

[15] 28.8.1936, "Commentarii 1935/36."

[16] Cf. "Man kann im gleichen Hause sehr verschieden leben, man kann es durch verschiedene Türen betreten. Was ich mit meinem 'konstruktiven Denken' eines neuen Römischen Reiches im Jahre 1933 betrat, war aber nicht einmal das Haus der Politik; sondern eines der vielen öffentlichen Häuser falscher Sprachlichkeit. Ich war wirklich 'zu bösen Häusern' gekommen," 12.6.1946, *Tangenten*, p. 472.

[17] Unpublished letter of 14.5.1962 to Gustav H. Heimo. Cf. "Daß ich hier in der österreichischen Heimat infolge meiner vor neun Jahren schon Anfang 1937 abgebrochenen einstmaligen Sympathien zur Welt des Nazismus nunmehr die größten Schwierigkeiten habe,...," 2.5.1946, *Tangenten*, p. 441.

[18] 27.8.1936, "Commentarii 1935/36."

[19] *Studie*, p. 56.

[20] Ibid., p. 58.

[21] E.E. Noth, a personal friend of Doderer, is mistaken in his assessment of the reasons why Doderer did not publish at this time. What he says may be true of the final version of the novel, but it is certainly not applicable to "Die Dämonen der Ostmark:" "Or la partie essentielle de ce livre était déjà terminée en 1937, mais une publication était impossible dans le Troisième Reich. Car, chose extraordinaire, et apparemment contradictoire, en considérant les antécédents politiques de l'auteur, ce roman 'anti-idéologique' est radicalement et totalement anti-totalitaire, et très nettement 'anti-antisémite,'" "Monsieur 'Vienne,'" *Les Nouvelles Littéraires*, 28 January 1965. Gertrud Seidmann also misinterprets the reasons for the non-publication of the novel at this time: "The first part, the work of seven years, reached his publishers in 1938: but its publication had to be deferred indefinitely, for its background was an account of the events leading to the abortive Vienna revolution of 1927; its message, an unambiguous rejection of 'that devastating form of modern stupidity'..., the thinking according to ideologies; its most striking feature, a social and psychological realism, out of place among 'gleichgeschaltetes Schrifttum,'" "Heimito von Doderer," *Modern Languages*, 40, no. 2 (June, 1959), 53-56 (p. 53).

[22] *Der Spiegel*, 5 June 1957, p. 56.

[23] 5.8.1944, *Tangenten*, p. 92.

[24] *Die Wiederkehr der Drachen*, p. 293.

[25] *Commentarii*, p. 72.

[26] "Aus dem Quellgebiet der 'Dämonen' Heimito von Doderers. Anmerkungen zu

Tagebuchaufzeichnungen des Autors aus dem Jahre 1951," *Literatur und Kritik*, no. 80 (1973), 578-98 (p. 598).

²⁷*Die Wiederkehr der Drachen*, p. 287.

²⁸ *Erinnerungen*, p. 189.

²⁹ Draft of a letter of 29.8.1951 in "Commentarii VI," Ser.n. 14.080. Quoted by Schröder, *Untersuchungen*, p. 402. In his reply to Ernst Erich Noth, who had asked him about his Nazi interlude, Doderer said: "L'écrivain en moi n'avait jamais été affecté," E.E. Noth, "Heimito von Doderer," *Cahiers du Sud*, 51, no. 380 (1964), 187-96 (p. 195).

³⁰ See "'Die Dämonen:' totaler Roman und antirevolutionärer Traktat," *Literatur und Kritik*, no. 80 (1973), 599-608 (p. 600).

³¹ "Quellgebiet," p. 582. Quoted by Schröder, *Untersuchungen*, p. 404.

³² Ibid., p. 405.

³³ "Kritische Überlegungen zum Wirklichkeitsverständnis Doderers." Published in *Heimito von Doderer 1896-1966. Symposium anläßlich des 80. Geburtstages. Wien 1976* (Salzburg: Verlag Wolfgang Neugebaur, 1978), 61-81 (p. 80).

³⁴ See *Der Spiegel*, 5 June 1957, p. 57.

³⁵ 24.8.1951, *Commentarii*, p. 67.

³⁶ "Anhang," *Die Wiederkehr der Drachen*, p. 304.

³⁷ Karl Hopf links up Doderer's idea of "apriorische Geographie" to Aquinas's concept of *materia signata*. See "Von der Strudlhofstiege zum Grenzwald. Die Funktion der Topographie in den Romanen Heimito von Doderers," *Österreich in Geschichte und Literatur*, 16 (1972), 436-57 (p. 442).

³⁸ 26.4.1921, "Journal 1. Heft (ab Herbst 1920)." Published in the "Nachwort," *Frühe Prosa*, p. 388.

³⁹ *Doderer lesen. Zu einer historischen Theorie der literarischen Praxis. Essai* (Salzburg: Verlag Wolfgang Neugebaur, 1978), p. 8.

⁴⁰ "Scylla und Charybdis. Der junge Doderer zwischen Journalismus und Fachwissenschaft," in *Symposium*, 9-24 (p. 14). I also do not subscribe to Schmid's belief that Doderer's studies at the Institut für Österreichische Geschichtsforschung between 1948 and 1950 were prompted by a desire to prove that he was capable of successfully completing the course. Schmid claims that Doderer undertook these studies, "um zu beweisen, daß auch ein Literat den extremen Rigiditäten des legendären Wiener Kurses standhalten könne," *Doderer lesen*, p. 8. I believe that he went to the Institut in order to prepare himself intellectually for resuming work on *Die Dämonen*.

⁴¹ Cf. "Nicht hatte sich hier ein Roman zu Divertimento entfaltet, sondern umgekehrt: ein Divertimento war zum Roman entartet, wenn ich so sagen darf," unpublished letter of 12.12.1960 to Dietrich Weber, 525/25. See also Weber, *Studien*, pp. 64 and 275.

[42] When he was working on *Der Grenzwald* Doderer said of *Das Geheimnis des Reichs* that it was composed "in kleinen geschlossenen historiographischen Blocks," 4.8.1965, "Commentarii XX," published in *Frühe Prosa*, p. 377. In *Der Grenzwald* Doderer endeavored to achieve the complete integration of private and public happening.

[43] 18.6.1963, "Commentarii XVIII," Ser.n. 14.096/97, published in the "Anhang" to *Der Grenzwald*, p. 243.

[44] *Roman No. 7* marks yet another stage in Doderer's attempt to resolve the problem of how to treat historical content in a work of literature: "Es (R 7) ist mein erstes unabhängiges Werk. Die 2. Wirklichkeit (DD) konnte nur in statu nascendi dargestellt werden, der folgende Strom von Faktizität ist ohne Substanz, ist nur Schlamperei: 1939-1945 war um nichts mehr als das. Jedes chronikalische, fortsetzungsmäßige, inhaltlich vorausbestimmte Festlegung muß von R 7 weit ab bleiben, also kein Einfluß der Zeitgeschichte nach 1929 auf das Buch," 13.8.1958, "Nachtbuch," Ser.n. 14.102. Also: "Ich muß mich hier vollends frei machen von jedem Bezug zu Zeitalter und Chronik, zum historischen Roman: R 7 ist a-historisch. Es ist mein erster ganzer Umgriff um ein gehabtes deperceptives Sein," 2.11.1958, "Commentarii XIII."

[45] "Autobiographisches Nachwort," *Das letzte Abenteuer*, p. 126.

[46] Ibid.

[47] "Menschen auf der Strudlhofstiege. Spectrum Austriae im Roman," *Wort und Wahrheit*, 6 (1951), 771-75 (p. 771).

[48] Tape No. 3 in the Dokumentationsstelle für neuere österreichische Literatur.

[49] "Commentarii 1935/36."

[50] Unpublished draft of speech in "Skizzenbuch 34," 28./29.3.1951, Ser.n. 14.143.

[51] 17.8.1953, *Commentarii*, p. 229.

[52] "Down a Steep Place...A Study of Heimito von Doderer's 'Die Dämonen,'" *Forum for Modern Language Studies*, 7, no. 1 (January 1971), 76-82 (pp. 79-80).

[53] "Es steht mir nicht über die künstlerischen Qualitäten des Werkes zu urteilen, wohl aber darf ich für mich in Anspruch nehmen über die Schilderung rings um den 15. Juli auszusagen, als Einer, der damals mithandeln mußte, mitsah und auch mitlitt. Ich kenne keine literarische Würdigung dieses Unglückstages, die gerechter wäre als die Ihre, die von einem Einfühlsvermögen Zeugnis gibt, das aufrichtig verwundert," unpublished letter of 12.12.1958, 525/11-1.

[54] 23.1.1953, *Commentarii*, p. 186.

[55] With respect to the demands of the workers for "proletarische Klassenjustiz," G.E.R. Gedye points out that the Schattendorf shooting was "the fifth occasion within two years that Fascists had shot down Socialists and gone scot-free," *Fallen Bastions*, p. 37.

[56] 19.7.1956, *Commentarii*, p. 542.

[57] 16.12.1953, ibid., p. 258.

58 21.7.1936, "Commentarii 1935/36."

59 11.12.1944, *Tangenten*, p. 257.

60 15.12.1944, ibid., p. 260.

61 Frank Trommler remarks on the fact that in the chapter "Das Feuer" Doderer ascribes a political function to metaphor: "Er weist der Metapher selbst politische Funktion zu und macht dies am Ende der 'Dämonen' anschaulich, als eine alte Frau mit Milchflaschen von Gewehrschüssen niedergestreckt wird und Milch und Blut auf die Straße rinnen. Mit 'Rot-Weiß, Milch und Blut' beherrscht die Metapher selbst die Szene, aus ihrer Bedeutung 'blühenden Lebens und gesunder Jugend' in die grobe Stofflichkeit zurückgeworfen," "Doderers Moral der Sprache," p. 293.

62 6.7.1942, *Tangenten*, p. 134.

63 Reininger, "'Die Dämonen:' totaler Roman und antirevolutionärer Traktat," pp. 607-08.

64 *Der habsburgische Mythos in der österreichischen Literatur* (Salzburg: Otto Müller Verlag, 1966), 295-303 (p. 297).

65 "Doderers erste Wirklichkeit," in *Symposium*, 41-60 (p. 46).

66 Ibid.

Appendix I

1 This typed list of characters for the novel is to be found in the folder "Materialsammlung R VII und DD." The typescript is undated, but the list was probably made at about the same time as the "Aide-mémoire" in 1934. In the typescript deletions are made with a pencil-line through the word or words to be removed. In this Appendix additions are indicated inside square brackets, deletions inside italicized brackets. Some changes were obviously made at a much later date in blue pencil. These changes will be indicated in the notes.

2 These changes were made in blue pencil, probably in 1951.

3 Deleted in blue pencil.

4 Underlined in pencil.

5 Added in blue pencil. Leonhard was not added to the novel until 1952.

6 Deleted in blue pencil. A blue pencil line points to Angelika's name in the "1. Gruppe."

7 "Witwe" is added in blue pencil.

8 Deleted in blue pencil.

9 Written in pencil, deleted in blue pencil.

10 Deleted in blue pencil.

[11] Added in blue pencil.

[12] From "Zwischenfiguren" onwards is written in ink, deleted in blue pencil.

Appendix II

[1] Reininger entitles the chapter in which he deals with the "Aide-mémoire" "Ein Plan zur Fortsetzung—Das Problem des Antisemitismus," *Studie*, pp. 50-53.

[2] Added in pencil.

[3] The numbers inside square brackets in this Appendix are the page-numbers of the typescript of the "Aide-mémoire."

[4] Levièlle: Doderer accents Levielle's name in this fashion in the "Aide-mémoire," but not consistently. In the "Namenverzeichnis" he uses the spelling "Lévièlle." In "Die Dämonen der Ostmark" he uses the version "Lévielle." In the notes to "Die Dämonen der Ostmark" which he made in 1951 he decided that the definitive spelling of the name would be without accents: "Levielle ist *immer* ohne Accent zu schreiben." An undated entry in "Studien Va" for 1930 gives the following information about Levielle: "Levielle: Er hat natürlich einmal Lévy geheissen und stammt irgendwo 'aus Polen,' sagen wir mal aus— Monasterzyska. An ihm ist alles *unecht*, außer seinen schmutzigen Geschäften, auch seine Liebe zu F.R. ist nur eine zurechtgelegte Pose, die er sich dann am Ende selbst glaubt, obwohl ihr ein utilitärischer Beischuß nie fehlte. Als die Sache aufflog, liebte er sehr die Märtyrerpose des verkannten Freundes und mit unerhörter Brutalität behandelten alten Mannes. Er sieht aus wie der alte Dr. Max F., nur größer: Ein auf 'Lord' stilisierter Jud. Er ist ausgesprochen sentimental, natürlich nur an der Oberfläche und in zweckdienlicherweise. Er verdankt seine Karriere, außer seiner Perfidie, dem Umstand, daß er 'elegant' aussieht (zurechtgemacht ist) und eine gewisse 'Lord-Hafte' Würde sich angewöhnt hat. Bessere Menschen erkennen natürlich das Elende seiner Physiognomie (so wie beim alten Fürst), Mischlinge und Juden haben zu ihm eine mehr-weniger bewußte Seinsverwandtschaft, und das dumme Pack fällt hinein, weil ihm jeder physiognomische Takt fehlt."

[5] Written in the margin in red pencil is "Fach." This refers to the fact that Levielle kept the evidence of Quapp's inheritance in a secret drawer in his writing-table, from which it was stolen by Kajetan's "gang" on the morning of 15 July 1927.

[6] This last sentence is crossed out in pencil, and the corrections are also in pencil. There are pencilled brackets around "am Schluß des 14. Kap." Doderer originally intended that Levielle should actually be brought to trial for his fraudulent dealings. However, he later discarded this idea and considered that the loss of his position as the trusted adviser of Friederike Ruthmayr was punishment enough for Levielle. He did not actually steal from Quapp's inheritance, indeed, he invested the money quite profitably. His crime was to suppress the fact of the existence of Ruthmayr's will and to fail to carry out his duties as its executor. By 16.7.1935 Chapter 11, "Die Sache mit Altschul," is already Chapter 14.

⁷ The words "großen Reiterschlachten" are crossed out in pencil, and written in pencil in the upper margin is "erst gegen *Ende* gefallen." However, in "Die Dämonen der Ostmark," pp. 261-62, and DD, p. 225, Ruthmayr is described as "Gatte der Friederike Ruthmayr, Gutsbesitzer und Reserverittmeister, 1914 in Galizien gefallen." One wonders why and when Doderer decided to move back the date of Ruthmayr's death. The change in date does create one anomaly. On her return from the Opera on the evening of the "Massen-Umtrunk," Friederike Ruthmayr takes a book from her late husband's library (DD, p. 115). The book in question is Benedetto Croce's *Theorie und Geschichte der Geschichtsschreibung*, which was not translated into German until 1915. Thus, if Ruthmayr was killed in 1914 he could not have acquired the book before his death.

⁸ The introduction in the 1950s of the character of Claire Charagiel as Quapp's natural mother requires changes to be made to this account of Quapp's birth. The new version is to be found in DD, pp. 1065-66.

⁹ The word "alten" is scored out in pencil, and written in pencil in the R.H. margin is "damals noch jungen."

¹⁰ There is a pencilled x after "heute," and written in the L.H. margin is "x der alte Herr starb vor 1914." He later moved Eustach von Schlaggenberg's death forward to 1926, and inserted a sentence to this effect in the chapter "Die Entstehung einer Kolonie I": "Man muß hier wissen, daß nicht ganz ein Jahr vorher Kajetans Vater, Herr Eustach von Schlaggenberg, auf seinem Herrengute in der Südsteiermark gestorben war," DD, p. 63.

¹¹ The phrase inside brackets is deleted in pencil.

¹² After "Allianz," pencilled x. In margin: "x Zeitungskonzern."

¹³ After "herauskam," pencilled x. In margin: "x Die (illegible) ließ L. allerdings glatt verschwinden."

¹⁴ After "worden," pencilled x. In margin: "t.m. Gach."

¹⁵ Doderer was obviously undecided about the spelling of Camy von Schlaggenberg's maiden-name. In the "Namenverzeichnis" the spelling is Schedik. In the "Aide-mémoire" the original spelling was Schädik, and in the "Commentarii 1935/36" in the extract titled "Im Spital zum deutschen Geist" the spelling is Schadik.

¹⁶ The last part of the sentence, "um zwei...herzustellen," is enclosed in pencilled quotation marks, inside pencilled brackets.

¹⁷ This opening part of the sentence is underlined in pencil, and the paragraph is not indented.

¹⁸ The phrase "zweifellos ein völliger Idiot war" is underlined in pencil.

¹⁹ By 21.7.1936 the two parts of the novel are "Der Eintopf" and "An der Wasser-scheide."

²⁰ The phrase "die generative Aufgabe mit zu erfüllen" is underlined in blue pencil and written in blue pencil in the margin is "da ist *viel* einzuwenden!"

[21] The phrase "in sich einen Regress auf die Pubertätserotik provozieren" is underlined in pencil.

[22] The phrase "mitten in die Siebenschein'sche Verwandtschaft" is underlined in pencil.

[23] The phrase "stößt hier auf seinen wesentlichen Gegner Levièlle" is underlined in pencil. Cf. the following remark in the March 1939 review of the "Aide-mémoire": "S. 11 (ff) Schlaggenberg stößt in der (illegible) Welt der DD auf seinen wesentlichen Gegner (Levielle). Dieser Punkt als eines der wesentlichen nächsten C[ompositions]–Glieder zu klären! ff! s. auch 15," "Commentarii 1939/40/41."

[24] This sentence is scored out. Doderer probably considered that he would be laboring the point to have two episodes in the novel concerned with the stealing of an incriminating document.

[25] No definite date is given in the "Aide-mémoire" for the starting-point of the novel. Part I is going to end around 28 March 1927, which is the date of Levielle's second visit to Schlaggenberg. Part II will start in March 1927, with the "Gründungsfest" and will end, as is indicated here, with the events of July 1927. Part III will start in the fall of 1927 and will end in 1932.

[26] Underlined in pencil.

[27] The phrase "die Zerlegung der Gesellschaft" is underlined in pencil.

[28] Doderer read Dostoevsky's novel *The Possessed* in 1931, in the German translation published by Piper Verlag. He later claimed that in order to examine the structure of the novel he took it apart and laid it out on three tables. Cf. *Der Spiegel*, 8 June 1957, p. 54.

[29] "Zerfällung" is underlined in pencil.

[30] Doderer read Spengler in the 1920s: "Spengler/Untergang, etc. I beendet," 16.11. 1922, "Journal 2. Heft," Ser.n. 14.062. References to Spengler also occur in later diaries. Schröder considers that Spengler exerted a considerable influence on Doderer. See *Untersuchungen*, p. 308.

[31] The phrase "bereits damals" is underlined in pencil. Cf. "Schon 1933 wußte ich, daß ich meine Handlung ein Jahr noch vor dem Antreten der neuen Epoche würde schließen lassen," 21.7.1936, "Commentarii 1935/36."

[32] As on page 1 of the "Aide-mémoire" the second part of the title, "der Ostmark," has been removed.

[33] "Fleisch mit Augen" and "Idiotenhölle" were mentioned as possible chapter-headings in an undated entry for 1930 in "Studien Va." In DD "Idiotenhölle" introduces a section of Schlaggenberg's "Chronique Scandaleuse," DD, p. 680.

[34] After "Negria" there is a pencilled cross and written in the bottom margin is "Gesellschaft zur Verbreitung von Schrecken aller Art." There was a mention of the "Organisation Negria" in "Studien Va" in 1929: "Organisation 'Negria.' 'Verein schwarze Hand' (Terrororganisation zur Erzeugung öffentlicher Skandale)." In the early stages of development of the novel "Negria" was merely the name of this rather dubious

organization, but in *Die Strudlhofstiege* the character of Dr. Boris Negria is introduced and it is mentioned that he gave his name to the "Organisation Negria," *Die Strudlhofstiege*, p. 11.

[35] There is a red pencil line in the margin alongside this paragraph, the latter part of the preceding paragraph, and the first sentence of the following paragraph, and written in red pencil is: "alles in Einheit der Zeit 1927."

[36] In DD the "Empfang" takes place on 23 June 1927, in keeping with the changed temporal structure of the later version of the novel. This episode did not form part of "Die Dämonen der Ostmark," which ended with the table-tennis evening at Siebenscheins' on 14 May 1927. Friederike's "Empfang" finds its place in Part III of the novel, DD, pp. 1126-35, and is also mentioned in the "Ouvertüre," ibid., pp. 18-19. The content of the scene corresponds very closely to the outline given here in the "Aide-mémoire," although it must have been written around twenty years later. This would seem to suggest that Doderer made reference to the "Aide-mémoire" when he was working on the chapter "Kurze Kurven II" in which the "Empfang" takes place.

[37] In the margin alongside this sentence is written in pencil "Ouvertüre." However, in the 1955 version of the chapter the orchestra is playing the march from the *Tales of Hoffmann*, and not the music from *Der Rosenkavalier*, the opera to which Geyrenhoff went with Friederike on the evening of 14 May 1927. The change in the choice of music may be intended to reflect the change which their relationship had undergone in the intervening two months.

[38] Cf. "Die DD m.d.H.!" and "'Die dicke Dame' mit dem Herzen suchen," undated entries in "Studien Va."

[39] This phrase is doubly underlined in red pencil.

[40] Cf. the following remark in the review of the "Aide-mémoire": "S. 17, Mitte und unten, sowie 19 Mitte: Dieser ganze Punkt des Ersatzes Schlaggenberg durch Stangeler bei Friederike erscheint psychologisch als mindestens von einiger Fraglichkeit," "Commentarii 1939/40/41." Even in 1939 Doderer has not discarded the idea, but is having doubts about its psychological motivation. There is as yet no suggestion that Geyrenhoff will become Friederike's suitor. The three words "bringen als Friederike" are underlined in pencil.

[41] This sentence is underlined in pencil.

[42] There is a large pencilled question-mark alongside this last sentence, and written in pencil at the end of the paragraph is "B-Cra-1930/31."

[43] The character of Gyurkicz was based to a certain extent on a friend of Doderer, Béla Faludy. The following remark about Gyurkicz appears in "Studien Va": "Giurkicz. Seine Vergangenheit ist ebenso dunkel wie die Lévielles. Er wechselt im entscheidenden Augenblick hinüber (ebenso wie die Glöckner, Neuberg, Holder)...Im Geistigen O, weil im Grunde jüdisch," undated entry.

[44] In pencil in the margin: "er heißt Géza von Orkay."

[45] The phrase inside brackets is deleted in pencil.

[46] There is a large question-mark in the margin. Clearly Doderer has not yet worked out a detailed chronological structure for the later parts of the novel.

[47] The phrase "in einer den Methoden Gyurkicz seltsam verwandten Art" is underlined in pencil.

[48] This sentence is underlined in pencil. There are also heavy lines drawn in ink down the margin alongside this section of the manuscript.

[49] The phrase "sondern an einem anderen" is underlined in pencil.

[50] From "daß Friederike..." onwards is underlined in pencil.

[51] From "ihn und Quapp..." onwards is underlined in red pencil.

[52] The word "wessen" is underlined in ink.

[53] The phrase inside brackets is deleted in pencil.

[54] The phrase "in keiner Weise mehr getroffen" is underlined in pencil.

[55] In the margin in pencil: "x) Hiezu siehe ergänzende Note am Schluß," but the note itself does not seem to exist.

[56] There is a red-pencilled x after "geknüpft," and in the margin written in red pencil is: "durchaus nicht—hätte so werden sollen aber René versagt—oder, wenn man will, er gerät in eine andere Kausalkette: Herzka-Williams-Gontard." This note was obviously made after Doderer resumed work on the novel in 1951.

[57] Doderer mentions the "Affaire Malik" on several occasions, but does not give any detail as to what exactly is involved in it.

[58] This remark about the collapse of the Bodencreditanstalt is deleted, because Doderer decided later to have Levielle disappear from the scene before the events of July 1927. "Der Kammerrat verläßt Wien, er übersiedelt ganz nach Paris. Morgen [30. Juni 1927] reist er schon," DD, p. 1134.

[59] This sentence is underlined in pencil.

[60] This sentence is scored out in pencil and written in pencil in the margin is "gut!"

[61] The two words "erachten ist" are underlined in red pencil and written in the margin in red pencil is "ohne es zu sein."

[62] The first great event is presumably the burning of the Palace of Justice, but it is mentioned much less frequently in the "Aide-mémoire" than is the collapse of the Bodencreditanstalt.

[63] Doderer has added a pencilled acute accent to the first "e" of Levielle, and a grave accent to the second.

[64] Pencilled note in margin: "Tochter Dr. Trapps."

[65] The word "Dezidierens" is underlined in pencil and a pencil-line joins it to "???," written in pencil in the top margin.

[66] From "welche" to "können" is underlined in pencil.

[67] The phrase "gelingt es ihm" is scored out in red pencil, "wiederzugewinnen" is underlined in red pencil, and in the margin is written in red pencil "gelingt nicht," underlined in red.

[68] The word "nicht" is underlined in pencil. It is not clear at this point just what Renate's role was to be.

[69] The word "erst" is underlined in pencil.

[70] By 1936 Schlaggenberg's disappearance from the Viennese scene has been moved forward to Part II. He does not disappear completely from the ranks of "Die Unsrigen," but keeps in touch by letter.

[71] The word "Zentrierung" is underlined in pencil, and there is a red line through the first six lines of this paragraph. In the margin is written in pencil "diese gehen nun entgegen," followed by a small diagram and an illegible word.

[72] This is a reference to Gütersloh. There is a pencilled x after "Lehrer" and written at the foot of the "Aide-mémoire" is "x Albert Scolander." Doderer frequently referred to Gütersloh in his diaries as Scolander.

[73] A reference to Doderer's *Der Fall Gütersloh*.

[74] The word "Kopie" is underlined in pencil.

[75] The phrase "Das neue Reich" is underlined in pencil, and a pencilled arrow points to "bei Reden und Aufsätzen," which is written in red pencil at the foot of the manuscript. Doderer gave a speech on the theme of the emergence of a new Germany in Gütersloh's studio on 1.7.1932. The last section of the "Aide-mémoire," twelve lines of the manuscript, is heavily crossed out in red. This was after the resumption of work on the novel in the 1950s, when Doderer had rejected his National Socialist past.

Bibliography

This bibliography lists only the material, published and unpublished, consulted in research for the book. It also updates the more complete bibliographies to be found in the following works:

Schmidt-Dengler, Wendelin, "Bibliographie. Sekundärliteratur zu Heimito von Doderer," *Literatur und Kritik*, no. 80 (1973), 615-20.

Weber, Dietrich, *Heimito von Doderer. Studien zu seinem Romanwerk* (Munich: C.H. Beck, 1963).

Wolff, Lutz-Werner, *Wiedereroberte Außenwelt. Studien zur Erzählweise Heimito von Doderers am Beispiel des "Romans No. 7"* (Göppingen: Kümmerle Verlag, 1969).

I. Primary Material (Published)

Unless otherwise stated, the place of publication is Munich and the publisher is Bieder-stein Verlag.

Commentarii 1951 bis 1956. Tagebücher aus dem Nachlaß, ed. by Wendelin Schmidt-Dengler (1976).

Das Geheimnis des Reichs. Roman aus dem russischen Bürgerkrieg (Vienna: Saturn-Verlag, 1930). Also in *Frühe Prosa*, pp. 219-357.

Das letzte Abenteuer. Erzählung. Mit einem autobiographischen Nachwort (Stuttgart: Reclam, 1953). Also in *Die Erzählungen*, pp. 386-449, but without the "Nachwort."

Der Fall Gütersloh. Ein Schicksal und seine Deutung (Vienna: Haybach Verlag, 1930). Also in *Die Wiederkehr der Drachen*, pp. 39-109.

Der Grenzwald. Roman No. 7. Zweiter Teil (Fragment), ed. by Dietrich Weber (1967).

Die Bresche. Ein Vorgang in vierundzwanzig Stunden (Vienna: Haybach Verlag, 1924). Also in *Frühe Prosa*, pp. 7-91.

Die Dämonen. Nach der Chronik des Sektionsrates Geyrenhoff. Roman (1956).

Die Erzählungen, ed. by Wendelin Schmidt-Dengler (1972).

Die Merowinger oder die totale Familie (1962).

Die Posaunen von Jericho (Zürich: Arche Verlag, 1958). Also in *Die Erzählungen*,   pp. 154-89.

Die Strudlhofstiege oder Melzer und die Tiefe der Jahre. Roman (1951).

Die Wasserfälle von Slunj. Roman No. 7. Erster Teil (1963).

Die Wiederkehr der Drachen. Aufsätze, Traktate, Reden, ed. by Wendelin Schmidt-Dengler (1970).

Ein Mord den jeder begeht. Roman (Munich and Berlin: C.H. Beck, 1938).

Ein Umweg. Roman aus dem österreichischen Barock (Munich and Berlin: C.H. Beck, 1940).

Ein Weg im Dunklen. Gedichte und epigrammatische Verse (1957).

Frühe Prosa, ed. by Hans Flesch-Brunningen (1968).

Grundlagen und Funktion des Romans (Nuremberg: Glock und Lutz Verlag, 1959). Also in *Die Wiederkehr der Drachen*, pp. 149-75.

Meine neunzehn Lebensläufe und neun andere Geschichten (1966).

Repertorium. Ein Begreifbuch von höheren und niederen Lebens-Sachen, ed. by Dietrich Weber (1969).

Tangenten. Tagebuch eines Schriftstellers 1940-1950 (1964).

Articles

"Bekehrung zur Sprache. Ein Selbstporträt," *Welt und Wort*, 7 (1952), p. 125. In *Meine neunzehn Lebensläufe* under the title "Gedanken zum Selbstbildnis," 69-72.

"Es geht uns alle an," *Die Kultur*, 8, no. 148 (February 1960), p. 3.

"Innsbrucker Rede. Zum Thema Epik," *Akzente*, 2 (1955), 522-25.

"Offener Brief an Baron Kirill Ostrog," *Plan*, 2 (1947/48), 398-402. Also in *Die Wiederkehr der Drachen*, 126-32.

"Von der Unschuld im Indirekten," *Plan*, 2 (1947/48), 2-14. Also in *Die Wiederkehr der Drachen*, 111-25.

II. Primary Material (Unpublished)

Doderer's *Nachlaß* is now in the Österreichische Nationalbibliothek, catalogued, as a new acquisition, under the "Series-nova-Handschriften," "Codex Vindobonensis. Series nova 14.043-14.356." Some of his correspondence, mainly letters to him although there are also some from Doderer to relatives and friends, have also been acquired by the Nationalbibliothek, but not all of them have been catalogued. Those which have been catalogued and which are cited in the book are followed by their catalogue number.

Ser.n.	14.051/53	Die Dämonen, Probetexte und Entwürfe, Ms I-III
	14.054	Die Entstehung einer Kolonie
	14.061	Journal 1. Heft (ab Herbst 1920)
	14.062	Journal 2. Heft (ab Oktober 1921)
	14.063	Journal 3. Heft (ab Februar 1923)
	14.064	Journal 4. Heft (ab 1.4.1924)
	14.065	Journal TBS (1925 bis Juli 1926)
	14.067	Journal TB-TBS 1930/31
	14.068	Journal TB-TBS, 12.9.1931-3.3.1932
	14.069	Journal TB-TBS (Übungen ab 4.3.1932)
	14.070	Journal TB-TBS (Übungen ab 22.8.1932)
	14.071	Journal TB-TBS (Übungen ab 22.3.1933)
	14.072	Commentarii 1934, II/III
	14.073	Commentarii 1935/36
	14.075	Commentarii 1939/40/41
	14.076	Carnet rouge 1941/42; 1944/45
	14.080	Commentarii VI 1951
	14.081	Commentarii VII 1952
	14.082	Commentarii VIII 1953, I und II
	14.083	Commentarii IX 1954
	14.084	Commentarii X 1955
	14.085	Commentarii Xb 1955
	14.086	Commentarii XI 1956
	14.087	Commentarii XII 1957
	14.088	Commentarii XIII 1958
	14.089/90	Commentarii XIV 1959
	14.091	Commentarii XV 1960
	14.092/93	Commentarii XVI 1961
	14.094/95	Commentarii XVII 1962
	14.096/97	Commentarii XVIII 1963
	14.098/99	Commentarii XIX 1964
	14.100	Commentarii XX 1965
	14.101	Commentarii XXI 1966
	14.102	Nachtbuch 1954-1958
	14.123	Skizzenbuch 1935/II
	14.129	Skizzenbuch 25
	14.130	Skizzenbuch 26 1941/II (1942) (1943)
	14.143	Skizzenbuch 34 1951
	14.148	Skizzenbuch 39 1956
	14.174	Studien 1. Heft
	14.175	Studien 2. Heft (ab Jänner 1921)
	14.177	Studien Va
	14.182	Epiloge des Sektionsrates Geyrenhoff
	14.184	Roman-Studien IV (Dämonen)

14.188	Materialsammlung R VII und DD
14.189	Konvolut mit Zeichnungen
14.207	Notizheft 1951
14.208	Notizheft 1952
14.209	Notizheft 1953
14.210	Notizheft 1954
14.211	Notizheft 1955
14.212	Notizheft 1956
14.238/40	DD Roman-Studien I-III, "Die Dämonen der Ostmark"
14.242	Reden und Aufsätze (Ms No. 7 [Reden] a)
14.247	Commentarii Dezember 1934

III. Secondary Material (Books)

Bachem, Michael, *Heimito von Doderer* (Boston: G.K. Hall, 1981).

Fischer, Roswitha, *Studien zur Entstehungsgeschichte der "Strudlhofstiege" Heimito von Doderers* (Vienna: Wilhelm Braumüller Universitäts-Verlagsbuchhandlung, 1975).

Liewerscheidt, Dieter, *Satirischer Anspruch und Selbstpersiflage in Heimito von Doderers Roman "Die Merowinger"* (Cologne: private publication, 1976).

Reininger, Anton, *Die Erlösung des Bürgers. Eine ideologiekritische Studie zum Werk Heimito von Doderers* (Bonn: Bouvier Verlag, 1975).

Schaffgotsch, Xaver, ed., *Erinnerungen an Heimito von Doderer* (Munich: Biederstein Verlag, 1972).

Schmid, Georg, *Doderer lesen. Zu einer historischen Theorie der literarischen Praxis. Essai* (Salzburg: Verlag Wolfgang Neugebaur, 1978).

Schröder, Hans Joachim, *Apperzeption und Vorurteil. Untersuchungen zur Reflexion Heimito von Doderers* (Heidelberg: Carl Winter Universitätsverlag, 1976).

Weber, Dietrich, *Heimito von Doderer. Studien zu seinem Romanwerk* (Munich: C.H. Beck, 1963).

Wolff, Lutz-Werner, *Wiedereroberte Außenwelt. Studien zur Erzählweise Heimito von Doderers am Beispiel des "Romans No. 7"* (Göppingen: Kümmerle Verlag, 1969).

IV. Secondary Material (Articles)

Anon., "Doderer. Der Spätzünder," *Der Spiegel*, 5 June 1957, 53-58.

Barker, Andrew, "Closely observed trains—some thoughts on Heimito von Doderer's use of the railway theme," *Forum for Modern Language Studies*, 10 (1974), 357-64.

_____ "Heimito von Doderer and the meaning of memory," *German Life and Letters*, 32, no. 1 (October 1978), 30-39.

——————— "Heimito von Doderer and the 'Science' of Physiognomy," *New German Studies*, 5 (1977), 91-109.

——————— "'Kammern der Befangnis'—An Aspect of Thought and Image in the Work of Heimito von Doderer," *Modern Austrian Literature*, 14, nos. 1/2 (1981), 25-43.

Barthofer, Alfred, "Leonhard Kakabsa: Success or Failure? Marginalia to a Key Character in Doderer's Novel *Die Dämonen*," *Forum for Modern Language Studies*, 14 (1978), 304-15.

Boelcskevy, Andrew, "Spatial Form and Moral Ambiguity: A Note on Heimito von Doderer's Narrative Technique," *German Quarterly*, 47, no. 1 (1974), 55-59.

Buddeberg, Else, "Schreibe, als ob du allein im Universum wärest," *Deutsche Beiträge zur geistigen Überlieferung*, 7 (Heidelberg, 1972), 160-239.

Christophe, Jean-Pierre, "Heimito von Doderer ou la réhabilitation du roman," *Revue d' Allemagne*, 3 (1971), 903-15.

Doppler, Alfred, "Historische Ereignisse im österreichischen Roman," *Österreich in Geschichte und Literatur*, 13 (1969), 503-16.

Fink, Humbert, "Österreichisches Zweigestirn. Die Erzähler Gütersloh und Doderer," *Der Monat*, 15, no. 176 (May 1963), 61-66.

Hamburger, Michael, "Über Heimito von Doderer," *Literatur und Kritik*, 1, no. 6 (1966), 1-8.

Haslinger, Adolf, "Doderers Weg in den Grenzwald," in *Heimito von Doderer 1896-1966. Symposium anläßlich des 80. Geburtstages. Wien, 1976* (Salzburg: Verlag Wolfgang Neugebaur, 1978), 83-95.

Heydemann, Klaus, "Doderers Divertimenti," *Sprachkunst*, 6, no. 2 (1975), 346-61.

Hopf, Karl, "Die Romane Heimito von Doderers," *Österreich in Geschichte und Literatur*, 11 (1967), 204-18.

——————— "Von der Strudlhofstiege zum Grenzwald. Die Funktion der Topographie in den Romanen Heimito von Doderers," *Österreich in Geschichte und Literatur*, 16 (1972), 436-57.

Ivask, Ivar, "Psychologie und Geschichte in Doderers Romanwerk," *Literatur und Kritik*, 3 (1968), 213-17.

Jones, David L., "Proust and Doderer as Historical Novelists," *Comparative Literature Studies*, 10 (March 1973), 9-24.

——————— "Proust and Doderer. Themes and Techniques," *Books Abroad*, 37 (1963), 12-15.

Kruntorad, Paul, "Heimito von Doderer. Analogia entis," in *Die zeitgenössische Literatur Österreichs*, ed. by Hilde Spiel, *Kindlers Literaturgeschichte der Gegenwart* (Zürich and Munich: Kindler Verlag, 1976), 164-74.

Liewerscheidt, Dieter, "Heimito von Doderer: 'Die erleuchteten Fenster'," *Wirkendes Wort*, no. 1 (1976), 3-26.

Magris, Claudio, "Doderers erste Wirklichkeit," *Literatur und Kritik*, no. 114 (1977), 209-26. Also in *Heimito von Doderer 1896-1966. Symposium anläßlich des 80. Geburts tages. Wien, 1976* (Salzburg: Verlag Wolfgang Neugebaur, 1978), 41-60.

_____ "Neubarock und Ostwind," in *Der habsburgische Mythos in der österreichischen Literatur* (Salzburg: Otto Müller Verlag, 1966), 295-303.

Noth, Ernst Erich, "Heimito von Doderer," *Cahiers du Sud*, 51, no. 380 (1964), 187-96.

_____ "Monsieur 'Vienne'," *Les Nouvelles Littéraires*, 28 January 1965.

Pabisch, Peter and Alan Best, "The 'total novel:' Heimito von Doderer and Albert Paris Gütersloh," in *Modern Austrian Writing. Literature and Society after 1945* (London: Oswald Wolff, 1980), 63-78.

Pfeiffer, Engelbert, "Heimito von Doderer in Döbling," *Literatur und Kritik*, no. 123 (1978), 158-70.

Politzer, Heinz, "Heimito von Doderer's 'Demons' and the Modern Kakanian Novel," in *The Contemporary Novel in German*, ed. by Robert H. Heitner (Austin and London: University of Texas Press, 1967), 37-62.

_____ "Zeit, Wirklichkeit, Musik im Werk Heimito von Doderers," in *Das Schweigen der Sirenen. Studien zur deutschen und österreichischen Literatur* (Stuttgart: J.B. Metzlersche Verlagsbuchhandlung, 1968), 70-78. Also in *Merkur*, 22 (1968), 426-32.

Reininger, Anton, "'Die Dämonen:' totaler Roman und antirevolutionärer Traktat," *Literatur und Kritik*, no. 80 (1973), 599-608.

Riedtmann, Meret, "Heimito von Doderer und die Wissenschaft vom Leben," *Wort in der Zeit*, 2 (1956), 607-14.

Schmidt-Dengler, Wendelin, "'Analogia entis' oder das 'Schweigen unendlicher Räume,'" in *Gott in der Literatur*, ed. by Gottfried Bachl (Linz: Oberösterreichischer Landesverlag, 1976), 93-107.

_____ "Aus dem Quellgebiet der 'Dämonen' Heimito von Doderers. Anmerkungen zu Tagebuchaufzeichnungen des Autors aus dem Jahre 1951," *Literatur und Kritik*, no. 80 (1973), 578-98.

_____ "Die Anfänge des Falles Gütersloh," *Literatur und Kritik*, no. 68 (1972), 472-79.

_____ "Die Thematisierung der Sprache in Heimito von Doderers 'Dämonen,'" in *Sprachthematik in der österreichischen Literatur des 20. Jahrhunderts* (Vienna: Hirt Verlag, 1974), 119-34.

_____ "Heimito von Doderer. Grammatica locuta causa finita. Tagebucheintragungen des Autors zur Sprachtheorie aus den Jahren 1951 bis 1956," in *Austriaca. Beiträge zur österreichischen Literatur. Festschrift für Heinz Politzer zum 65. Geburtstag*, ed. by Winfried Kudszus and Hinrich C. Seeba (Tübingen: Max Niemeyer Verlag, 1975), 406-22.

_____ "Heimito von Doderer. Notationen einer wesentlichen Biographie. Aus den 'Commentarii 1951,'" *Jahresring* 74/75, 65-74.

_____ "Heimito von Doderers 'Jutta Bamberger.' Entstehung, Aufbau, Thematik," *Zeitschrift für deutsche Philologie*, 89, no. 4 (1970), 576-601.

_____ "Heimito von Doderers schriftstellerische Anfänge. Anmerkungen zu unbekannten Publikationen des Autors," *Österreich in Geschichte und Literatur*, 16 (1972), 98-109.

_____ "On the Posthumous Papers of Heimito von Doderer," *Books Abroad*, 42, no. 3 (1968), 368-71.

_____ "Scylla und Charybdis. Der junge Doderer zwischen Journalismus und Fachwissenschaft," in *Heimito von Doderer 1896-1966. Symposium anläßlich des 80. Geburtstages. Wien, 1976* (Salzburg: Verlag Wolfgang Neugebaur, 1978), 9-24.

_____ "Zum Nachlaß Heimito von Doderers. Probleme der praktischen Philologie heute," *Jahrbuch der Grillparzer-Gesellschaft*, Series 3, 13 (Vienna, 1978), 127-40.

Schröder, Hans Joachim, "Kritische Überlegungen zum Wirklichkeitsverständnis Doderers," in *Heimito von Doderer 1896-1966. Symposium anläßlich des 80. Geburtstages. Wien 1976* (Salzburg: Verlag Wolfgang Neugebaur, 1978), 61-81.

Seidmann, Gertrud, "Heimito von Doderer," *Modern Languages*, 40, no. 2 (June 1959), 53-56.

Slawik, Franz, "Literatur von Innen. Heimito von Doderer und das Selbstverständnis der modernen Literatur," *Literatur und Kritik*, no. 114 (1977), 227-41.

Strebl, Laurenz, "Der Doderer-Nachlaß in der Österreichischen Nationalbibliothek," *Biblos*, 21, no. 1 (1972), 17-25.

Strelka, Joseph, "Die Tiefe ist außen oder Doderers Romantheorie," *Acta Germanica*, 5 (1970), 215-26.

Sulke, Franz, "Menschen auf der Strudlhofstiege. Spectrum Austriae im Roman," *Wort und Wahrheit*, 6 (1951), 771-75.

Swales, Martin W., "Ordnung und Verworrenheit. Zum Werk Heimito von Doderers," *Wirkendes Wort*, 18, no. 2 (1968), 96-130.

_____ "The Narrator in the Novels of Heimito von Doderer," *Modern Language Review*, 61, no. 1 (1966), 85-95.

Toman, Lore, "Posthume Einladung zum Dichter Heimito von Doderer," *Modern Austrian Literature*, 14, nos. 1/2 (1981), 97-100.

Trommler, Frank, "Doderers Moral der Sprache," *Colloquia Germanica* (1971), 283-98.

_____ "Für eine gerechte Doderer-Fama," *Neues Forum*, 15 (1968), 781-84.

_____ "Doderer und Gütersloh," in *Roman und Wirklichkeit. Eine Ortsbestimmung am Beispiel von Musil, Broch, Roth, Doderer und Gütersloh* (Stuttgart: Kohlhammer Verlag, 1966), 133-67.

Watt, R.H., "'Der Einbruch von unten:' an Austrian Syndrome of the Inter-War Years?," *German Life and Letters*, 27, no. 4 (1974), 315-24.

Weber, Dietrich, "Doderers Ästhetik des Glücks," in *Heimito von Doderer 1896-1966. Symposium anläßlich des 80. Geburtstages. Wien, 1976* (Salzburg: Verlag Wolfgang Neugebaur, 1978), 25-40.

_____ "Heimito von Doderer," in *Deutsche Literatur seit 1945 in Einzeldarstellungen,* ed. by Dietrich Weber (Stuttgart: Kroner Verlag, 1968), 77-102.

Williams, C.E., "Down a Steep Place...A Study of Heimito von Doderer's 'Die Dämonen,'" *Forum for Modern Language Studies,* 7, no. 1 (1971), 76-82.

_____ "Heimito von Doderer," in *The Broken Eagle. The Politics of Austrian Literature from Empire to Anschluß* (London: Paul Elek Ltd., 1974), 132-45.

V. Secondary Material (Dissertations)

Barker, Andrew, "The Individual and Reality in the Works of Heimito von Doderer" (unpublished dissertation, Edinburgh University, 1976).

Batke, Peter A., "Autobiographical Elements in Heimito von Doderer's *Die Dämonen*" (unpublished dissertation, University of North Carolina, 1979).

Boelcskevy, Andrew, "Rhetorische Darstellungsmittel in Heimito von Doderers Roman 'Die Strudlhofstiege'" (unpublished dissertation, University of Pennsylvania, 1970).

Christophe, Jean-Pierre, "Le procès de l'humanisation dans l'oeuvre romanesque de Doderer" (unpublished dissertation, University of Nancy, 1976).

Dollenmayer, David B., "The Novel and History: Roth-Musil-Doderer" (unpublished dissertation, Princeton University, 1977).

Falk, Thomas H., "Heimito von Doderer's Concept of the Novel. Theory and Practice" (unpublished dissertation, University of Southern California, 1970).

Haberl, Franz-Peter, "Theme and Structure in the Novels of Heimito von Doderer" (unpublished dissertation, Cornell University, 1964).

Hauer, Margarete, "Studium zum Aufbau von Heimito von Doderers Roman 'Die Dämonen'" (unpublished dissertation, University of Vienna, 1975).

Hesson, Elizabeth C., "Heimito von Doderer's *Die Dämonen*: its Genesis, Structure and Purport" (unpublished dissertation, Oxford University, 1981).

Jaffe, William W., "Studies in Obsession: Otto Weininger, Arthur Schnitzler, Heimito von Doderer (unpublished dissertation, Yale University, 1979).

Kastner, Siegmund, "Thomismus und Roman. Studien zu Heimito von Doderers Roman 'Die Dämonen' in Zusammenschau mit den 'Commentarii 1951 bis 1956'" (unpublished dissertation, University of Vienna, 1977).

Lidén, Ulla, "'Saltus grammaticus.' Studien zu Heimito von Doderers Sprachauffassung in Theorie und Praxis unter besonderer Berücksichtigung der 'Tangenten' und des 'Repertorium'" (unpublished dissertation, University of Stockholm, 1970).

Mitchell, M.R., "Heimito von Doderer as a Social Novelist" (unpublished dissertation, Oxford University, 1970).

O'Bryon, Patrick W., "Responses to the Urban Challenge: The Search for Home in the City in the Twentieth-Century German Novel" (unpublished dissertation, Princeton University, 1976).

Rieser, Hannes, "Doderer und Gütersloh. Metaphorik und 'totaler' Roman" (unpublished dissertation, University of Salzburg, 1968).

Ryan, Ingrid W., "Zur Funktion und Bedeutung des Zufalls in Heimito von Doderers Roman 'Die Dämonen'" (unpublished dissertation, University of Oregon, 1980).

Stengel, Elisabeth, "Die Entwicklung von Heimito von Doderers Sprachstil in seinen Romanen" (unpublished dissertation, University of Vienna, 1963).

Swales, Martin W., "Heimito von Doderer and the Return to Realism" (unpublished dissertation, Birmingham University, 1963).

Ulmer, Ann C., "A Doderer *Répertoire* with an Essay on Characterization in his Novels" (unpublished dissertation, Yale University, 1973).

VI. General

Edmondson, C. Earl, *The Heimwehr and Austrian Politics 1918-1936* (Athens, Georgia: University of Georgia Press, 1978).

Frank, Joseph, *The Widening Gyre. Crisis and Mastery in Modern Literature* (New Brunswick, N.J.: Rutgers University Press, 1963).

Gedye, G.E.R., *Fallen Bastions. The Central European Tragedy* (London: Victor Gollancz, 1939).

Johnston, William M., *The Austrian Mind. An Intellectual and Social History 1848-1938* (Berkeley, Los Angeles, London: University of California Press, 1972).

Kitchen, Martin, *The Coming of Austrian Fascism* (London: Croom Helm Ltd., 1980).

Kraus, Karl, "Der Hort der Republik," *Die Fackel*, nos. 766-70 (October, 1927).

Stadler, Karl R., *Austria* (London: Ernest Benn Limited, 1971).

Index